THOSE NAVY GUYS AND THEIR PBY's
THE ALEUTIAN SOLUTION

This book
is dedicated to
our shipmates who didn't come back.

CONTENTS

PHOTO DIRECTORY

Cover photo from National Archives

ACKNOWLEDGEMENTS

Many people were involved with me in my experiences during the early days in Patrol Wing Four and during the days of the Aleutian Campaign. And there were many things happening in other parts of the world which had a bearing on what we did or did not do. *Those Navy Guys and Their PBY's* is meant to be a composite picture of the events, people and places making up my Navy life during the period of 1940 to 1943. It is an expanded version of a few chapters of *Kedging through Airpockets*, which is the story of my twenty years in the Navy. To write *Those Navy Guys and Their PBY's* I needed help.

My thanks go to several old shipmates who shared their memories of those days. My interviews with Dick Babbitt, Bill Brady, Al Birchman, Boyd Peer, Captain Carl Amme, Captain M.E. Johnson and Captain W. M. Dickey enabled me to write of many incidents, some of whose details had escaped my memory. We do not agree to this day on all details, and I have written my account with the knowledge that, were they writing it, there could be some slight differences.

I also owe a debt of gratitude to Robert Brown, Joe Segar, Bob Wallenstien and Bill Brady for allowing me to use some of the photographs which appear in this book. Bill Brady has kept this project going through his encouragement and promotion efforts.

Admiral James S. Russell's help, hospitality and encouragement have been of great assistance in my efforts. His library of documents relating to the Aleutian Campaign and his other material involved with those times and places are a gold mine to a writer. His conversations provided me with the command point of view of VP-42's actions, which is understandably different from the ordinary aircrewman's perception of the same actions. I must also thank him for allowing me to use some of his photographs in my book.

The many authors whose writings have touched on the actions of Patrol Wing Four and related incidents in other parts of the world provided me with the information necessary to tie my experiences in with the big picture of World War II. Appropriate footnotes and the bibliography list the publications and authors.

The war diary of VP-42 and the history of Patrol Wing Four provided by the Naval Historical Center enabled me to cite dates and places of some incidents in which I was involved but whose details I could not always recall.

Special thanks must go to my wife, Pat, who edited what I have written. Her expertise has greatly improved the readability of the book.

FOREWORD

Just prior to and in the early days of World War II, Elmer Freeman and I served in VP-42, a navy aircraft squadron equipped with "Catalina" flying boats. Our primary mission was reconnaissance, but we could carry and use bombs, torpedoes and depth charges. Elmer began as a member of the squadron beaching crew, but gradually worked up to the very responsible position of aircraft flight engineer, while I served as squadron commander of VP-42.

I had graduated from flight school as Naval Aviator No. 3495 in 1929. In those early days of naval aviation it was Navy policy to assign young aviators successively to different types of naval aviation in the fleet in order to broaden their horizons. Thus I had flown float planes from battleships, landplanes from aircraft carriers, and flying boats from the surface of the sea.

In June 1941 I found myself again assigned to flying boat duty, having served in that type of duty ten years before. After I joined my squadron in Seattle, we flew to Alaska and on out the Aleutian chain of islands to Kiska. In Kiska harbor we joined our seaplane tender, USS *Williamson*, and based on her for two weeks while we made many local flights to Attu at the western end of the chain and to Adak in the east.

The only permanent inhabitants in this vast area were about sixty Aleuts who lived on the shore of Chichagof Harbor, at the east end of Attu Island. Several of the islands—notably Kiska, Amchitka and Adak— had shacks spaced a day's walk apart for fox trappers who came in January or February and departed in March or April. Constantine Harbor on Amchitka had on its shore a deserted village.

After about two weeks we moved our base to Dutch Harbor on Unalaska Island where a new Naval Air Station was under construction. Our squadron was the first to be hauled out of the water on the new ramp there.

While at Dutch Harbor we made many local flights examining Adak, Atka (a village with about forty Aleuts), Umnak (with Aleuts in Nikolski village at the west end), and Unalaska Island (which had not only a very good natural harbor at Dutch, but also good shelter at Chernofski Harbor to the west and at Beaver Inlet to the east). Flying east we looked at the old whaling station on Akutan and crossed over Unimak Pass to the end of the Alaskan Peninsula. Crossing Unimak Pass we looked over the spacious roadstead in Cold Bay, then landed in Dolgoi Bay in the Pavlof Islands group where we based on our tender for two days. Finally, after a look at Chignik, we settled down at the Naval Air Station Kodiak for a period of intensive training until October 1941 when VP-41 flew up from Seattle and took over our beat.

Pearl Harbor Day (7 December 1941) found us enjoying Sunday off in the Seattle area. Notified of the Japanese attack, we opened the Orange War Plan and established the spider web of patrols off the coast which covered the crippled ships returning from Pearl Harbor.

In January 1942 we had enough trained crews in VP-42 to double the strength of the squadron and we became a twelve-plane Catalina squadron, equipped with—joy of joys—the amphibious version of the Catalina, the PBY-5A. With it we could land in the water, lower our wheels, and taxi up a ramp under our own power to a parking apron. This eliminated the difficult maneuver of a beach approach, having men in waders attach beaching wheels and being hauled out of the water and up a ramp backward by a tractor. Alternatively we could land on an airfield and operate as any landplane. In "going amphibious" two small penalties were involved: increased weight from the two side wheels, the nose wheel and their retracting mechanisms, and decreased buoyancy of the hull caused by the wheel wells. Water-borne, the amphibian sat a little deeper in the water than the flying boat.

From the end of January until late May 1942, VP-42 served as the only reconnaissance squadron covering the Alaskan seas. The magnitude of the task can be visualized by the distances involved. From the sheltered Inside Passage through the many islands of southeast Alaska, passing through Icy Strait and Cross Sound and taking departure from Cape Spencer, there are roughly 1,000 nautical miles of open sea to Unimak Pass at the end of the Alaskan Peninsula, on the route to Nome. From Unimak Pass down the Aleutian chain of islands to Attu at its western end is another 1,000 nautical miles. Keeping track of what was going on in this vast sea area was truly a task of herculean proportions.

Besides our at-sea reconnaissance there remained the job of training additional aircraft crews and performing heavy maintenance on our aircraft. To meet these requirements we established our main base at Naval Air Station (N.A.S.) Kodiak, halfway across the Gulf of Alaska, and deployed two aircraft to N.A.S. Sitka and four aircraft to N.A.S. Dutch Harbor. Duties at these two "advanced" posts were exchanged approximately monthly. As we set up the patrols from Sitka and Dutch Harbor, I flew in company with the two planes to Sitka and the four planes to Dutch Harbor, in order to have first-hand knowledge of conditions under which our planes would be operating and to insure a smooth transition from the VP-41 personnel in place to the VP-42 flyers who were taking over.

An episode in Dutch Harbor is illuminating. Inspecting the Dutch Harbor "line shack" which was used to store waders and other gear used by the beaching crews and which served as shelter for the beaching crews, I noticed a chart pinned up on the wall. It was a plot of morale against time, time plotted horizontally and morale vertically. I noted a steady decline in morale, but at one point it broke and went upward, causing a small hump in the morale curve. When asked what happened at that point, our VP-41 escort replied, "Oh, a shipment of beer arrived!" After that small change, the morale curve continued to fall until it crossed the zero base line and continued on down the wall—and across the floor! I did what I could to speed VP-42's take-over of the Dutch Harbor line shack. It was a relief to know that beach handling of our amphibians would be very much easier than handling VP-41's seaplanes.

Having completed the foregoing few paragraphs of orientation for the reader, let me comment more directly on Elmer Freeman's good work in this book, *Those Navy Guys and Their PBY's*. His is the story of a farm boy who came into the Navy because he liked sea service and flying. Intent on serving his country in wartime and fired by the indomitable spirit of American youth, he was pioneering one of our nation's last frontiers.

He finds humor in the most trying circumstances. A case in point occurred when, as a junior flight engineer in a crew ferrying a new Catalina amphibian from Kodiak to Cold Bay, he unknowingly refueled an already fueled airplane. This added weight to a heavy load of plumbing the pilot had accepted as cargo for Cold Bay. After the airplane struggled successfully to get into the air, a course was laid for Cold Bay. It was eventually discovered that this new airplane had its radar hooked up backwards. Land known to be on the starboard hand appeared on the radar as being to port. By the time the navigation was unscrambled and a successful let-down made at Cold Bay, the engines were eating well into the fuel supplied by the second, and inadvertent, refueling.

Fighting in the Aleutians was a battle not only against the Japanese enemy but also against the Aleutian weather. In our twelve-plane squadron, VP-42, which I had the honor to command from June 1941 through October 1942, we lost three planes to direct known enemy action and five due to weather.

The loss of an airplane did not always mean the loss of its crew. A case in point occurred on the first day of attacks from the Japanese aircraft carriers. When Dutch Harbor broadcast that it was under attack in the early morning of 3 June 1942, Lt. Lucius Delandville Campbell and his crew were manning one of our PBY-5A amphibious flying boats moored to a buoy in Akutan Harbor, site of the old whaling station. About 150 miles out from Akutan Campbell ran into the Japanese force—two aircraft carriers, two heavy cruisers, and about four destroyers. As he got out his radio report giving his position and the composition of the enemy task group, Campbell was engaged by the ZERO fighters of the carriers' combat air patrol.

In consideration of time and the damage sustained in his brush with the ZERO's—one man with a superficial wound, numerous bullet holes in his airplane, and his rudder control wires shot away—Campbell decided to return to his dispersal base at Akutan. Fifty miles from Akutan both engines ran out of fuel and quit. Campbell lowered the nose of his aircraft and made an instrument let-down through approximately 6000 feet of cloud with no rudder and no power. At an altitude of roughly 300 feet the surface of the open sea became visible. He pulled the nose of the aircraft up and made a successful landing in the open sea.

Safely down on the sea, Campbell and his crew busily engaged in plugging bullet holes in the hull and in bailing. Immediately upon landing, Campbell had his radioman re-broadcast the contact report as to the location and composition of the enemy raiding force. As luck would have it, both contact reports were garbled in their encryption or decryption and were never fully understood at headquarters in Dutch Harbor or Kodiak. A Coast Guard patrol boat picked up Campbell and his crew. Their tow of the bullet-riddled Catalina became unmanageable as it slowly filled with seawater. Finally the towline was cut and the airplane was allowed to sink. Thus we lost an airplane, but gave thanks to the Almighty for the survival of the seven-man crew.

The World War II experiences we lived through in VP-42 and its parent organization, Navy Patrol Wing Four, together with our brothers-in-arms in the Eleventh Army Air Force, generated many life-long friendships. Even today, fifty years later, well-attended reunions are held about every three years. We owe Elmer Freeman a debt of gratitude for recording many of the events which transpired as we fought the Japanese in Alaska. His easy-going style in writing and the "tongue in cheek" humor with which he treats even some near desperate situations make good reading.

James S. Russell
Admiral, U.S.N. (Retired)

PREFACE

When one thinks of the role flying boats have played in the history of Naval Aviation, it would be hard to begin anyplace else but with the NC-4, which flew across the Atlantic Ocean in 1919. In the 1920s and 1930s there were other flying boats, built by Curtiss, Sikorsky, Douglas, Martin and Consolidated. The planes were products of imagination and good old American engineering know-how. The Consolidated PBY was, and still is, a prime example of the art of building a flying boat.

But where did the people come from who were the pilots and crews that operated these boats with wings? Were they recruited from special aeronautical institutions which turned out superior aviation-type students? Hardly. They came from the farms, towns and cities all over America, and most of them had never had anything to do with airplanes before they entered the Navy. All had requested assignment to Naval Aviation because they wanted to be around airplanes. Some volunteered because they wanted to fly. Others volunteered because they wanted to maintain the planes and equipment. Each wanted a piece of the action in Naval Aviation.

The pilots were trained at the Navy's Flight School at Pensacola, Florida. To understand how Navy Mechanics, Radiomen, Ordnancemen and Metalsmiths learned their trades and became aircrewmen or ground-crewmen, it is helpful to follow their paths of training from their apprenticeship forward. This book is an attempt to do that. Ours was not a structured, schoolroom environment. It was a daily routine of learning on the job—whatever job was assigned to us—learning to carry out orders until we knew enough to be on our own and make the right decisions. The advent of World War II forced us to learn a lot faster than any of us thought we could.

Although some of our training took place in Seattle, we were always aware that our eventual destination was Alaska and the Aleutian Islands. The Navy gave us PBY's to fly and we figured that was the best flying boat there was for the job we had to do. In 1941 and 1942 our operations in the Aleutians were constant exercises in survival. The weather was an ever-present threat and during 1942 the Japanese caused us no end of trouble, but we managed to accomplish the missions assigned to us. How we began and how we eventually fought in the Aleutian Campaign is the story of *Those Navy Guys and Their PBY's.*

Elmer Freeman
ADJC, U.S.N. (Ret)

Chapter 1

PBY Patrol Squadron, VP-41 Sitka Operation

THE BIG FLYING BOAT banked smoothly into its final approach over the floating bridge across Lake Washington. As the plane descended, floats disengaged themselves from the ends of the wing, moved downward on mechanical arms and locked into place beneath the wingtips. The aircraft levelled off a few feet above the lake's surface, then settled to the water a few hundred yards offshore from Sand Point Naval Air Station. The scene was a familiar one to the residents around the lake in the summer days of 1940.

As the plane turned to taxi toward the shoreline, the sun flashed over its tail showing the red checkerboard pattern. On the concrete ramp toward which the plane was taxiing, a watchful, white-hatted sailor shouted, "Red tail on the water!"

A dozen more sailors of the Beach Crew answered the call by trotting to various spots in the vicinity of the ramp, taking up their stations for the ritual of beaching the flying boat. Half the men were in swimming trunks and the rest wore dungarees.

There was no doubt about who was in charge of this operation and what he was. Only a Boatswain's Mate could give orders in the tone this Beachmaster was using. An aircrewman hustled out of the waist blister of the plane, climbed to the top of the wing and made his way out to the port wingtip. Another crewman streamed a large cone-shaped canvas sea anchor, securing its lines to a snubbing post inside the port waist.

The plane taxied toward the beach two hundred yards to the left of the ramp, then, aided by the drag of the sea anchor and the pilot adjusting his throttles, turned ninety degrees to port and taxied toward the ramp on a course parallel to the beach. The starboard wingtip float, raised out of the water by the man's weight at the opposite end of the wing, passed over a Beach Crewman in swimming trunks standing hip deep in the water. He reached up and placed a hook through a ring on the float, and six men in dungarees ran along the beach with a long line fastened to the hook. This action and the continued drag of the sea anchor caused the plane to spin around in the water; it ended up nose out to the lake, with the tail in position right over the ramp.

As the pilot cut his engines, an aircrewman in the port blister tossed a heaving line toward the ramp. He took a turn with the line around the snubbing post inside the plane while a couple of Beach Crewmen caught the line and slowly pulled the big flying boat back toward the ramp.

Two men, waiting with the tailwheel gear, moved underneath the tail, fastened it in place and hooked a towline to the heavy-duty towing fitting near the tailwheel. A tractor at the head of the ramp slowly took a strain on the towline and pulled the plane backward so that the tailwheel was touching bottom. The two main beaching gear assemblies for the sides of the plane were rolled into the water, each handled by a pair of swimmers, and attached to the sides of the hull. Each main beaching gear assembly had a set of dual wheels mounted on a heavy steel post about as tall as a man. The tires were not only inflated with air, but they also contained enough water to achieve negative buoyancy so that the handlers could force the wheels under water while attaching the gear to the hull. When the main gear handlers called, "Starboard gear secured," and "Port gear secured," the beaching operation was complete and the plane was ready for towing.

On orders from the Beachmaster the tractor got under way and pulled the plane up the ramp. With the last few drops of water dripping from its hull, the VP-41 PBY was towed to a parking spot.

To the casual observer the routine appeared quite simple. But in reality it was precisely orchestrated. A foulup on any movement of the operation could allow the aluminum hull of the flying boat to be severely damaged on the concrete ramp. The Beachmaster operated like a combination of symphony conductor and surgeon, controlling his crew's actions with vigorous arm motions and sharply barked orders. Those of us in his crew didn't make a move without his order or permission. A well-run Beach Crew was a necessary part of each PBY squadron.

In 1940 Patrol Wing Four was based at the Sand Point Naval Air Station in Seattle, Washington. A Patrol Wing was made up of a number of Patrol Squadrons numbered to indicate that they belonged to that particular wing. Patrol Wing Four had four such squadrons, VP-41, VP-42, VP-43 and VP-44. The "V" indicates heavier-than-air, as opposed to lighter-than-air (blimps for example); "P" indicates patrol; the first digit indicates the wing.

VP-41 and VP-42 were equipped with PBY-5's, which were the latest model of patrol bomber, built by Consolidated Aircraft Company in San Diego. These planes were hull-type (flying boat) seaplanes, with a single "parasol" wing, retractable wingtip floats and two engines. The parasol wing was set above the hull and connected by a cabane strut. This large strut not only supported the wing but also housed the flight engineer's station, where all of the engine instruments and related equipment were located. The nose of the plane housed the bombardier's station and a thirty-caliber machine gun; behind the nose was the cockpit for two pilots; further aft were the navigator's table and the radioman's station. In the center portion of the hull, directly beneath the flight engineer's station, there was an Auxiliary Power Unit, a small 2-cycle gas engine, for furnishing electricity when the main engines were not running, and there was a two-burner hotplate for cooking. Aft of that were the bunk compartment and then the waist compartment. There were port and starboard plexiglass blisters at the waist. These blisters could be opened to allow rigging and firing of two fifty-caliber machine guns, one to either side. Toward the tail section was the tunnel hatch in the bottom of the hull, which could be opened and was armed with a thirty-caliber machine gun. Bombs were carried under the wing, and the bomb racks could be converted to carry aerial torpedoes.

For part of the year VP-41 and VP-42 shared the same hangar at N.A.S. Sand Point, Seattle. During the summer months the squadrons alternated moving north to Alaska. In the late 1930s it was assumed that no PBY squadron could survive winter flying operations in the Alaska area and only summer operations were possible. Old hands who had been in VP-16 and VP-17 (which eventually became VP-41 and VP-42) talked about operating from tenders at Kodiak or Sitka in past summers, but bases had not yet been built in those places in 1940.

There was a lot of friendly rivalry between VP-41 and VP-42, with competition between the Beach Crews, the Flight Crews and the Maintenance Crews. Disparaging remarks were traded constantly. Unfortunate perpetrators of foulups were immediately taken in hand by squadron-mates and given an extra dose of training to make sure there was no repeat of the error.

When I reported to Patrol Wing Four, I was assigned to VP-41 in the Beach Crew. That was the normal assignment for a Seaman Second Class when first joining one of these squadrons. We had the job of launching and beaching our PBY's, as well as taking care of all the equipment used for the job. Our boss was a First Class Boatswain's Mate named Evans. He ruled his crew with an iron hand and considered it his personal mission in life to try to make decent sailors out of the miserable lot put under his care. He was of the school where a sailor did the job right or he kept on doing it until he learned how to do it right.

In August 1940 Hitler's armies were dominating Europe. Hirohito's forces were dominating China. And Admiral Yamamoto was thoughtfully studying a chart of Pearl Harbor aboard his flagship.[1]

Completely oblivious to all of these global happenings, I was busily laying out six lengths of manila line on the seawall overlooking Lake Washington near our Beach shack one day that August. The squadron had completed the 1600 muster for the day, the duty section had posted the watches and the liberty sections were all happily donning their dress blues in preparation for a night on the town. All except me.

Marlinespike seamanship has to do with knots and splices and otherwise caring for lines for all the various uses in the Navy. Our Boatswain's Mate was big on training his crew in marlinespike seamanship.

Earlier in the day Boats had assigned several of us to make up some seaplane tiedown lines. This job consisted of cutting the lines to the proper length, putting an eye-splice in one end and a whipping at the other end. When Boats came by to inspect the finished tiedowns, all of them passed but mine. "Those damned things look like a gob of week-old spaghetti." Now, when I heard a verdict like that, I knew the sentence was going to be close behind. "After muster you stay here and undo this mess, get more line, and make up six of these things. When you're finished, the Duty Section Leader will look at them. If they are done right, he may let you have your liberty card. If they aren't, you just keep doing them until he says you can secure."

Learning the basic skills was often just a little painful for young sailors. And it may seem hard to relate making a proper eye-splice to becoming a Flight Engineer in a flight crew. But the fact of the matter was that if anyone didn't learn to do a good job for the Boatswain's Mate, it was assumed that he more than likely wouldn't do a good job for anyone else either. Boats got to know us all pretty well, and he knew what our aspirations were. When it came time to assign a few people from the Beach Crew to Flight Crews, Engineering Shop or Radio Shack, it was pretty important to have a good recommendation from him.

As I say, it was a little painful. Hitler, Hirohito and Yamamoto had their worries, but at that particular time and place my only concern was to make six decent eye-

---

[1] Hiroyuki Agawa, *The Reluctant Admiral: Yamamoto and the Imperial Navy*, trans. John Bester (Tokyo: Kodansha International, Ltd., 1979), 193.

splices. Who wants to spend his whole Navy career in the Beach Crew? I guess the treatment worked. About one month later Boats assigned me the job of teaching a couple of new guys how to make eye-splices.

All in all, a job in the Beach Crew was quite pleasant. I spent a good deal of the time in swimming trunks working around the ramp and on the beach during the summer. When the weather became colder we used neck-high waders to perform our tasks around the planes in the water. It was a learning experience, but it was fun, and actually, there was a good deal of excitement for most of us in just being a part of a PBY squadron operation.

Although we were in the beginning stage of duty in Naval Aviation, we had high hopes for the future. We made it a point to observe closely what the aircrewmen who were regular members of flight crews did, anticipating that at some future date our opportunity to be assigned to a flight crew would come too. When our Beach Crew operations went well for a couple of days, Boats was generally in a pretty good mood. That was usually when a couple of Beach Crew members requested his permission to ask a flight crew plane captain to let them go out on a flight with his crew.

The first flight I made was in the fall of 1940. The Chief Petty Officer who was the plane captain told me that I had one duty during the flight—stay out of the way of his crew carrying on their regular duties. The fact that I was considered excess baggage didn't diminish the thrill of flying one bit that day.

VP-43 and VP-44 operated from a different hangar than ours and were equipped with the older model Consolidated aircraft known as P2Y's. They were also seaplanes but were biplanes, having the lower stub-wing about midway up the sides of the hull and the higher wing attached above it with struts. The two engines were mounted between the wings. Although these squadrons had some sort of rotation to Alaska, too, VP-41 and VP-42 weren't involved with their operations very much.

In addition to the four seaplane squadrons, there were also two ships assigned to Patrol Wing Four, USS *Williamson* and USS *Teal*. USS *Williamson* was one of the old four-piper destroyers of World War I vintage. *Williamson* had begun her career as DD 244, built in 1916 or 1917, but in 1939 she had been converted to a Seaplane Tender. This meant that one boiler, one fireroom and two stacks had been removed and replaced with tanks for hauling aviation fuel. She also had stowage for bombs and ammunition, as well as some spare parts for our aircraft.

The other ship, USS *Teal*, was a converted sea-going tug and was fitted out so that she could do some limited duty as a seaplane tender.

A few hundred yards around the beach from the ramp used by VP-41 and VP-42 there was a non-military flying boat handling dock. From time to time the huge Boeing China Clipper landed in Lake Washington and eased into the dock for servicing. We were always fascinated by the mammoth size of that plane. It was another part of the Lake Washington scene in 1940.

From time to time the squadrons had advance base exercises. *Williamson* went to sea, anchored in a selected bay along the coast and set up a seadrome for the aircraft. This consisted of marking out landing areas with buoys for the planes to land and then planting other buoys where the planes could moor.

When planes needed fuel, they slowly taxied to the fantail of the ship. With the ship's crew and the plane crew working together, the plane was held as steady as possible as it was fueled and otherwise serviced.

There were no aviation personnel on permanent assignment to the ship, so

Formation of VP-41 PBY-5's over Puget Sound area—January 1941 (note checkerboard tail markings)   (National Archives)

Five-Plane formation of VP-41 PBY-5's — January 1941

(National Archives)

Consolidated P2Y-3 Flying Boat. Earlier models had engines mounted between wings.

(National Archives)

1940 Aerial view of N.A.S. Seattle with Lake Washington in background

(National Archives)

USS *Williamson* (AVD-2) — PatWing Four Seaplane Tender

(National Archives)

USS *Teal* (AVP-5) — PatWing Four Seaplane Tender

(National Archives)

squadron personnel would be temporarily assigned when the ship was operating with aircraft, to assist with fueling and handling. The squadron personnel also helped with setting out the seadrome and running boats to and from planes moored at buoys.

One of the safety precautions always followed when our PBY's were taking off and landing was the presence of a crash boat in a nearby area. The boat was equipped with fire fighting equipment and other rescue equipment and was always ready to rush to any crash or other disabling mishap to assist the plane crew. In Lake Washington the boat operated from the station boathouse, but at an advance base the boat was furnished by the ship.

I had enlisted in the Navy at the age of 19, in late 1939, coming from New England, North Dakota, a small farming community in the southwest part of the state. The Navy had turned me down for enlistment a year earlier because I had two bad teeth. The dentist was able to fill one but had to pull the other. That left me one tooth short of the required number. However, when the Germans marched into Poland on 1 September 1939 and the president declared an emergency, the physical requirements for enlistment in all the services were changed enough so that I passed the physical for the Navy. Upon completion of my boot training at Great Lakes Naval Training Station I was assigned to Aviation Machinist's Mate School at San Diego and, after twelve weeks of school and a short tour of temporary duty in VP-12 at San Diego, had received orders to Patrol Wing Four.

These were exciting times to be in the Navy. Throughout most of the 1930s the Navy had been pretty stagnant. Little new construction had taken place. Recruiting new personnel was at a trickle. Advancement for people in the Navy was at a snail's pace. But eventually somebody recognized that Hitler's and Hirohito's plans might involve more than Europe and China. America was looking at two oceans which might have to be defended.

In 1940 there were new ships and new airplanes being built, and thousands of new people were being trained to man them. As the Petty Officers who had been waiting so long began to be promoted, there were vacancies to be filled. A vacancy for Third Class Aviation Machinist's Mate was what I hoped to fill. That was the first step toward becoming a plane captain. As I became familiar with the operations of our squadron, it seemed to me there were a few people whose status was just a cut above all the others. They were all Chief Petty Officers; all were Aviation Machinist's Mates. They were the Plane Captains. Each plane had an assigned crew and the man in charge was the Plane Captain.

Of course the skipper, exec and all the other officers were senior in rank and, as pilots, held the actual command positions aboard our PBY's. But a pilot can't be a pilot unless he has an airplane which will fly. The Plane Captain was responsible for maintaining the aircraft on the ground so that it was always ready to fly. And he had to have his crew trained to man all of the stations except pilot and navigator spots aboard the aircraft when it was in the air. It seemed to me that being a Plane Captain would be the greatest job in the Navy. Sometimes, when I thought of how many years it would be before I could hope for such a position, it seemed like an impossible dream. I could only keep doing a good job and hope to get promotions when I became eligible. Maybe I would make it and maybe I wouldn't, but it was worth trying.

The ordinary path of advancement was from Apprentice Seaman to Seaman Second Class, then Seaman First Class and Third Class Petty Officer. But I, among others, got a break. Those of us who had attended Aviation Machinist's Mate School were notified that we would eventually be allowed to take the test for Third Class without having to make Seaman First Class. We had to fulfill certain squadron requirements in order to be declared eligible for promotion. Every one of us went about his daily duties with a Third Class Course Book sticking out of his hip pocket. If we got a ten-minute break we studied and young sailors with their noses buried in their books was the common order of the evenings in the barracks. The senior Petty Officers held classes for us. Our immediate superiors were on our tails constantly. Nobody wanted the guy who worked for him to be the only one who flunked the exam for advancement. It would make him look bad.

The first hurdle came in December 1940. I became eligible and passed the exam for Third Class Aviation Machinist's Mate. Actual advancement came a month later, in January 1941. The "Machinist's Mate" part of the rating came from the days when there were no Aviation ratings in the Navy. General service Machinist's Mates were assigned to aviation duty to fill the job of mechanics. Later, when Aviation became a full-fledged part of the Navy, the word "Aviation" was added, and the winged propeller was designated as the rating insignia for Aviation Machinist's Mates. To most people in the Navy we were known as "AMM's" or Aviation Mechs.[2]

With the advancement in rating also came the much-desired assignment to a flight crew. It was only a part-time training assignment, but it was a start. The flight crew was made up of three pilots, who were officers, a Chief Petty Officer as plane captain, two other Aviation Mechs, a couple of radiomen and perhaps an ordnance-man. The Chief had the task of teaching us our flight duties, how to maintain the aircraft on the ground and water and how to be a credit generally to the Navy as sailors. Now I was one of the guys who streamed the sea anchor or tossed the heaving line. And nobody was more critical of these actions than my Beach Crew buddies with whom I still worked part time.

If done properly, handling the heaving line was a simple and routine proce-dure—stand in the port blister, toss the weighted end of the line a distance of 25-30 feet and take a turn around a snubbing post with the other end. But there were a number of things which could go wrong and become very embarrassing.

If one forgot to hang onto one end of the line the whole thing ended up lying in the water with the Boatswain's Mate muttering bad things about "airdales." If the line was not coiled properly, the weight got half way out and a tangle of line fell in the water half way to its intended receiver. But the worst problem occurred whenever the thrower got a coil of line around his ankle. The Beach Crew man caught the weighted end and began pulling—and the thrower had to avoid being upended while getting untangled. A few apprentice aircrewmen found themselves with one leg out of the blister, hanging on for dear life as the Beach Crew hauled away, using the unfortunate leg to replace the snubbing post.

Our squadron, VP-41, consisted of six PBY seaplanes and about 150 people to fly and maintain them. One of the first ground duties I learned was fueling the plane.

The routine for fueling usually involved moving the plane to the fueling pit after it had been beached, stationing a man on top of the wing to handle the fuel hose, having someone on the ground to supervise and having another man in the fuel pit to operate the valves when all was in readiness to pump fuel. With the fueling

---

[2]The original "AMM" designation was changed to "AD" in the 1950s. To identify specialties further an "R" or "J" was added to signify "Reciprocating" or "Jet" engines.

completed, the plane was moved into the hangar, and the next plane in line went through the same routine.

The First Class Mech on our crew had shown me several times how to open the fuel-tank filler cap, place the fuel strainer over it, place the strainer nozzle in the hole, release the center valve in the strainer and call for the man in the pit to start pumping gas. He always stressed that the center valve in the strainer had to be released so that the gas could go through the strainer. If the valve wasn't released, the strainer would fill up and overflow all over the top of the wing.

The day eventually came when I was on top of the wing alone and we were fueling the plane. The Chief was standing down below, just aft of the trailing edge of the wing, where he could see me and also be in position to give orders to the man in the pit. The fuel hose was passed up to me, and I proceeded to get the strainer in position over the tank filler and insert the hose. Finally, I gave the signal to the Chief that I was all ready. He told the man in the fuel pit to start pumping. And he did. As soon as the fuel started coming, I knew I was in trouble. I had forgotten to release the center shut-off valve.

The Chief was standing right under the trailing edge of the wing. The strainer filled up in about a second and overflowed onto the wing. The lowest part of the wing was the trailing edge, and fuel was flowing down and over the edge in about two seconds—on top of the Chief's head. I was trying to get the fuel stopped by yelling at the top of my lungs and finally did succeed, but not before the Chief was soaked with gas.

The crew behind us, waiting to fuel, thought the scene was the funniest thing they had ever seen. By this time I had the strainer valve open, which did absolutely nothing to help the situation. I had never felt so alone in my life, standing there waiting for the Chief to take off on me. What he did was calmly walk to the sea wall, hop off and walk into Lake Washington.

Further astonishing me, he sloshed around for a minute or two, came out on the beach, disrobed down to his scivvies, and deliberately took up his former station. "Freeman, do you think you can do it right this time?" And I did.

In a minute or two the First Class took over and the Chief disappeared into the hangar. We finished fueling and nobody had to tell me to get soap and water and scrub every trace of fuel off the top of the wing. We eventually got our plane parked in the hangar, and I saw the First Class talking to the Chief, now decked out in a clean uniform. When the Chief patted his shirt pocket and shook his head, I knew what was happening. The First Class came over and told me to forget my liberty card for awhile. I knew that it would be in the Chief's pocket for an undetermined length of time.

Later, when I talked to the First Class I said, "I suppose the Chief will hate me forever for running gas all over him."

"Naw. He'll tolerate a mistake like that—once. But Lord help you if you ever do it again. He'll get you transferred to some harbor tug in Whangpoo, China."

I had no idea where Whangpoo, China was, but it didn't sound as if it was a good place to be, and I made a solemn vow to mend my ways.

Maybe there was some regulation against the Chief's depriving me of liberty without due process. But when anyone has pulled as stupid a stunt as I'd pulled, he doesn't argue. He is just grateful that they have done away with keelhauling and the forty lashes with the cat-o-nine-tails. After ten days I checked for my liberty card, but it wasn't there. About two weeks after the incident it finally showed up.

Two months later our squadron moved to a new base at Sitka. Those of us not in regular flight crews rode the *Williamson* up the Inside Passage to our new base. The Navy base at Sitka was pretty primitive compared with the facilities at Seattle. The ramp was about twice as steep as the one at Sand Point, and it was a real pull for our tractor to haul a plane up the ramp. We double checked all of our towing gear after every launch and recovery. The fact that we were operating from salt water, rather than the fresh water we were used to in Lake Washington, meant that we had to douse each plane with fresh water from hoses as we towed it over the top of the ramp. The combination of aluminum-hulled flying boats and salt water has always been a source of concern because of the corrosion which can occur.

At first we had only partial use of the hangar at Sitka because it was still under construction. But there was progress every day on the construction, and eventually we had a pretty complete seaplane facility.

Although I spent a lot of time working in the Beach Crew, I was assigned to fly about once a week, becoming qualified to take a turn at manning the flight engineer's station and standing lookout watches. Sooner or later there would be an opening in a flight crew and I figured I was ready for the third mech spot.

About once a week some of us aspiring mechs were assigned to work on a plane's engines with a flight crew performing a 30-hour or 60-hour check. A routine thing like changing spark plugs was a super experience for those of us waiting for our chance to show the world what great aircrewmen we could be. There were a few pretty tedious jobs to be done too. Painting rivets was one of those. Armed with a paper cup of zinc chromate, a primer compound, and a one-eighth inch paint brush, one of us examined the row upon row of rivets for any sign of corrosion. The least sign called for a tiny swipe of the brush. Nobody can appreciate the number of rivets in a PBY flying boat hull until he has put in a few hours painting rivets.

The ever-present crash boat had an additional duty at Sitka. There were times when the takeoff and landing area had stray logs floating around. Before each landing and takeoff the crash boat made high speed sweeps, zigzagging the full length of the area looking for logs and removing any that were found.

A new thing we had to cope with was the tide. Sitka has about twelve or thirteen feet of tide and that is a lot of water running in and out of the channel. At full low tide we couldn't even beach a plane. Our ramp ended a couple of feet short of the water at low tide and there was no way to tow a plane up on it. If a plane landed during a low tide, he had to moor to a buoy until there was enough water to get him up on the ramp. At high tide practically the whole length of the ramp was under water.

The tides affected not only beaching the planes but also loading and unloading liberty-boats at the dock. In order to go on liberty, for example, we had to catch a boat across the channel to the town of Sitka. At high tide it was an easy step from the dock into the boat, but when the tide was out we had to climb down a ladder of about ten steps to reach the boat. A few sailors had a tough time with that ladder when returning from liberty, having imbibed a bit past their capacity.

Sitka was a preview of the kind of operations our seaplane squadrons would be seeing for the next three years. Move into a new base. As soon as it gets to be liveable, move on out to another new base. The town of Sitka was not very impressive although it did seem quite prosperous. Fishing seemed to be the main industry in the area but the civilian workers who were building the Navy base added a lot to the economy. For recreation we did a little drinking in the saloons of Sitka, we did a little mountain

1941 Aerial view of N.A.S. Sitka on Japonski Island

(National Archives)

1941 Aerial view of N.A.S. Sitka with town of Sitka in background

(National Archives)

1941 view of hangar and parking ramp, N.A.S. Sitka

(National Archives)

climbing on the mountain behind Sitka, and we played a little poker.

As far as I know, there has always been a Navy regulation against gambling on ships and stations. From a practical standpoint, enforcement of this regulation was usually up to the commanding officer. In situations like Sitka, there was little or no enforcement. Every night we had a poker game going in the head. Lights out was at 2200 in all the barracks. But the lights in the head were never turned out.

One night, at about midnight, the usual poker game was going on in the head when in walked the Duty Officer, Ensign Jack Litsey, and the Master-at-Arms. In Sitka this wasn't exactly a cause for alarm, but Mr. Litsey was telling the Master-at-Arms to make a list of the names and rates of all of us. Suddenly it appeared that things were getting serious. When he had the complete list, he took out a piece of paper and began comparing the list with the piece of paper. Then he called off six names and told us to get our seabags packed. The Master-at-Arms was instructed to get our hammocks out of storage and give them to us.

Hearing this, we were certain we were in for a "Bag and Hammock Drill," a punishment sometimes used in the Navy. It consisted of loading the complete seabag and hammock on one's shoulder and marching up and down an assigned area until told to stop.

When we had completed packing and gotten our hammocks rigged around our seabags, the Master-at-Arms told us to leave them by the office and report to the Duty Officer at the hangar. Still wondering what was going to happen, we arrived there at about 0200. My friend, R. M. Jones, was the other AMM3c in the group and we were mumbling to each other, trying to figure out what in the world was happening to us. There was a sleepy-eyed yeoman going over a set of orders with the Duty Officer. It turned out that a dispatch had come in, instructing our squadron to transfer six men, in specified rates, to VP-42 in Seattle. There was a Destroyer, *Kane*, leaving Sitka at 0700 and this six-man draft was to be aboard for the run to Seattle. There would be a boat at the pier at 0530 to take us out to the ship.

We never did know why we were needed so urgently in Seattle. But the PatWing Four dispatch from Seattle was our ticket for a ride back down the Inside Passage. The poker game furnished the Duty Officer with the exact people he needed. He didn't even have to wake anyone up. And when the squadron mustered at 0800 that morning, we were long gone to Seattle.

Chapter 2

VP-42 in Seattle,
Williamson in the Aleutians

HAVING BEEN IN VP-41, I found joining VP-42 just a bit difficult. Having so recently been so critical of everything VP-42 did, it was a little unsettling now to find myself a member of the squadron. It was tough to swallow all of those snide remarks I had made about their operations. But in reality, there wasn't much difference between the two squadrons. Of course, within a couple of weeks VP-42 was my squadron, and we did everything better than anybody else did. We got a new skipper in VP-42 just about the time I checked in. Lieutenant Commander James S. Russell relieved Lieutenant Commander Alan Nash as Commanding Officer.

The Naval Air Station, Sand Point, was a wonderful base for duty. There was a handsome brick building which housed our barracks, mess hall and auditorium and had a small BX in the basement. There was another brick building which contained the Station offices and Wing administrative offices. We had good, well-built hangars for our planes, Squadron offices and workshops. I don't think I ever heard any complaints about being assigned to Naval Air Station, Sand Point. The chow was good and the discipline was reasonable. We were a pretty happy crew.

Seattle was not only the home base for VP-42; it was also a super place for liberty. I had spent about six months in San Diego in Aviation Machinist's Mate school and as a temporary member of VP-12 before coming to PatWing Four. The place was packed with sailors. Even though the main units of the Pacific Fleet had been moved to Hawaii in 1940, there were still a fair number of ships, besides the many shore installations in San Diego, meaning quite a large population of sailors in the area.

Not long after the fleet moved to Hawaii, VP-11 and VP-12 were also moved to Hawaii from San Diego. To fill the need for patrol squadrons in San Diego, VP-43 and VP-44 were transferred from Seattle to San Diego. There were very few ships based in Seattle, and with only VP-41 and VP-42 left in Patrol Wing Four, there weren't enough sailors in the Seattle area to cause much of an increase in population. That made for good liberty.

Seattle had many attractions. There were some fine golf courses to be played in the city. The Seattle Rainiers were competing in the Pacific Coast League, and there were great ball games to watch. The Palomar Theater always had a good movie running, and in addition to the movie they also ran good vaudeville acts. Then there was the Trianon Ballroom where the big bands played. Every couple of weeks they had a change of bands. Tommy Dorsey, Jimmy Dorsey, Gene Krupa, Jan Garber, Stan Kenton—they all played the Trianon. We had a Navy boathouse on the base where we

19

1938 Photo of N.A.S. Seattle seaplane hangars, parking ramp and PBY's

(National Archives)

1941 Aerial view of N.A.S. Seattle showing runway layout   (National Archives)

could check out small motor boats or sailboats and go boating on Lake Washington. That was where I first tried my hand at sailing.

But no liberty in Seattle was complete without a visit to First Avenue. That's where the real action was. The Music Hall, a nightclub on First Avenue, was headquarters for VP-41 and VP-42 sailors. If you were looking for anybody who was on liberty, you looked there first. They had a bar and booths and tables. There was a dance floor and a guy who could play anything on the huge theater organ there. A beefy bouncer at the door checked ID cards and once in awhile forcibly ushered a couple of would-be prize fighters out into the street. And there were girls.

These girls worked at department stores and banks; they worked at Boeing and the telephone company. They came from all over Seattle and liked to dance and have a couple of beers as much as we did. The Music Hall was a kind of meeting place. From there we would go to the Trianon or maybe the movies.

When the Air Station theater advertised the weekly movie as "Dawn Patrol," all of us aspiring aircrewmen made it a point to see it. It was a World War I story of American and German flyers fighting over Germany and France. The sneering German pilot was always picking on the young American pilots who were on a first flight over enemy territory. Sometimes they were shot down and survived the crash. But the ultimate tragedy occurred when the young American pilot was "shot down in flames." He always died in that kind of crash. Of course, eventually the seasoned, experienced Squadron Commander finally got that sneering German one on one in a dog-fight and shot him down in flames.

From then on we used "shot down" to describe minor disappointments. When we experienced a serious setback we were "shot down in flames." Within a matter of months the expression would take on a much more serious meaning for us. In the meantime it generally referred to everyday setbacks.

Wheeler Rawls was a southerner. For him the Civil War was only a temporary setback and the Confederacy would certainly rise again. In tribute to his background and attitude he naturally picked up the nickname, "Rebel."

Ol' Rebel Rawls had been dating a young lady for a couple of months and they had had wonderful times on their dates. Then one fine evening the young lady introduced Rebel to her girl friend. Well, Rebel instantly became enamored with the girl friend and when he could speak to her alone, he asked her for a date. It was the wrong thing to do.

He not only didn't get a date, but the girl told her friend what had happened and they both told him what a lousy, two-timing scoundrel he was, and for him to get out and stay out and never speak to them again. All Rebel could say when he related his problems to us was that he had been "shot down in flames."

Like Rebel Rawls and just about all the other sailors, I had my own setbacks. One day I decided to shop for a Mother's Day gift for my mother. She always liked religious gifts, so I went to a religious supply store. I kind of browsed around for awhile and finally stopped at a table to look at some things. A girl came over to see if she could help me. She was absolutely stunning. I began fumbling around with the things on the table and promptly forgot why I was even in the store. She suggested a small prayer book for Mother's Day and I bought it. It could have been a Webster's Dictionary, and I wouldn't have noticed. When she made out the sales slip and I paid her, she looked up at me and said, "Thank you." And I walked out of the store in a daze.

That sales slip had a little square on it for the clerk's name. Her name was Rose.

I had to see Rose again. Every time I had the chance I went shopping in that store. I bought a rosary and then a Bible. I bought a crucifix and then a picture. And I always worked it so Rose waited on me. I don't think she was too surprised when I finally got up the nerve to ask her for a date. But that Friday night was a bad night for her, and she couldn't go. So the gift purchasing went on and on. Pretty soon I had about half a seabag full of religious articles, but no date. Finally, after I had bought one of almost everything in the store, I went in one day and Rose wasn't there. When a lady had waited on me and I was about to leave, I nonchalantly asked where Rose was. "Oh, she went to Pennsylvania to stay with her grandmother. She's going to college there this fall."

All of my relatives were impressed with the Christmas gifts I sent out that year. That was the first time I ever got my Christmas mailing done in August. It's better to have loved and lost than never to have loved at all.

While my experience with Rose took the wind out of my sails, it was not bad enough to dampen my enjoyment of Seattle. The Music Hall closed at midnight. Sometimes we weren't ready to go back to the base at midnight. There was an all-night cafe almost directly across the street from the Music Hall, and a half dozen of us would continue the night's festivities there. I suppose they had a menu, but we never looked at it. We just ordered ham and eggs. They didn't serve beer in the cafe so once in awhile one of us had the foresight to have a pint of bourbon hidden under his jumper so we could sweeten the coffee. They weren't exactly blind to what was going on and always gave us the high sign if the Shore Patrol showed up at the door. We got to know the couple who ran the place quite well. To us they were Ma and Pa Russell.

At four o'clock in the morning Russell's cafe closed for one hour of cleaning. Ma Russell would chase us all out the door. There were a few times when we took our cups of coffee with us and sat on the curb until they reopened at five. If we had to be back to the base, we were again kicked out by six so we would have time to catch the bus back to Sand Point.

In addition to its many attractions Seattle offered some of the most spectacular scenery I had ever seen. When you have spent most of your life on the plains of North Dakota, you can't get used to seeing Mount Rainier or Puget Sound. Anthony Duesing, from Kansas, and I used to buy round-trip ferry rides on the Kalakala over to Bremerton and back just to look at the scenery. For a young sailor on liberty, it just doesn't get any better than Seattle. Wherever we were, we always hoped to get back and fight the "Battle of Seattle."

Because of the similarity in our situations—trying to become mechs in flight crews—some of us had much in common and thus tended to spend more time together than with others in the squadron. We had flown a few training flights in our PBY's and were hooked on the thrill of flying. There was no job, no matter how menial or how difficult, that we wouldn't take on as long as it got us a flight in one of our planes. We just loved to fly.

Two of the guys with whom I became friends were Al Birchman and A. K. "Dick" Babbitt. They were as opposite as two people could be. Birchman was reserved and quiet. Babbitt was outgoing and talked all the time. Both were good Third Class Mechs and both came from farm backgrounds.

Since Babbitt came from North Dakota, we had that in common, and it became our duty to defend our state in the usual arguments which came up about the merits of one's home state. It was great to have Babbitt on my side because he could talk anybody down.

Birchman came from nearby Tacoma, which made it convenient for him to visit home regularly. I accompanied him on a visit home one weekend and it was not hard to see how his quiet personality had developed. His family lived on a small farm just outside Tacoma and in the time I was there I never heard anybody raise his voice once. It was the quietest liberty I ever spent.

Of course, we weren't on liberty every night. The squadron was divided into four duty sections, which meant we caught the duty every fourth night. The more junior people could count on being assigned to "Roving Patrol" sentry duty around the hangar on duty nights. This meant that one man was assigned for every four hours of the night from 1600 until 0800 walking around the outside of the hangar and making rounds inside the hangar among the planes parked there. In 1940 we stood these watches armed with a night stick. But during 1941 there were numerous reports of sabotage around the country and we began standing our watches armed with a forty-five. If anybody entered the area he was to be challenged with the age-old words, "Halt, who goes there!" Then when the person gave his name—"Advance and be recognized!"

One night Dick Babbitt was on Roving Patrol on the 0000-0400 watch. He had made his round of the outside of the hangar and came inside to walk his pattern among the planes. Just about the time he got to the middle of the hangar one of the beaching gear tires on a plane behind him suddenly blew out with a loud "BANG!" Always alert and ready for action, Babbitt swung around, drew his forty-five and yelled, "Come out of there, you son-of-a-bitch, or I'll blow your head off!"

"Halt, who goes there," might be good enough in polite company, but when there was a crisis it called for something a little stronger.

The bunk room where off-duty sentries and the Section Leader slept was only a few feet away from the action and the sudden shattering of the silence had all hands grabbing for their pants and grumbling, "What the hell happened?" Nobody rushed to Babbitt's assistance because they had heard enough to let them know that it might be dangerous to go wandering out into the hangar. Finally the Section Leader managed to get to the light switch and turned on all the hangar lights, revealing Babbitt aiming his forty-five at the waist hatch of the plane and repeating his command to the would-be saboteur at the top of his lungs. Finally the Section Leader inspected the plane and determined that it was a blowout which was the offender. Babbitt then continued to walk his post in a military manner. The aroused people from the bunk room went to the Engineering Shop and put on a pot of coffee. There wouldn't be any more sleep after that ruckus.

When VP-42 received orders to move to Kodiak, I didn't have a permanent spot in a flight crew. That meant I would make the move as a temporary member of the crew of the USS *Williamson*. When a squadron moved, it meant moving everything but the hangar. We crated shop equipment. We packed files and records. We boxed up spare armament and ammunition. Finally we loaded it all aboard the ship and got underway for Kodiak.

Williamson was berthed at a pier at N.A.S. Sand Point, on Lake Washington. Going to sea was a scenic voyage. We steamed along the lake and past the University of Washington through a sort of canal into Lake Union. After passing through Lake Union we eventually entered the Ballard Locks which allowed passage out to Elliott Bay. After several hours we passed through the Straits of Juan de Fuca, past Cape Flattery, finally reaching the open sea. Then we set a direct course for Kodiak.

It appeared to me that when *Williamson* was built the ship-designers overlooked the fact that there was going to be a crew living aboard. Berthing compartments were crammed like sardine cans. Finding enough bunks for a couple of dozen passengers was hopeless. We had been hauling our hammocks with us since boot camp and now we knew why. The Master-at-Arms showed us various spots where hammocks were to be strung and told us that they could be put up at 1900 and were to be stowed by 0700. A few of us who were immediately assigned to underway watches did manage to find some sleeping space below decks, but there was little doubt that this wasn't going to be a luxury cruise.

Because of the "Machinist's Mate" being part of our rating, those of us who were Third Class were assigned to the "Black Gang," the Engineering Division, for duty. I ended up standing watches as after-throttleman in the aft engine room. The after throttle controlled the port screw, while the forward throttle controlled the starboard screw. The starboard screw was the control screw. There was a large brass wheel at my station, the after throttle control. My job was to keep an eye on a round brass plate with a single hand on it, called the "telltale indicator." This device indicated whether or not the screws were turning at the same speed. If the hand moved either way I had to turn my throttle control one way or the other to adjust the speed of my screw to synchronize it with the starboard one. When verbal orders were required, our orders came from the bridge through a "speaking tube." Somebody up there rang an electric bell, like a doorbell, to get our attention, and yelled down to us through a tube. We put an ear to our end of the tube and listened to the order and yelled back an acknowledgement. World War I ships did not have much high technology.

We did not have an inclinometer in our engine room, but we did have a half-inch steel bolt hanging from a piece of cord tied to an overhead pipe. As the ship rolled the suspended bolt indicated the degree of roll. There were a couple of pencil marks on the bulkhead behind the bolt showing the extremes of rolls in the past. By the time we reached Kodiak we had come very close to setting some new marks.

The importance of doing a good job on my watch became apparent to me after my first watch. Some guy in the deck force who had been standing a helmsman watch on the bridge asked, "Who in hell was on the after throttle on the 8 to 12 last night?" It seemed that my inability to keep the screws synchronized and my chasing the telltale indicator by overadjusting kept the poor guy on the wheel working his tail off to keep the ship on course.

My friend, Al Birchman, stood watches in the fireroom. We had a rough passage. Our new duties were tough enough to handle, but we also battled high seas and storms all the way to Kodiak. When we got there, the storm was so bad we couldn't even get into the harbor. We spent the next two days being beaten and battered by the sea as we went around in circles outside the harbor. There was green water breaking over the weather decks all the time. Whenever the watch changed, every four hours, we had to make the exciting trip from or to our watch station. That meant a trip of a hundred feet across the open deck. You watched for a big one to break over the ship and then when she rolled away from it, you got a few seconds to make a dash for it before the next big one came along. Of course, when your watch was over you had the same fun and games getting back. The romance of the sea wears a little thin after about seventy-two hours of that.

I got a barked shin, a bruised arm and a small bump on the head in all of this. That was about par. But on one mid-watch, Birchman had about all the bad luck a guy could stand. First, he somehow burned his arm lighting off some burners. He got that greased up and bandaged and continued his watch. Then on his way back across the deck after his watch, his timing was a little bit off and he came close to going overboard. When he reached the safety of the bunk compartment, it was, of course, dark. While trying to stow his clothes up beside his bunk, he stuck his hand into a fan. Then, just about the time he was crawling into his bunk, the ship took a vicious roll and threw him across the compartment, landing him on his shins on a foot locker. He didn't even try to get up again. He rolled under a mess table, wedged himself between two table legs, and spent the rest of the night sleeping on the steel deck. Compounding all of these miseries was the fact that he was seasick. Although Birchman was a quiet and patient man, he was close to coming unglued that night.

When the storm was finally over, we entered Kodiak harbor and off-loaded all of the squadron equipment. Most of the VP-42 people moved ashore to the base, but a few of us were assigned to stay aboard ship to assist in servicing our planes when they operated from the *Williamson* at a later date. After a couple of days in Kodiak we headed back out to sea for an exploration trip to the Aleutian Islands.

The Bible tells us that God created the world in six days and rested on the seventh. I really believe that when quitting time came on the sixth day, He had the whole job completed except for the Aleutian Islands. He really intended to put in an hour or so the next morning finishing the job, but He never got around to it. There is something about the Aleutian Chain which closely resembles the chaos which the Bible describes as the condition of the earth before God put things in order.

The winds are like no others on earth. You can be leaning into a 50-knot head wind and in a second it will change direction and hit you in the back. The incessant fog makes you wonder if the sun will ever shine again. There's rain. There's snow. There's sleet. Sometimes they come one at a time. Sometimes they come all at once. On rare occasions the fog will clear long enough so you can see a smoking volcano on an island. Flat areas of the islands are just plain mud.

In 1941 the Navy's charts of the Aleutians were inadequate and needed updating and correcting. The *Williamson* was to do some of that on this voyage. Our Captain, Lieutenant Commander Frederick N. Kivette, was also scouting out likely-looking bays where we might set up for seaplane operations if we needed to. We'd steam along for awhile, then we'd lie dead in the water and lower a whaleboat and take the skipper ashore. He did a little exploring and we'd take him back to the ship, pick up the boat and move on. When the ship stopped, someone always asked the question, "Where in hell are we?" Eventually one of the ship's Quartermasters who was familiar with the navigation for the day would tell us. Not that it made much difference. We visited such islands as Umnak, Amukna, Seguam, Atka and Adak. They all looked pretty much the same. The one which was different from the rest was Bogoslof Island.

Bogoslof Island, about one mile in diameter, is located by itself, about 100 miles north of Umnak in the Bering Sea. When we went ashore there, we were greeted by the entire population, all sea lions. There were thousands of them. Big ones and little ones, they paid little attention to us, and we didn't bother them. The skipper got the information he wanted, and we returned to the ship and moved on.

Although we didn't see much of the sun during our voyage, the weather was mostly calm. There was just enough of the high-wind and blowing-rain kind of weather to make us appreciate calm seas and dry weather. We were only troubled by fog a couple of times but a low overcast persisted throughout our voyage.

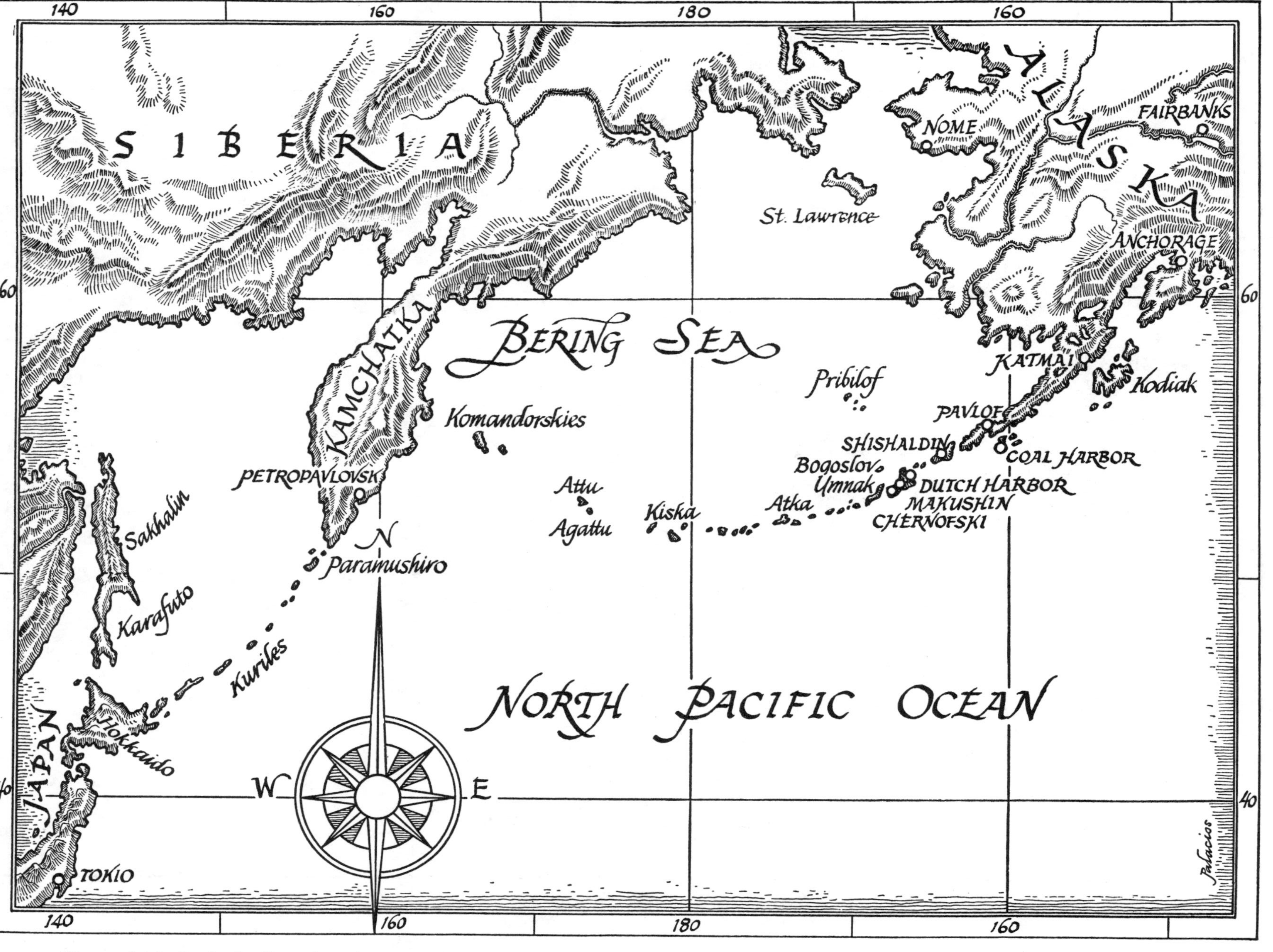

Chart of Alaska including the Aleutian Islands

(Henry Holt and Company, Inc.)

Chart of Alaska including the Aleutian Islands

(U.S. Geological Survey)

Finally we dropped anchor in a harbor at an island called Kiska, put our boats in the water and set up a seadrome. With crews of six in each of our two whaleboats we planted buoys to mark a landing area and in an adjacent area we placed several mooring buoys. It was as part of this work force that Birchman and I began getting some experience in running a 26-foot motor whaleboat. Under the supervision of a boatswain's mate we hauled loads of buoys, cables and anchors out to the seadrome area and planted them in the specified locations. It took a full day's work to prepare the area to the skipper's satisfaction.

The next day our VP-42 planes came flying in and we commenced playing mother hen for a flock of PBY's. Some of the servicing was performed by boat with the planes tied up to mooring buoys. Fueling was done at the fantail of the ship.

With the fueling detail waiting on the fantail of the ship, a plane would taxi slowly into position. A mooring line was then fastened to the bow of the plane and two long bamboo poles, fitted with padded "U" ends and manned by six sailors each, were thrust toward the bow of the plane or the leading edge of the wing to port and starboard. Finally, with the mooring line fast to the ship and the bamboo poles fending the plane off the fantail, the pilot cut his engines. The fuel hose was passed to the plane crew and they checked their oil. There was always lots of hustle and bustle as we replenished water and food supplies and needed parts for the plane crew.

During our boat trips back and forth from ship to planes we heard some discussion of the merits of Kiska's harbor. Although we were blessed with good weather during our operations, it was the general opinion that if the wind kicked up it probably would make things pretty miserable. The mouth of the harbor appeared to be wide open to the elements. We felt that perhaps it would be wise to search out a more protected base of operations the next time we came this far west in the Aleutians.

Little did we imagine the scope of activity which would take place in Kiska harbor in less than a year—activity which indeed forced us to seek a different base of operations in the area.

After several days of operations the planes headed back to Kodiak, and *Williamson* retrieved all of its seadrome equipment and went to sea again. It had been a busy and interesting time. I had been aware in a general way of how a Seaplane Tender operated, but after participating in the work of setting up a seadrome I would always have an appreciation for the detailed work required to bring about a successful advance base operation. It seemed to me that *Williamson* did well enough at its assigned mission, but we came up a little short trying to berth flight crew personnel. It was a good thing that they didn't mind camping out in their planes. As long as we kept them supplied with food and water they seemed to be happy with their lot, although it struck me that they might get pretty fed up with that routine after a week or ten days.

Life aboard the *Williamson* had its lighter moments. When a ship is at sea its fresh water supply is all made from sea water by an evaporator system. The boilers must have fresh water and the crew consumes whatever is left after the boilers are supplied. There is never any excess and most of the time there is a shortage. Wherever possible, salt water is used in the plumbing system of the ship.

The enlisted men's head in the after deck-house of the *Williamson*, for example, had fresh water showers and sinks but used salt water in the toilet facilities. The toilet setup consisted of a large, slightly sloping trough along the outer bulkhead equipped with five seats next to each other at the upper end and an open part of the trough at the lower end. Usually there was a roll of toilet paper provided near each seat. And there was a porthole right above the valve where the water entered. If the weather was decent the porthole was open for ventilation. This situation offered the opportunity for the "Phantom Firebug" to strike.

Sometimes during the day there was a waiting line to use the various facilities in the head. Usually during these busy times the seats were all occupied by sailors in deep meditation. Seasoned hands on the seats kept a weather eye out when someone departed from a seat to see that he wasn't carrying a wad of toilet paper with him, for they were well aware of the risk of complacency. The Phantom Firebug could strike at any time.

Every now and then some jokester would depart from the head and when he got outside on deck he eased around to the porthole over the incoming stream of water. Then he lit off a large wad of toilet paper, reaching in to drop it into the water. When the flaming missile floated rapidly down the full length of the trough, passing beneath the posteriors of those unfortunates seated thereon, all hell broke loose. All kinds of loud and profane references to the ancestry of the perpetrator were made, and vows were made to remove his genitals and nail them to the mast. But the villain was long gone. The Phantom Firebug had struck again.

Nobody ever actually witnessed the dastardly deed being done and nobody could be sure just who the culprit was, but generally a likely suspect was picked out. Fortunately the abuse was kept on a verbal level and all the victims thereafter watched for a chance to even the score. A goodly number of the crew of the *Williamson* had their buns singed at least once.

After about ten days of exploration we steamed into Dutch Harbor and anchored. Although Birchman and I had been casually checked out as coxswain and engineer on a motor whaleboat during the voyage, our formal skills were a bit lacking and became exposed in an unfortunate incident in Dutch Harbor. The coxswain on a motor whaleboat stands at the stern, surrounded by a small railing, and operates the tiller. The engineer is a little forward of the coxswain and down in the bottom of the boat, where he runs the engine from commands given by the coxswain. Birchman was the coxswain and I was the engineer. Most of the time we had a seaman from the deck force as bowhook, the man up at the bow of the boat.

The coxswain has a bell with which he is supposed to signal to the engineer. There are four signals: one bell, two bells, three bells and four bells. They translate into these commands: one—ahead, two—stop, three—back down, and four—full speed whichever way you are going. With seasoned boat crews these bell signals are second nature, and they are experts at landing at a dock, clearing a dock and maneuvering in dense boat traffic. Birchman and I were no experts. Our training mainly consisted of leaving the ship and running the bow of the boat up in the sand on an island and returning to the ship. Now and then we ran a work boat with a crew aboard to drop or pick up seadrome buoys. Our signals were almost always verbal. Birchman would say, "Kick 'er ahead," or "Back 'er down," or "Pour on the coal." It was sloppy seamanship, but it worked for the type of operation we were used to.

When *Williamson* anchored in Dutch Harbor that day, the skipper had to go ashore. The Captain's gig was a motor whaleboat just like the one we had used on our trips back and forth to the islands. But it had a smarter paint job, and there was a canvas canopy up forward to shelter the Captain from the weather. There was a designated crew assigned to man the Captain's gig whenever it was called away. When the gig was called away that day in Dutch Harbor, the coxswain and engineer were in a pinochle game.

Birchman and I were lounging nearby, looking at the scenery (or lack thereof), and the gig coxswain called for us to man the gig. It was surprising to us, but no big deal, because the gig was the same kind of boat we were used to running. How this switch in crews got past the Officer of the Deck I'll never know, but in a couple of minutes we had the gig alongside and the Captain stepped aboard. He gave us the order to make the boat landing at Dutch Harbor, and we departed from the ship.

Now, we were smart enough to know that in this situation we should be using the bell signals. It was simple enough getting away—one bell to move away from the accommodation ladder and clear the ship, then four bells for full speed ahead. There wasn't much of anything at Dutch Harbor, so it wasn't hard to spot the boat landing. Getting alongside the landing was another matter.

When we were about 200 yards from the landing, Birchman gave me one bell, and I slowed it down. From where I was I couldn't see anything up forward, because of the canopy. I tried to visualize how our approach was going and anticipated two bells, for stop. All of a sudden he gave me three bells, to back down. I did a stop and then kicked it into reverse, but the moment of confusion was our undoing. There was a loud crunch as we hit the landing head-on. There was an officer standing there waiting to meet the Captain. The bowhook went flying off the bow and landed in a heap, but he hung onto the bowline, and the officer stepped in to help him out and see if he was injured.

With no vision forward, the Captain had no warning of what was happening. He ended up bouncing off the thwart and tumbling to the bottom of the boat. When he finally regained his feet, he was pretty mad. "Who taught you two how to run a boat?" And after he had looked over the canopy up forward and assured himself that we were not in a sinking condition, "Take me back to the ship." While trying to get turned around we managed to back into a log boom floating near the landing. When we got to the ship and got tied up alongside, Captain Kivette went steaming up the accommodation ladder. Pretty soon the Officer of the Deck called down to us to tie the gig up to the boat boom and report to the Quarterdeck. When we got there he had the gig crew standing at attention and he turned to us. "You are dismissed." It could be that he sneered a little when he said "You." Happily, we didn't hear anything more about the incident, but I'm sure others did.

For whatever reason, Birchman and I were not called on to run a boat for the rest of the voyage. A few days later we steamed into Kodiak and moved from the ship to the barracks and rejoined our squadron-mates who had already commenced flying operations from the new base.

Chapter 3

Kodiak, Pearl Harbor Day,
Tongue Point

IT WAS NICE TO BE BACK among our squadron-mates and experience the spaciousness of the berthing and messing facilities ashore, but we would not soon forget our Aleutian cruise aboard *Williamson*. Some of those islands we visited were only insignificant dots on the chart in August 1941. Within a short year many of them became important centers of activity for us.

The hangar at Kodiak was still being built, but the barracks and mess hall were complete, and the launching ramp and parking apron were ready to use. The Navy docks where *Williamson* and another Navy ship were moored were near the ramp. There was an ancient-looking ship tied up at one of the docks displaying the name *Victoria*. We were told that the *Victoria* was permanently parked and served as a barracks for the civilian workers who were employed by the contractor building the base.

At this stage of building, the base did not have an Enlisted Men's Club. Somehow, though, we did have a brig. It was located in the basement of the barracks and was quite modern. It had one large cell and one small cell, both enclosed with the latest system of steel bars. The cells even had electrically operated doors that clanged ominously when they were closed, as if this were planned for death row.

Since we were not in need of brig facilities at this time, it was decided that the space should be used for something else. It became the barber shop and the Enlisted Men's Club. The barber operated during working hours, and after working hours the duty storekeeper sold beer. The beer joint was in the large cell. We scrounged a couple of mess tables and some benches and used a shipping crate for a bar. The mess hall furnished us with a washtub full of ice every day and even gave us some cheese and crackers once in awhile. It wasn't the Ritz, but it was a nice snug harbor for us beer drinkers.

There was also an added advantage for the Master-at-Arms. When he declared beer drinking hours over at midnight, he and the storekeeper moved the stock of beer into the small cell. Then he gave us about ten minutes to clear the area, at which time he merely slammed the doors closed, and whoever wasn't out stayed there until 0600, when he let us out to go to work. At first, waking up in the brig was quite a shock, but after awhile we got used to it.

Being assigned as a regular Third Mech in a crew, I got to know a PBY intimately. Now and then we made a particularly rough landing and popped a few rivets in the bottom of the hull. This allowed tiny fountains of sea water to spring up in the bottom. One of my jobs on these occasions was to scramble from stem to stern with my head

32

in the bilges. I was equipped with a bundle of quarter-inch dowling sticks, sharpened like pencils. I stuck one of these in each hole where a rivet was missing to plug the hole. When we were beached, I retrieved all of my little sticks and the Metalsmiths replaced the rivets.

I got plenty of flight time operating out of Kodiak. Our Commanding Officer, Lieutenant Commander Russell, always had reasons why we should be getting out there on more flights. One reason was for gunnery practice: we had guns and we had to know how to use them. Another reason was training for bombing.

On gunnery practice days the uninitiated observer would have considered the preparations a bit unusual, but it was just another phase in our training. Our .50 caliber machine guns were designed to be loaded with magazines (cans) of sixty rounds. There were six cans for each of the guns. When we prepared for gunnery practice, the ordnancemen took belts of .50 caliber ammo and dipped the tips of the slugs into various colors of paint. With the paint still tacky, the ammo was loaded into the cans and they were placed in the planes. At the same time, one or two planes were being equipped with reels mounted in the tunnel hatch section. The reels were wound with about 200 yards of steel cable, which could be released through the tunnel hatch and rewound when desired. Sleeve-targets were then made ready alongside the reels. These sleeve-targets were made of light canvas and were about thirty feet long and three feet in diameter.

The original .50 caliber equipment in the early PBY's had been the old standard twin-spade-grip models with an open ring sight. But in the later model planes we had modified .50 caliber guns which featured a padded shoulder rest at the rear of the gun for the right shoulder, and a hand hold for the left hand attached part way down the barrel. The sight was an electric telescopic one which had a lighted "mil-ring" in it for sighting. The gunner's cheek rested atop the breech area with his right eye against the sight. The position of the right hand allowed for charging the gun and pulling the trigger. Most gunners agreed that the newer model gun could be held steadier than the old spade-grip models during firing.

Each gunner was assigned a certain color of paint-tipped ammo to use and these assignments were duly recorded. When the planes were airborne and had flown to a designated area for gunnery, the tow-plane reeled out a sleeve, and the gunners prepared to commence firing. Various kinds of runs were made, parallel, crosswise, high and low. Each gunner fired his designated color and quota of ammo as the various runs were made, and targets were changed by the tow-plane. When the exercise was completed, all planes returned to the base, and the sleeves were spread out to count the scores. If a slug hit the target, the colored paint left a ring around the hole. It was a sad day, indeed, when you had fired a couple of cans of ammo and your color didn't show up on any of the sleeves.

The "Pursuit Curve" was always a big point of discussion in conversations involving gunnery. The theory was that any fighter attacking a plane such as a PBY from the beam aft (which probably would be the most likely point of attack) had to follow a precise geometric curve in order to bring his guns on the target. Most people agreed that this was probably true. Our problem was to figure out just how to use this knowledge in order to make our own gunnery more effective. Nobody wanted to be solving complex mathematical problems when we were under attack, so the general opinion was to pick a point of aim a bit ahead of the attacker and let him fly into it. On blackboard diagrams it seemed to be the way to go. We got practically no experience even sighting at a pursuing fighter aircraft and never did have any way of really firing at such a target.

Ground training for bombing included exercises with the Norden bombsight for the pilots, who handled the bombardier's job. The training device was a ten-foot high tower affair built out of pipe. It was equipped with wheels and powered by an electric motor with a cord a couple of hundred feet long. The Norden bombsight was installed on a mounting pad atop the tower and the bombardier was seated in a position to operate the bombsight. A small plumb-bob was connected to the release mechanism near the bottom of the tower and was dropped on signal from the bombsight.

Although the Norden bombsight itself was a highly classified piece of equipment, we became accustomed to seeing the training device slowly moving across the hangar deck on a course to intercept a moving target. When the tower approached the target we stopped whatever activity we were engaged in and watched to see how successful the bombing run had been.

On flying days when we were practice bombing we loaded the planes up with 100 or 500 pound waterfill bombs. These were hollow metal cylinders with a bomb tail attached. After the bombs were filled with water, the ordnancemen loaded them on the plane bomb racks. Then the planes flew out and climbed to 8,000 or 10,000 feet, made drops on the bombing target and were scored by ground observers. Although our primary mission was patrol work, we needed to know how to attack an enemy installation as well as defend ourselves if attacked by an enemy.

As a result of our occasional flights out over the Bering Sea we became conscious that the coast of Russia was much closer than it was from mainland United States. It was not uncommon to sight Russian vessels in these northern waters. I recalled that the Russians were considered "bad guys" in the late thirties, but at the present time world politics had changed around to where the Russians were now "good guys." There was some sort of arrangement called "Lend Lease" being set up and the U.S. was considering "lending" Russia some war equipment.

One day in late September we were informed that we were to be visited by some Russian PBY's. The story was that they were on their way to Washington to negotiate some of the Lend Lease equipment for themselves. Since they were expected to arrive late in the afternoon, after normal secure time, the Duty Section was alerted to take care of beaching and servicing the Russian planes. After they had landed in Woman's Bay and were taxiing toward our ramp there was much speculation about whether or not our beaching gear would fit the Russian planes. We need not have been concerned, though, because the beaching gear fit as if their PBY's had been made in the U.S.A. They appeared to be identical.

When the Russian planes had been parked at the head of the ramp they began to unload. We were dumbfounded. Twenty-two guys unloaded from one plane and twenty-three from the other. We normally carried seven or eight. The Commanding Officer of N.A.S. Kodiak was on hand to greet the V.I.P.'s and show them to their quarters. The Mechs and Radiomen then turned to, servicing their aircraft with the assistance of our Duty Section. We had considerable difficulty because of the language problem. But we had Malinoski and Krinitski, who spoke Polish. Evidently there is enough similarity between Russian and Polish to allow for some understanding between the two. With much pointing and gesturing we managed to give them the assistance they needed.

The big crisis came when they wanted to gas up and informed us they needed

Formation of VP-42 PBY-5's over Alaska — August 1941

(National Archives)

VP-42 PBY-5 over Alaska glacier—August 1941

(National Archives)

Beach crew beaching PBY-5 at Woman's Bay, Kodiak

(Courtesy of Joseph Segar)

so many liters. Our truck measured in gallons and the metric system was something we boned up on for exams and promptly forgot thereafter. Finally someone came up with a Third Class Aviation Machinist's Mate course book which contained a conversion table. With a pad of paper and pencil we calculated the gallons-vs-liters problem, and the Russians did the same thing. The gas truck driver was a bit impatient with all of this, but we wouldn't start pumping gas until we and our visitors came up with the same answer.

An interesting thing we observed was that they used copper wire for safety wiring when working on their engines, and carefully straightened and reused each piece. Instead of the roll of steel wire we generally had in a tool box, they had a supply of copper wires of varying lengths and seemed overly careful to choose the proper length wire for the job at hand so there would be no waste. Because we used our steel wire which tended to break after one use, we always discarded any used wire and used new wire for each job.

Our Russian visitors seemed comfortable in our barracks as if they were accustomed to the same type of accommodations. But a difference became apparent when all hands prepared to observe taps. Of course we disrobed down to our regulation white Navy scivvies. But we were awed by the array of pink, yellow, blue and other colored scivvies the Russians wore. I am sure they were commenting on our uniformity while we were attempting to ignore the invasion of color. We had always heard that there was a certain dullness in the Russian way of life. That may have been true in some respects, but it certainly did not hold true in the underwear department.

The Russians departed the next morning. As they flew across the Gulf of Alaska toward Sitka they sighted a submarine and sent back a radio report on it. While we scrambled to get three PBY's launched, Base Communications was confirming that there were no U.S. submarines operating in the area. Although we spent several hours searching the area, we sighted nothing. As we were to find out later, submarines are allergic to being spotted from the air. If she were Japanese, as we suspected, she would be all the more determined to stay out of sight. Her lookouts must have been goofing off to have let the Russians sight them.

Before our tour of duty at Kodiak came to an end we made a few flights out to another new base, at Dutch Harbor. It wasn't much of a base yet, but there was enough there for some limited operation of PBY's.

In October 1941 we were back in Seattle with our training schedule still of prime concern. We took part in a really tragic bombing exercise that fall in the area of the San Juan Islands. It was a grim reminder that even "training" exercises can be deadly when things go wrong. We had three planes flying in "V" formation carrying out a mock attack on one of the islands, while an Army fighter outfit from Payne Field was acting as the defending unit. The bombing run was being made from an altitude of 5,000 feet while the Army P-36's came in from a higher altitude, made the intercept and carried out an attack on our PBY's, diving right through our formation.

A standard defense maneuver in this situation was to descend to an altitude of 100 feet as quickly as possible to deprive the attackers of the opportunity of making a run from below us. The P-36's made another run at us from above while we descended. By the time they made a third run we were right down on the water. All but one of the P-36's pulled out above us, but one came right through the formation a third time. There was no room to pull out and he crashed head on into the water.

The pilot's body was thrown clear and was observed floating in the wreckage

1940 view of N.A.S. Dutch Harbor site before construction of base   (National Archives)

Aerial view of N.A.S. Dutch Harbor in May 1942 (note sand spit)

(National Archives)

PBY in for 60-hour check at N.A.S. Seattle (note workstands)   (National Archives)

Army Air Corps Curtiss P-36

of his plane, so one of our planes landed and recovered the broken remains. When we returned to N.A.S. Sand Point an ambulance and group of medics quietly offloaded the dead pilot's body and proceeded to return it to his unit at Payne Field.

When we moved back to Seattle in October 1941, VP-41 had moved north to relieve us and were operating out of Sitka and Kodiak. One afternoon we were notified that Lieutenant Commander F. B. Johnson, the skipper of VP-41, was flying toward Seattle with the bottom of his plane bashed in. It seems he had hit a log on takeoff from Sitka but managed to get airborne. Because major repairs would be necessary he decided to come to Seattle, rather than try to get back in at Sitka.

When he appeared over Lake Washington practically our whole squadron assembled along the sea wall to watch him land. When he touched down he was on course right at our ramp and kept the power on and the hull on the step all the way in, trying to avoid having his plane sink in the middle of the lake. He finally cut the throttles just before he ran the plane right up on the ramp. The bottom had been in pretty bad shape from hitting the log, but hitting the concrete ramp finished it completely. After the hull settled into the shallow water the lifting sling was attached to the fittings on top of the wing and the "Mary Ann" (a crane on a barge) moved into position to lift the plane up so we could attach the beaching gear. The plane was then towed directly to the Assembly and Repair shop to have a new bottom installed.

In Seattle the VP-42 flying routine continued as always, but the move from Kodiak had made the liberty much better. The Music Hall alone had more bright lights than the whole town of Kodiak. And along with the good liberty I was happily assigned to a regular flight crew job.

I was Third Mech on a crew, which included another Third Class Mech named Walrath; Tom Harper was the Chief in charge. He never let up. If we weren't flying, we were working on the plane. Whenever we got the plane up to his expectations, he had us studying. He had waited sixteen years to make Chief, and he couldn't see anybody wasting time when some studying could result in an advancement in rating in the expanding Navy. Largely because of his unrelenting work on us and with us, Walrath and I made Second Class on 1 December 1941, less than a year after making Third Class. A few years before, that would have been impossible. But this was 1941, and we had a whole new ball game. My pay went to $72 a month. Because I was in a flight crew I received 50% extra, or $36. I felt extremely prosperous with a monthly paycheck of over $100. Plane Captain still seemed a long way off, but certainly I had gotten closer than seemed possible a year earlier.

On the day I made Second Class, the Imperial Japanese Navy was planning a real hardball game. On that day they made the final decision to attack Pearl Harbor. Vice Admiral Nagumo had his fleet at a predetermined position in the Pacific and was awaiting further orders. The next day he received the orders. It was in a Japanese code but it meant, "Proceed with the attack on Pearl Harbor." He set course for the launch point for his carrier aircraft.[1] Admiral Yamamoto studied his chart of Pearl Harbor back in Japan and began the days of waiting for the report of the attack. If it was successful, Japan might buy enough time to consolidate her advances in the Orient before the U.S. and England could stop her.

In Seattle, VP-42 continued training. When Sunday, 7 December, rolled around, I was on liberty in Seattle. A civilian friend and I were listening to the radio as we drove

---

[1] John Costello, *The Pacific War* (New York: Quill, 1981), 122.

along looking for a place to eat a late breakfast. Suddenly the program was being interrupted and the announcer was talking about Pearl Harbor being attacked. Pretty soon he was saying that all personnel of Patrol Wing Four should report back to their base immediately. Bill, who had spent an enlistment in the Navy, headed the car toward Sand Point and said, "We'd better get you back to the base right now."

When I got to the hangar, the Duty Officer was getting a flight crew together. The duty flight crews had already been launched and were searching off the coast. The Duty Section had a plane parked at the head of the ramp, loaded with depth charges and ready to launch. Within a few minutes we had a crew together, manned the plane and were launched. Since we were short-handed I went out as Second Mech. I guess nobody else thought much about it, but it struck me that promotions were coming my way about as fast as I could handle them. As we lifted off from Lake Washington and headed out to sea, we knew that this was no drill. We searched the ocean as we had never searched before, but at the end of ten hours we landed back on Lake Washington, having seen nothing and hoping we hadn't missed anything we should have seen.

Admiral Nagumo had long since sent his message of success to Admiral Yamamoto and had his fleet headed west at flank speed.

When the Beach Crew pulled us out of the water that night, I couldn't believe the scene. It was like a beehive. There was activity everywhere. The squadron had received orders to move operations to Tongue Point, Oregon, at the mouth of the Columbia River. Trucks were being loaded with all of our equipment. Planes were being fueled and worked on, and there were still some planes on the water, coming back from patrol and awaiting their turn to be beached.

The trucks spent half the night getting to Tongue Point. The next morning we took off for patrol from Seattle and landed in the Columbia River at the end of the day. Our skipper and a couple of other planes landed in Ucluelet, a bay up on the west coast of Vancouver Island. They operated from there for a few days, tended by *Teal*, but then had to move to Tongue Point because of the lack of maintenance support.

We flew out of Tongue Point for six weeks, until Consolidated Aircraft Company could equip us with PBY-5A's. They were the new amphibian model, with retractable wheels, so we could fly from the water or operate from runways.

Even though we still only had six planes, we needed more than six crews to handle the heavy flight schedule. When the new crews were formed, I was designated as the regular Second Mech on Chief Joe Romero's crew. Our Plane Commander was Lieutenant Norman Garton.

Within a few days after we started flying out of Tongue Point, we received orders to meet a convoy headed our way from Pearl Harbor. One of our planes was to meet the convoy about 700 miles out and start an anti-submarine patrol around it. We would continue the patrol until the convoy reached Bremerton.

The convoy turned out to be a group of ships damaged at Pearl Harbor but able to get underway to the States for repairs. It was good to see the *Tennessee* steaming along in the convoy. I had a good friend aboard.

During the first couple of weeks after 7 December there was a fear that a carrier task force was planning an attack on our Pacific Coast. Our planes were spread pitifully thin trying to patrol the whole west coast, but we had every one of them out there searching all day every day. Eventually the fear of carrier plane attack gave way to the evident danger from enemy submarines. The city of Santa Barbara, California, was actually shelled by a submarine and there were reports of similar shellings along the west coast of Canada.

Operations from Tongue Point really launched us into a wartime operation schedule. The urgency of the situation demanded as many planes as possible in the air every day. Our routine of taking off from the Columbia River before daylight every morning so that we could be 100 miles at sea at first light was risky. Our crash boats had to make sweeps of the take-off area constantly to assure that there were no logs or other floating debris because hitting even a small log on a take-off run could tear the whole bottom out of a PBY. It was always a big relief to take off or land without hitting a hidden obstacle.

A minor irritation in our operations at Tongue Point was the launch and recovery ramp. Periodically there would be a forty-knot wind roaring down the Columbia gorge and blowing onshore at our ramp. When that happened it was too risky trying to beach a plane and those planes waiting for recovery had to taxi around to the lee side of the point and moor at buoys until the wind subsided.

One of the final things a flight crew did when securing their plane after a flight was to tie the plane down. Each plane carried a set of tie-down lines plus a few other lengths of line for various uses in mooring boats or securing cargo. I had a habit of showing off my very limited roping skills when we were tossing the lines around in preparation for installing tie-downs. If the tractor was parked nearby I could usually toss a loop over the seat or perhaps catch a 55-gallon drum sitting alongside the ramp. I even had a little rope-spinning act. I could spin a large loop around myself, jump out of it, keep it spinning and sometimes end up by jumping back into the loop.

One of our pilots, a Chief AP named Lou Campbell, observed this routine a couple of times and finally commented that there had to be a showoff in every crowd. He mentally filed the scene away to be recalled when it could be of use to him.

One day when we came in from our patrol the onshore wind at the ramp was too strong for the beach crew to handle us and we were ordered to taxi around the point and moor to a buoy. One end of the mooring cable on a PBY is permanently attached to the keel under the water line. When the other end is shackled to a buoy and the plane swings free on the cable, the whole thing ends up under water. This arrangement requires the addition of an extra line from the buoy to the plane which is kept above the water line and is used for pulling the plane up to the buoy. This extra line is called a "Lizard."

Our guy handling the mooring duties up at the bow failed to secure the "Lizard" and lost it over the side. He had gotten the actual mooring cable attached to the buoy properly but had "lost the Lizard," which meant that he got it secured to the buoy but dropped the free end into the water as the plane swung back from the buoy.

Since the plane was securely moored and not in danger of going adrift, the engines were shut down and a boat came along side and hauled most of the crew ashore. Chief Campbell, myself and a radioman were left aboard as plane-watch. Lt. Garton's last word to us was to get busy and recover the Lizard.

Chief Campbell was not long in coming up with a super idea. "Freeman, here is going to be your chance to go down in history. Get back aft and grab one of those lines you are always throwing around. Climb up there on the bow and see if you can throw a loop over that buoy so we can pull ourselves up to it."

Somehow I had a feeling that my prowess with a lasso was not going to be equal to the task, but there was nothing to do but give it my best try. When I got up on the bow I knew I was in trouble. Even though we were on the lee side of the point there was a good twenty knots of wind blowing. The distance was about twenty-five feet and I think I could have handled that with a few tries—but not against the wind. With the Chief and the radioman sitting up on the wing cheering me on I made throw after throw. My loop got out ten feet and the wind stopped it. Down in the water it fell.

Finally the Chief said, "Freeman, you will never replace Will Rogers throwing a lasso. We'd better give up on that idea. Get ready to start the engines and we'll see if we can get the job done that way."

Gratefully I stowed the line I had been throwing and climbed up in the tower to help with starting the engines. Once they were running, the Chief gently eased us up to the buoy so that the radioman could probe around the water with a boathook; he soon recovered the Lizard. I had my chance for immortality and blew it. It was a long time before I did my rope-spinning act again.

With the fears of attack by the Japanese running high during those mid-December days there were self-appointed coast watchers all up and down the Pacific Coast. Our squadron received a steady stream of submarine sightings, and I think we checked out every one we got. On Christmas Day, our crew had been out on patrol starting at dawn. We came back in about the middle of the afternoon and headed for the mess hall for Christmas dinner, a little late but nevertheless ready to enjoy it. We had just sat down to dig in when a messenger came running in with the word that we were to report back to our plane on the double.

Lieutenant Garton was already in the cockpit when we arrived at the ramp. I got aboard, climbed up in the engineer's tower and reported, "Ready to start engines, sir." We had no more than gotten them running than the beach crew was launching us. The rule was that the cylinder head temperatures should be at least 100 degrees for launching and 200 degrees for takeoff. The beaching gear was barely clear of the plane when Mr. Garton called on the intercom, "Ready for takeoff."

I came back with, "We barely have a hundred degrees cylinder head temperature, sir."

As we went to full throttle, he answered, "Fine. They'll be a lot hotter when I pour the coal on."

Lieutenant Garton had a reputation for raising the wingtip floats quicker than anybody else in the squadron. The signal system between the cockpit and flight engineer's station in the tower was a series of lights. When the pilot wanted the floats raised he switched the "up floats" light switch and a corresponding light flashed on in the tower so the mech knew when to hit the "raise floats" switch. When you flew with Mr. Garton you learned in a hurry that as soon as the engines reached full RPM you got a signal to raise the floats.

It didn't take a genius to realize that Lt. Garton was more in a hurry than usual on this takeoff, so I had my finger on the switch before he got to full power. Sure enough, the "up floats" light flashed on and I started the floats up. Before we got up enough speed to have aileron control we had a few anxious moments trying to avoid dropping a wingtip in the water, but finally we smoothed out and made our takeoff—possibly in record time. And we went looking for another submarine that wasn't there.

Christmas dinner was a bit stale when we got back. But some patriotic soul out there had the satisfaction of knowing that a submarine report brought fast action from Tongue Point.

In the middle of January 1942, the Consolidated factory had finally built enough PBY-5A's to start equipping our squadron. We flew our PBY-5's to N.A.S. Alameda and traded them for 12 new planes. On our way north we stopped at Seattle for a bit of training in the new planes.

During training we found that the added weight of the landing gear slowed us down a bit in flight, and the bulk of the main wheels in their wheel wells on either side of the hull slowed us down for water takeoffs. But nobody ever claimed any speed records for PBY's anyway. I always liked the story one of our pilots told about flying over Puget Sound one day when there was a 75-80 knot wind blowing. He headed dead into the wind and throttled back until his airspeed dropped below 75 and finally he was actually making negative ground speed. Not many planes can fly backward.

By the end of January our one-week training period was over. We loaded up and headed north for Alaska with ten new PBY-5A's. Although we had actually been assigned twelve planes, we had to leave two in Seattle so that new pilots could train in them before coming north. VP-41 moved from Kodiak to Tongue Point, taking over our patrols there and waiting to be equipped with PBY-5A's. As soon as they were equipped with their new planes they would also be returning to Kodiak.

Chapter **4**

VP-42 War Patrols
Out of Kodiak

WINTER OPERATIONS IN KODIAK were no picnic. It gets cold and it snows. It doesn't get so cold as North Dakota and there's less snow, but it is definitely wintertime. At Kodiak's latitude the winter days are short, with sunrise about 0900 and sunset about 1500. There was a hangar but it was not large enough to hold all of our planes. We learned to expect all hands to be called out almost every day to clear snow off the planes parked outside and also from the rest of the parking area. But once we got the snow cleared so we could launch our planes, there was pretty good flying weather.

Kodiak didn't have a runway yet but at least our PBY-5A's didn't require a Beach Crew wading around in the frigid waters of Woman's Bay. It was not uncommon to see the bay covered with a coating of ice. The amphibian options made quite a change in both our beaching and launching procedures. When we landed on the water, we merely lowered the landing gear and proceeded to taxi right up the ramp to a parking spot. When launching, we taxied down the ramp, raised the wheels, and were ready for takeoff from the water. Since wartime activities continued to expand the base at Kodiak, a runway became a necessity and eventually a good runway was built. But in the winter of 1941-42 we had to do without it. As bases gradually were built out to the west, we made good use of amphibious options. Some of the runways were pretty hairy for landing, but we learned to use them. And of course in the island-hopping operations we were destined to pursue, there was always a need for our Seaplane Tenders.

Kodiak did not have the greatest list of tourist attractions. It had been a fishing village for many years and only recently had been invaded by a crowd of contractor hands working on the new Navy Base. There was a stuffed Kodiak bear at the bank, with a washtub alongside it, showing the mammoth size of the bear's head. Once you had seen this attraction, that was about it for sightseeing. There were several bars which served a good selection of drinks and sold liquor by the bottle if you wanted it. When you had paid your respects to the bear, the next stop was a bar.

Enlisted men's drinking was limited on the base to beer, so we were always scheming to get a bottle of hard liquor past the Marine sentries who guarded the gate through which we had to pass going to and from Kodiak. At night a large floodlamp lighted about a hundred-foot circle—fifty feet on each side of the gate. One night two of us came up with an idea to outwit the Marines.

We bought a fifth of I.W. Harper in Kodiak and headed back to the base. When we were approaching the gate we stopped well out of the circle of the floodlamp. We

VP-42 personnel servicing PBY-5A at Kodiak—February 1942

(National Archives)

VP-42 Line Crew tying down PBY-5A at Kodiak—February 1942

VP-42 Winter operations at Kodiak—February 1942

(National Archives)

VP-42 PBY-5A dug out of the snow and ready to test the nose wheel at Kodiak — Winter 1942

(National Archives)

Comedian Joe E. Brown came to Kodiak to entertain us. L-R: Lt. Comdr. Russell, Joe E. Brown, Col. Charles Corlett.

(National Archives)

Arrival of PatWing Four at Kodiak, 18 April 1942. L-R: Comdr. L. E. Gehres, Lt. Perkins, Lt.Cmdr. Russell, Army Officer.
(National Archives)

Miller and Rasche stand VP-42 Gun Watch at Kodiak—February 1942

(National Archives)

Clearing the ice at Kodiak. Preparing to beach a PBY-5— Winter 1942

(National Archives)

Beaching PBY-5 amid floating ice at Kodiak—Winter 1942

(National Archives)

tied a two-hundred foot length of twine to the neck of the bottle and put the bottle down on the gravel road. Then we nonchalantly walked to the gate, paying out the twine behind us. The Marine passed us on through, and we strolled past the circle of light. When we got to the end of our twine, we were safely in the dark. Then we stopped and began to pull our bottle through the gate. The Marine was inside his little sentry house when we started the operation, and all was going well. Maybe he heard the scraping in the gravel, maybe it was something else, but before our bottle got to the gate he stepped outside. Our twine was too close to the sentry house, and he ended up standing on it. When you have a caper like this going, you can't wait all night for a Marine to move his foot. After about two minutes of waiting, we bailed out, leaving poor old I.W. Harper on the cold, cold ground. Marines are like that. They take advantage of poor, enterprising sailors.

Not long after our return to Kodiak, there was a shuffling of flight crew personnel. With ten planes to man and a heavy flight schedule to handle, more crews were needed.

Besides our officers, who were all pilots, we had a number of enlisted pilots. They had received the same training as the officers but, whereas the officers were designated "Naval Aviators," the enlisted pilots were designated "Naval Aviation Pilots." Even though they might wear the rating badge of Aviation Machinist Mate or Radioman, they wore wings and were generally known as "AP's." (Later, the Navy instituted the actual rating of AP.) Not long after the war started many of the AP's became Commissioned Officers. Some of them had years of flying experience but, as enlisted men, were restricted from becoming Patrol Plane Commanders. As soon as they were commissioned several of them were immediately designated as Plane Commanders. That provided some extra command pilots for new crews.

We had not gotten many new personnel since the war started, and most of the new enlisted people were unrated; they had no training in a flight crew. A few of the Chiefs were promoted to commissioned officer status and others were assigned to ground jobs in shops. When all of the reassignments had been completed, the assignment lists were posted and there were several new flight crews. Our crew was one of them.

I was made Plane Captain; Dick Babbitt (like me, from North Dakota) was Second Mech; and Bill Stallings (South Carolina) was Third Mech. Bud Townsend (Montana) was our First Radioman, and Ed Summers (Texas) was Second Radioman. Because of a shortage of pilots, we had about a half dozen enlisted men of various rates who had been trained in navigation. One of these guys, Pierson (Minnesota), was assigned to our crew as Navigator. Lieutenant W. M. Dickey (Texas) was our Plane Commander. The co-pilot for our crew seemed to change almost every flight. There were new Ensigns checking into the squadron and they weren't assigned as permanent crew members until they had been flying awhile.

There it was! "Freeman, E. A., AMM2c.....Plane Captain." One year earlier I wouldn't have dreamed that it could happen. The first feelings of exhilaration gave way to doubt and fear. My next thought was, "What in hell do I do now?" All I could think of was that our crew didn't even have a tool box, then—hell, we didn't even have a plane!

Looking further down the list I saw Birchman's name, also listed as Plane Captain on another new crew. When I voiced my thoughts to him he said he thought it might be a good idea to get together with our Plane Commanders for some answers.

Back—Cola, Ens. Burklow, Lt.(jg) McFarland, Lt.(jg) Yund, Reeves; front—Freeman, Pierson, Townsend, Taylor

(National Archives)

After three weeks at Atka and Adak: Rear—Lt.(jg) McFarland, Freeman, Ens. Burklow, Reeves, Lt.(jg)Yund; front—Taylor, Townsend, Cola, Pierson (National Archives)

**Freeman, E. A., AMM2c:
At Oakland to install radar**
(Freeman Collection)

Lt. W. M. Dickey at Umnak, 1942
(Freeman Collection)

**Freeman back at work in the
Aleutians** (Freeman Collection)

Fueling from USS *Williamson*, mid-May, 1942: 1. Lt. Dickey, 2. Townsend, 3. Cornie, 4. Stallings, 5. Freeman, 6. Kinney, 7. Segar
(Courtesy of Joseph Segar)

So I went looking for Lieutenant Dickey.

He spotted me coming across the hangar and we met right in the middle of the hangar deck. I saluted and he saluted back and then stuck out his hand. As we shook hands he said, "It looks like we'll be doing a lot of flying together." Then he explained that we would be outfitted with what we needed and that a plane would be assigned when we were scheduled to fly. The old idea of each crew being assigned to a certain plane was being modified. Operations would try to assign us to the same plane but at times we would have to go in whatever was available.

I don't know how Lt. Dickey felt when we prepared for our first flight together, but I was nervous. I had always had some Chief watching over me, but now the load had been shifted to me. Lt. Dickey was in his thirties, but not one of the enlisted members of the crew was over twenty-two. A mere fourteen months earlier most of us had been in the beach crew, with only a dim idea of why our training seemed to be so urgent.

We were accustomed to seeing Chiefs with sixteen or eighteen years of service as Plane Captains, and First Class Petty Officers with at least twelve years in the Navy as Second Mechs. They had hundreds or even thousands of hours of flight experience. They had had lots of peacetime years to make their share of mistakes. And their flying experience had been in less dangerous times when nobody was going to be shooting at them.

Now the skipper had no choice but to put crews together who were just learning their trade. All of us were ready and willing and hopefully able. But none of us had more than 200-400 hours of flying experience. Many of the older hands shook their heads when they read the list of new crews posted on the bulletin board.

We all knew we were past the stage of counting those colored bullet holes in canvas sleeves and filling waterfill bombs. We had all aspired to the positions to which we were now assigned, but we had not expected our aspirations to be fulfilled so suddenly. It was final exam time.

The Patrol Plane Commander's position was similar to that of the Captain of a ship. He had complete command of his plane and was answerable for all that went on. His skill as a pilot had been verified through various stages of proficiency checks and finally he was designated as "PPC." Although the Plane Commander's judgment was observed throughout his training, it might have been more difficult to be as sure of his judgment as of his flying skill. Lack of good judgment could have tragic results at times.

In late April 1942 the Wing Commander, Captain L. E. Gehres, visited Dutch Harbor to observe the operations of our three-plane detachment at that location. On 27 April our skipper, Lieutenant Commander Russell, and Captain Gehres made an early morning check on the weather and determined that severe icing conditions existed and scheduled operations should be delayed until the weather improved. At the Officers' Mess they were discussing the possibility of the Wing Commander's flying in one of the planes when they heard the unmistakable sound of PBY engines winding up for takeoff. Alarmed at the idea of someone ignoring the hazardous weather conditions, they took off at a run for the ramp. As they came in view of the harbor they saw the PBY's spray as it began its takeoff run.

Ensign Andy Smith was following the usual takeoff course, toward the harbor mouth. A long arcing sandspit protruded from the left shore. Ice buildup on the wing soon began to affect the PBY's performance. The plane finally got up on the step and lifted off the water—only to settle back down again. This was repeated several times, and each time the plane became airborne the slight cross wind carried it in the direction of the sandspit. Still the struggling PBY roared on. Finally it was headed right for the sandspit and became airborne in an apparent attempt to stay aloft and clear the narrow bit of land. The attempt failed. When the plane crashed to the ground the horrible cloud of black smoke told the tale of the tragedy unfolding.

The crash site was over a mile from the ramp, with no access road. Lieutenant Commander Russell climbed into another PBY at the head of the ramp, fired up the engines, rolled into the water and began taxiing on the step toward the scene. Captain Gehres took off at a run along the beach, headed for the cloud of smoke. The skipper got there first, with Captain Gehres puffing onto the scene a short time later.

The imminent danger of bombs exploding in the heat was soon neutralized when the men accompanying the skipper succeeded in getting lines on the bombs and dragging them away from the wreck. Six members of the crew, including Ensign Smith, were already dead, but two men were rescued from the flaming wreckage. With only a minimum of fire-fighting equipment available, there was very little anybody could do about extinguishing the fire. The plane became a charred mass on the sand spit.

Our crew, as it was on the flight schedule about every other day, had a sort of on-the-job training. VP-42 had an assigned area to patrol and all crews took their turns flying the various sectors, observing and reporting all ship movements. At this time we were supposedly dealing with friendly vessels. However, we never assumed they were friendly until they were proven so. Our experience on a day in mid-February 1942 was typical.

"Port waist reporting a speck on the horizon dead on the port beam." I had watched it for a half minute, making sure the speck was on the horizon rather than the plexiglass blister.

In a moment Lt. Dickey answered, "I've got it. Navigator, we are making a turn to port. Waist gunners open your blisters and rig out the guns. Man the bow gun."

The reporting and the orders which followed became standard procedure. And in sixty seconds, "Port gun rigged and ready." "Starboard gun rigged and ready." "Bow gun rigged and ready." The reports came in quick order from all stations. Stallings had the starboard gun, I was on the port, and Ed Summers was up in the bow. Babbitt was in the tower, Pierson was navigating and Townsend was on the radio and busily double-checking the recognition signals we would be using. Everybody perked up when we spotted something and headed in to check it out. It was a welcome break. From our altitude, 4,000 feet, the horizon probably was twenty-five miles away, so we would have a few minutes to prepare for our encounter.

As we closed in we could see that the vessel was a surface ship rather than a submarine and she was headed our way with a "bone in her teeth." The bow wave of a ship travelling at high speed resembles a bone being carried in a dog's mouth when viewed head-on. This guy was in a hurry.

"Looks like it might be the *Williamson*. She must be making thirty knots," was Lt. Dickey's guess.

"If she's making thirty knots it can't be the *Williamson*," I answered. "We damned near blew up the boilers trying to get to twenty-eight on a speed run last summer."

The profile, head on, did look like those old tin cans. When we closed in and got a side view there were two stacks. She turned out to be the *Reid*, one of the destroyers working out of Kodiak.

Sand Point, Alaska, in the Shumagin Islands

(National Archives)

Another fueling operation from USS *Williamson* at Sand Point

(National Archives)

"Must be in a hurry to get back to Kodiak for liberty to night," said Lt. Dickey. "I didn't know you had duty on the *Williamson*, Freeman. You are liable to be seeing some of your old shipmates one of these days."

Summers came back in the waist and blinked a recognition signal to the ship and they answered. We circled them once and went back to our regular search.

"You can secure all guns and close the blisters. Pierson, give me a heading to our original turning point."

We worked a little bit better as a crew on every flight and we talked about our flight performance when we weren't flying. It was a kind of crash course, but at the end of our six weeks of training, we were doing a creditable job as a crew. Most of the time we flew in plane number 42-P-12.

As Plane Captain and senior enlisted man in the crew, I had to make sure all hands knew when we had to fly and to which plane we were assigned. I had to make up the "Yellow Sheet," the itemized inspection form which was our guide for pre-flighting the aircraft. Each item had to be inspected and checked off, and the sheet finally signed by the Plane Commander. In flight I had the responsibility of assigning members of the crew to the various stations and rotating the watches during long patrols.

When we needed flight rations, I had to see that an order was turned in and that the groceries were on board before we launched. Curiously, although we never received any training in cooking, there was an assumption that any member of a flight crew could cook. At best this was only marginally true. In some cases the cuisine was pretty strange. Standard equipment included a coffee pot, two two-quart pans, one four-quart pan, a ten-inch frying pan and an assortment of plates, cups and silverware. Everybody took a turn. Some improved, some didn't. Hardly a complaint was ever heard, but nobody had the parental disrespect to compare our inflight meals with his mother's cooking.

At the end of a flight we had to report any problems to our maintenance department. They assigned people to help us take care of the "gripes" written up on the final section of the "Yellow Sheet." On advance base operations we pretty much took care of all of our maintenance ourselves. When you have to fly them and fix them too, the schedule can get to be pretty busy.

Our first advance base operation came about the first week in March in the Shumagin Islands, a small group of islands to the southwest of Kodiak and south of the Alaska Peninsula. We were to operate from the *Williamson*, which was anchored in a bay out there; she had a seadrome in place and was ready to take care of our service needs. By advancing our operation this far out, we could cover many more miles toward Japan on our patrols. There was a suspicion that the Japanese were preparing to launch some kind of move toward the Aleutians and the mainland of Alaska.

En route to the Shumagins we were to fly a search some 300 miles out to sea and return to the peninsula before joining two of our other planes who were to operate from *Williamson*. The weather was really bad, so we had trouble fixing our location at the end of our search. The charts we had didn't have much of any detail on the area, and we couldn't raise *Williamson* on the radio, so something had to be done to find out where we were. With the ceiling so low it was dangerous to go flying around and around in a mountainous area, hoping to spot our ship. Rather than take a chance of running into a mountain or wasting fuel, Lt. Dickey spotted a likely-looking bay, and we headed in for a landing.

There was a fairly stiff wind blowing, so we made a full stall landing. (In a rough sea the pilot gets down almost on the wave tops and gradually throttles back until the plane stalls out and drops on top of a wave.) With a promising-looking beach as our destination we started taxiing. I got up on the bow of the plane with a boathook and probed for bottom as we moved along. When I felt bottom it seemed firm enough and smooth enough to put the wheels down for an attempt at taxiing up on the beach.

When the wheels touched bottom, Lt. Dickey added enough power to pull us along, and in a minute or so we were parked high and dry on the beach. After tying the wings down to some big logs which had washed ashore, we continued to try to raise *Williamson* on the radio.

That didn't work at all, but wonder of wonders, a YP (Yard Patrol) boat from Kodiak pulled into our little bay to get out of the weather. When Lt. Dickey got up on top of the wing and asked them by semaphore where we were, we received no response. But in a couple of minutes they launched a small boat and a couple of guys proceeded to join our little beach party. They showed us exactly where we were. It turned out that we were right at the foot of Pavlof Volcano. With the ceiling so low we couldn't see whether the terrain was 800 or 8,000 feet high. Pavlof is almost 9,000 feet.

We were actually within about forty miles of our ship. With our present location determined, we thanked the YP boat folks and proceeded to try to get our plane back in the water. Hauling that monster around 180 degrees in the sand took all hands except the plane commander. He was applying full power to the port engine and kicking full right rudder to assist with the turning job. The rest of us were hauling on a line attached to the tail towing ring in a scene reminiscent of the old sailing ship days. Finally we got the nose headed back out toward the water, got all hands loaded back aboard, and were able to·taxi out until we were waterborne and could raise the landing gear. Then we took off and flew along under the soup to our anchorage with *Williamson*.

When we operated from a tender and left the plane tied up to a buoy, part of the crew went aboard the ship, but we always kept a crew of at least three aboard the plane. This plane-guard crew consisted of a pilot, a radioman and a mech. If a sudden storm came up or other emergency arose, there were enough people to get the engines started and keep the plane from going adrift. The night hours were divided into watches so there was always at least one person awake.

Working on the engines when the plane was tied up to a buoy was a real adventure. We were equipped with small workstands which could be hung from the leading edge of the wing and hooked to the speed-ring, or forward part of the cowling. The workstand itself, once rigged, was about a foot wide and five feet long. The idea was to hang one of these stands in place and then climb down over the leading edge of the wing, try to open the cowling around the engine, keep from dropping anything in the water, and finally get to the engine. If you dropped a tool, it was just one more addition to Davy Jones' tool box.

Our port engine didn't quite come up to full power on take-off one morning, and I decided to take a look at it when we returned from our patrol that afternoon. We were tied up to a buoy a few hundred yards from the ship. I got out the workstand and rigged it alongside the engine. Whenever we did anything around a seaplane tied up to a buoy, we wore our Mae-West life vests. They kind of got in our way sometimes, but we felt naked without them. These things can be inflated by blowing through a rubber hose, or in an emergency they can be inflated by pulling on a toggle which releases a little CO_2 bottle which does the inflating in an instant.

I proceeded to lay out some tools on the wing, where I would be able to reach them from the workstand, and started to climb down over the leading edge of the wing. Just about the time I was getting both feet on the stand, I got hung up with my Mae-West. To get free I jerked on it. The CO_2 toggle had caught in the rigging, and my jerk discharged the bottle. There is a whistling sound when this thing is discharged and it surprised me. I took a step backward—into thin air—and was paddling around the water. Boy, was it cold.

I paddled around to the waist hatch to try to get back in the plane. We never had the ladder out when we were at a buoy, so Summers was trying to help me climb in the hatch. I had almost made it when I slipped and fell back into the water and we started all over again. By the time we succeeded I was getting pretty numb. Summers signalled the ship to send a boat out for me, and they had one alongside in a few minutes.

When we finally got to the ship, I was shaking so badly I could hardly get up the ladder. They took me to sick bay, where a corpsman sized up the situation. His prescription was simple. He poured out about a tumbler full of brandy and said, "Here, drink this." I grabbed it with both hands and started drinking. The prescription worked. In a minute or so I started to feel warm somewhere around my stomach. As the warmth moved up my body, I managed to stop shaking. In ten minutes' time I was joking with the corpsman. Maybe I was a little jollier than the occasion called for, but he finally pronounced me cured and locked up the bottle. Now that's a first-class party-pooper.

Our flight operations were not very complicated. Lieutenant Dickey received the word on our assigned sector, the crew manned the plane and away we went. The members of the crew couldn't stray very far; they were aboard either the plane or the ship. Those coming from the ship were in charge of getting our grocery order for the day and whatever other supplies we needed from the ship. The plane-watch crew got the plane ready to go. When the boat arrived at the plane, they made a slow trip around it for a pre-flight inspection before the crew got aboard. Then we manned our stations, fired up the engines, took off and headed in the general direction of Japan.

Although we usually were assigned specific patrol or reconnaissance flights, it was always assumed that we were also searching for submarines along the way. Searching for submarines was like looking for the proverbial needle in a haystack. Trying to spot a submarine periscope sticking up in the North Pacific or Bering Sea was a tiring and frustrating experience. Sometimes we picked up a speck on the horizon indicating a vessel on the surface fifteen miles away, but by the time we arrived at the spot there was nothing to be seen. Our quarry had spotted us and had long since disappeared.

Our own submarines moved in and out of the base at Dutch Harbor at regular intervals and we might see one on the surface if we happened to be flying near the mouth of the harbor when he was entering or departing. But outside the harbor we could be sure he would be submerged and we would never spot him. Some of our submarines hung around Kiska harbor; others were out along the Aleutians looking for Japanese ships; sometimes they ranged all the way over to Japan hunting for targets. If U.S. submarines were operating where we were searching, our plane commander was furnished with a grid-chart showing where they were and what their movements would be. We always assumed they saw us before we saw them, and they had a signalling device with which they could fire colored flares to identify themselves so we

U.S. submarine passing through Unalaska Ferry Channel—May 1942

(National Archives)

wouldn't be dropping depth charges on them.

When we sighted a periscope cutting through the water, leaving its little telltale wake, we immediately started a depth-charge run on it, assuming that if it was U.S., he would fire a flare to let us know who he was. If we saw green smoke or red smoke or whatever color was proper for the particular time of day, we made our pass over the periscope without dropping our depth charges. But if no signal came up, we would blow a couple of holes in the ocean.

If we were on our way back to our base after a long patrol, we sometimes were running low on fuel and could not spend much time trying to search for or chase down a suspected sub. Then we sent an urgent report in and the command people made a decision on what to do next.[1]

Our first attack run had to be quick and accurate. There wouldn't be a second chance because by the time we could get back around for another run the target would be long gone. A few times we recognized our target as a large fish as we closed in on it and saved our depth charges. I suspect we blew up a couple of fish, possibly whales, along the way, but I like to think we shook up a few Japanese submarine sailors too.

Day after day the searching continued. We spent long hours looking at the ocean, hoping to spot any enemy movement and get a report back to the people who made the decision on what to do about it. We didn't do any high-altitude flying, often staying below 1000 feet for hours at a time. To see the water, we had to stay below the overcast or fog. And there always seemed to be overcast and/or fog. We had an oxygen system in our planes, but because of the nature of our operations we didn't even check to see if it was working properly. We just didn't get high enough to need it.

We carried very little personal gear with us. We had some spare scivvies and socks and an extra shirt or two and practically lived in our fleece-lined flight suits. Our laundry arrangements usually consisted of obtaining a bucket of water and some soap when we got aboard a ship, scrubbing the few dirty garments we had, and hoping we could get them dry before we were called away for our next patrol flight. Such was the life of PBY aircrewmen in the Aleutians.

---

[1]Here is a typical entry from the VP-42 War Diary, for 7 July 1942: "Lieut. Dickey returning from search reported possible submarine at 57°00 N, 163°55 W. Lieut.(jg) Lindgren departed in search of submarine. Results were negative" (Part 2: 9).

Chapter 5

Attack on Dutch Harbor, Kiska Occupation

IN APRIL 1942 VP-42 RECEIVED ORDERS to start sending one or two planes at a time down to the Naval Air Station at Alameda, California to have radar installed. Radar was supposed to enable us to look through fog and even see at night. Most of us had never heard of radar, which was invented by the English. At this point the United States was building and installing it as fast as possible. We departed on our hurry-up trip to N.A.S. Alameda for our radar installation, planning quick refueling stops at Kodiak and Seattle before spending three days at Alameda getting our new equipment.

When we were halfway between Kodiak and Seattle, we received a message telling us that Seattle was socked in and we should look for an alternate base along the coast of Canada. The nearest Canadian base was Aliford Bay, which was reporting clear weather. They granted us permission to come in and land at their base, so we headed on in. We found Aliford Bay to be a medium-sized seaplane base from which the Canadians were flying their Stranner seaplanes, evidently doing the same type of patrol work we did. As soon as we had tied up to a buoy, they had a service boat alongside ready to take us ashore.

We could not have asked for more gracious hosts. After an excellent dinner in their mess, the beer bar opened for business. Let nobody ever say that those Canadian Air Force guys do not know how to throw a party. They sang songs which were definitely not of the Sunday School variety and they loudly proclaimed stories which could never be repeated in the presence of one's mother. In the morning we got an all-clear message from Seattle and after a fine breakfast manned our plane and continued on our trip to Alameda.

After the radar equipment had been installed, Townsend and Summers got a crash course on how to operate it. Lt. Dickey sat in on these sessions so he would know how the equipment should perform. We had just time for a night's liberty in San Francisco and Oakland, and then we headed out for the Aleutians again.

Although there were weather reports from patrol aircraft out along the Aleutian chain, the reports were irregular and not as complete as was desired. Since the weather pattern was from west to east it was valuable to know what was happening weather-wise to the west. In the middle of May 1942 a ten-man weather team was put ashore on Kiska from one of our ships to establish a weather station and regularly report accurate weather observations from the western area of the Aleutians.

Not long afterward two VP-42 PBY's, piloted by Lieutenant Commander Russell and Ensign Coleman, unintentionally spent a few storm-tossed days in Kiska harbor

72

and were tended by *Williamson*, then by *Casco*, which had arrived with supplies for the weather station personnel. The two planes' stay in Kiska harbor came about as a result of extra-curricular activities assigned to our squadron.

Early in May Lieutenant Commander Russell, our skipper, had received word that Commander Paul Foster was to visit our area and was to be taken on an extended tour of the Alaska area as a personal observer for President Roosevelt. The skipper had flown to Sitka to meet Commander Foster and then spent several days visiting such places as Annette and Yakutat and finally flying to Elmendorf Field at Anchorage, where the party made a call on General Buckner, the Alaska Defense Commander.

While the party was at Anchorage word was received that one of our planes piloted by Lt. Ed Winters had failed to return from a patrol. Lieutenant Commander Russell departed from Elmendorf immediately, flying to Dutch Harbor to join in the extended search for the missing plane. After several days the search had to be given up, and the skipper was still at Dutch Harbor when Ensign Sammy Coleman flew in from Kodiak bringing General Buckner and Commander Foster. The two VIP's wanted to fly out along the entire Aleutian chain to get a first-hand look at the islands all the way to Attu. Even though General Buckner was reminded that all indications were that the Japanese were going to make a move into the Aleutians in the near future and it might not be wise for him to go along on the trip, he had his mind made up and so continued on west with the rest of the observer party. Ensign Coleman and Lieutenant Commander Russell piloted the two PBY's on the long flight to Attu.

Although the weather cooperated almost all the way, allowing close visual observation of the islands, it finally turned bad halfway between Kiska and Attu and the two PBY's had to turn around and return to Kiska harbor where *Williamson* was on station to service them. It was hoped the next day's weather would allow the party to complete their mission. That night the weather deteriorated into a howling Aleutian storm and changed the mission into one of survival rather than observation. After two days of being beaten and battered by the elements General Buckner and Commander Foster agreed to go aboard the *Williamson* and return to Dutch Harbor.

Casco steamed into Kiska harbor on the third day of the storm with personnel, equipment and provisions for the weather station. *Casco's* skipper was kind enough to agree to stay on the scene until the weather abated and the bedraggled PBY's could take off and get out of there. The two PBY's finally got off on the morning of the fifth day and returned to Dutch Harbor.[1]

By late May we were flying regularly out of Dutch Harbor. We combed the Bering Sea and the northern Pacific Ocean. We got to look at a lot of water when we spent ten hours a day searching. The new radar worked great. Townsend and Summers became more proficient with every flight. We couldn't find any Japanese ships, but we

---

[1]A bit over three years later it transpired that Russell (by then a Commander) was part of a survey party which went into Tokyo in the days immediately after the Japanese surrender in August 1945. The party questioned Japanese personnel and examined whatever documents they could find relating to the war. Commander Russell discovered photos and documents which revealed that a Japanese ship had been nosing around Kiska and Adak within days of his own storm-tossed sojourn in Kiska harbor. As had happened many times during the PBY's adventurous days in the Aleutians, the weather had prevented the two opponents from meeting each other.

The account of General Buckner and Commander Foster's being flown on the observation trip around mainland Alaska and the Aleutians is from a letter from Admiral James S. Russell, USN (Ret) to the author, dated 20 May 1991.

Diagram of day's flight, searching for missing PBY—14 May 1942 (Lt. Winters and crew)

(National Archives)

AIRCRAFT PLOTTING SHEET

MERCATOR PROJECTION   1° Lat. = 3 inches at mid latitude

Plotting Chart of search plan for missing PBY—14 May 1942 (Lt. Winters and crew)

(National Archives)

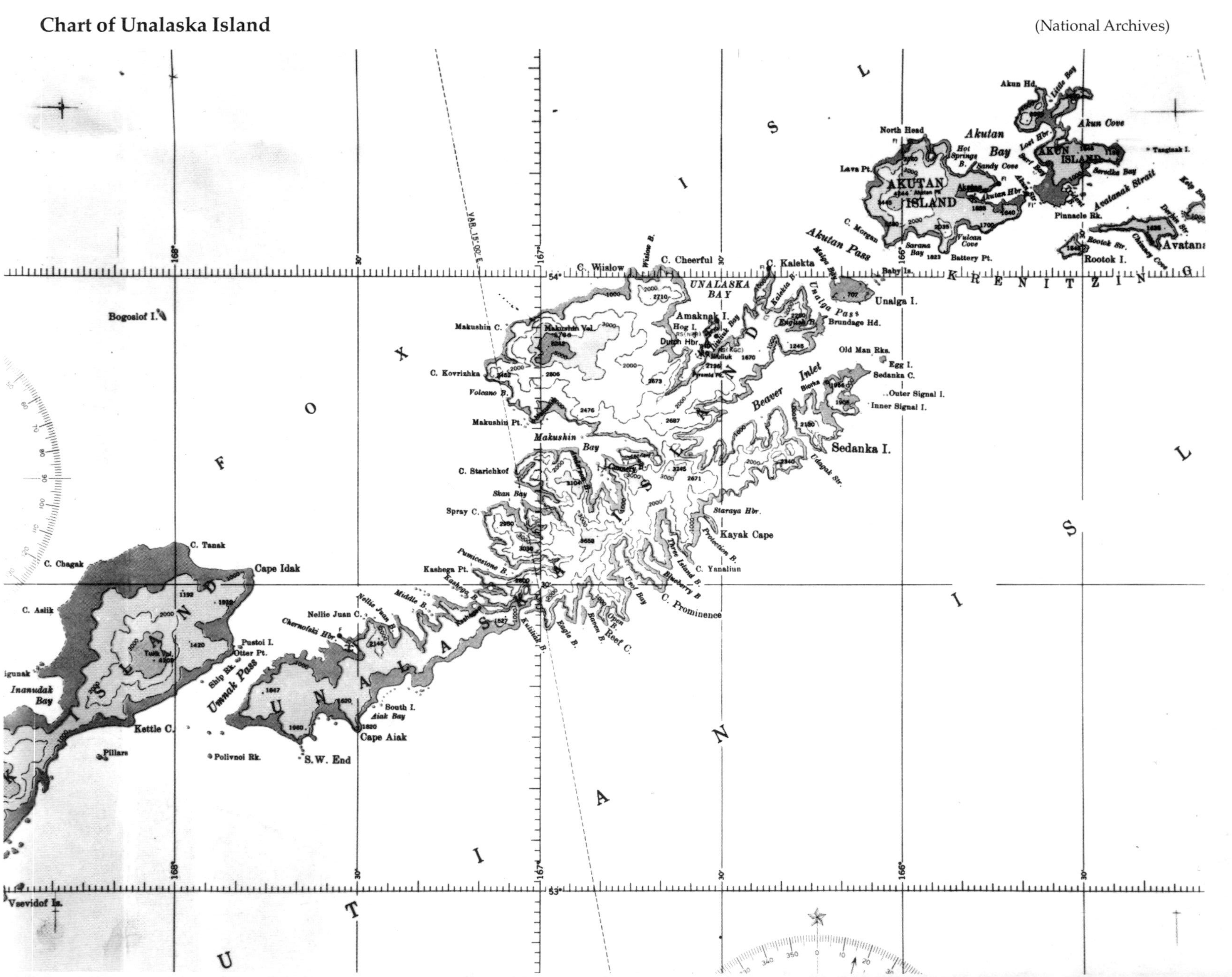

AKUTAN ISLAND
AKUN ISLAND
Akutan Bay
Akun Cove
Akun Hd.
North Head
Lava Pt.
C. Morgan
Hot Springs B.
Sandy Cove
Vulcan Cove
Sarana Bay
Battery Pt.
Pinnacle Rk.
Tanginak I.
Avatanak Strait
Rootok I.
Avatanak
Egg Bay
Akutan Pass
KRENITZIN ISLANDS
Baby Is.
Unalga I.
Unalga Pass
C. Kalekta
C. Cheerful
C. Wislow
Wislow B.
UNALASKA BAY
Amaknak I.
Hog I.
Dutch Hbr.
Iliuliuk
English B.
Brundage Hd.
Old Man Rks.
Egg I.
Sedanka C.
Outer Signal I.
Inner Signal I.
Sedanka I.
Makushin C.
Makushin Vol.
C. Kovrizhka
Volcano B.
Makushin Pt.
Makushin Bay
Beaver Inlet
Udagak Str.
C. Starichkof
Skan Bay
Spray C.
Staraya Hbr.
Kayak Cape
Protection B.
C. Yanaliun
C. Prominence
Three Island B.
Blueberry B.
Usof Bay
Reef C.
Raven B.
Eagle B.
Kuliliak B.
Kashega Pt.
Kashega B.
Pumicestone B.
Middle B.
Nellie Juan C.
Nellie Juan B.
Chernofski Hbr.
Pustoi I.
Otter Pt.
Ship Rk.
Umnak Pass
South I.
Aiak Bay
Cape Aiak
S.W. End
Polivnoi Rk.
Cape Idak
C. Tanak
C. Chagak
C. Aslik
Kettle C.
Pillars
Igunak
Inanudak Bay
Tulik Vol.
Vsevidof Is.
Bogoslof I.
FOX ISLANDS
UNALASKA ISLAND
ALEUTIAN ISLANDS
VAR. 15°00′ E.
76

Weather Crew stationed at Kiska: Back—Turner AerM2, Coffield CPhM, House AerM1, Lt. Mull, Eccles RM2, Yaconelli CPhoM, Courtney RM3; front—McCandless, Christiansen RM3, Winfry AerM3, Palmer Sea2, Gaffey Sea2 (Lt. Mull and Yaconelli were visitors from USS *Casco*)

(National Archives)

picked up a couple of Russian cargo ships plowing along in the Bering Sea.[2] As usual we had a problem getting some sort of recognition signal from them. We never could figure out whether they were stupid or just plain ornery, and we were sorely tempted to fire a few rounds across their bow. We logged over 200 hours in one month during this period, and our other crews were doing the same thing. The weather was lousy for aerial search, but we gave it our best shot.

By the end of May Admiral Yamamoto had a fleet headed in the direction of Midway Island some 1400 miles south of us. He also had a carrier task force headed toward the Aleutian Islands under the command of Admiral Kakuta.[3] This northern force, with carriers *Ryujo* and *Junyo*, was to carry out an attack on Dutch Harbor the day before the Midway attack was scheduled. Our Intelligence people knew all this and thought we should be able to find them. We ground out hundreds of hours looking for them. But in the end, the Aleutian weather was the toughest opponent either side faced.

During the night of 2 June 1942 Admiral Kakuta's carriers sneaked in within 200 miles of Dutch Harbor. Our crew had flown out of Dutch Harbor that night as part of the our squadron's round-the-clock search operations. On the morning of 3 June we were heading back in toward Dutch Harbor after an all-night search to the southeast. Suddenly the radioman picked up a message that Dutch Harbor was under attack. Next, there was a message for us to land in a bay about 100 miles short of Dutch Harbor and wait for further orders. All of our incoming planes were receiving the same sort of messages. We were implementing a dispersal plan designed to prevent the enemy from catching us with a whole group of aircraft in one place.

Around noon we received the all-clear message and proceeded on to Dutch Harbor. Some airplanes and buildings were wrecked, and the SS *Northwestern*, sitting at the dock, was putting up a plume of smoke.

One of the radiomen told us that *Gillis*, one of our tenders, had been leaving the harbor and had picked up a bunch of aircraft on her radar. She had sent a warning to alert the base, but there wasn't much time to get ready. Most of the guns were manned, but the attacking planes still did some damage. It was one of those screwy Aleutian mornings in Dutch Harbor when there was overcast all around, but right over the base there was a clear hole which went up several thousand feet.

A couple of VP-41's PBY's had been trying to take off from the bay when the attack came. A Japanese fighter strafed Ensign Jack Litsey's plane while he was still on his takeoff run, killed two people and set the plane on fire. Ensign Litsey managed to run his plane up on the beach, and all but two members of the crew got clear before it blew up. The other plane, Ensign Hildebrand's, got airborne with the Zeroes chasing him, but he got up into the soup and eluded them. This same crew got caught in a severe storm the very next night while shadowing the Japanese task force, and was never heard from again. My old buddy, Anthony Duesing was in that crew.

In the confusion of the attack communications became a bit mixed up and we had orders waiting for us to load up with gas and head out on a search to the north over the Bering Sea. We put in twelve hours looking for the Japanese carriers up there

---

[2]Technically the Russians were a neutral nation in the Pacific war, but we always had problems getting them to answer our recognition signals and were always prepared for hostile action when we encountered them at sea.

[3]Mitsuo Fuchida and Masatake Okumiya, *Midway: The Battle That Doomed Japan* (New York: Ballantine Books, 1958), 124.

USS *Gillis* **(AVD-12)**

(National Archives)

Aerial view of N.A.S. Dutch Harbor ramp and unfinished hangar—10 May 1942

(National Archives)

Japanese bomb hit near hangar at N.A.S. Dutch Harbor—3 June 1942

(National Archives)

Japanese bombs fall in harbor at Dutch Harbor—3 June 1942

SS *Northwestern* **and oil tanks burning after bombing attack at Dutch Harbor**

(National Archives)

Severely damaged SS *Northwestern* still smoking after attack

Smoke from warehouse, SS *Northwestern* and oil tanks—3 June 1942

(National Archives)

when, in fact, they were to the south of the Aleutians.

Lt.(jg) Jean Cusick's crew had flown out of Umnak on the night patrol on the night of 2 June and had seen nothing during the first seven hours of their flight. That wasn't surprising since the weather was stormy and the visibility was terrible. They hadn't even picked up anything on radar. When they were about 200 miles southwest of Dutch Harbor on their inbound leg they suddenly found themselves in the midst of the Japanese carrier attack planes heading toward their target.[4]

Attacked from all sides, Cusick's PBY had an engine shot out in a matter of seconds and was on its way down to a crash landing in another minute. The crew didn't even have time to get out a contact report. Although Cusick was wounded, all hands survived the landing and attempted to abandon the sinking plane, loading into the rubber life rafts. One raft sank and the three men in it were lost. The rest of the crew managed to get into the other life raft, but Cusick and one of the crewmen died of exposure within an hour. Lt.(jg) Wylie Hunt and two of the crewmen, Carl Creamer and Joe Brown, drifted helplessly in the stormy Northern Pacific until near noon. Then a Japanese cruiser steamed out of the mist and sighted them. They were picked up and subjected to repeated questioning for several days and even threatened with death. The Japanese finally gave up on the questioning and the three remained prisoners for the rest of the war.[5]

Lt.(jg) Lucius Campbell had mustered his crew on the morning of 3 June at 0400 and departed from Dutch Harbor at 0500, flying in 42-P-6, nearly an hour before the attack. He landed at Akutan Bay, one of our dispersal locations a short distance east of Dutch Harbor, to await further orders. At about 0730 he received a message ordering him to search a sector southwest of Dutch Harbor. Bill Brady, Campbell's navigator, laid out the navigation on his chart while the engines were started and the plane departed immediately.

At 0915 Campbell's crew picked up an aircraft on radar and sighted it a short time later, identifying it as an enemy scout. Pulling up into the cloud layer they lost him. At 1100 two enemy float-planes were sighted but did not attack. Finally at noon surface vessels showed up on radar twenty to twenty-five miles away, and very soon approaching aircraft were picked up.

A contact report was radioed back to all stations, but the message was so garbled by atmospheric interference that it was never received. The enemy fleet had been located, but nobody knew about it except Lt.(jg) Campbell's crew.

Shortly thereafter, Campbell's plane was under attack by fighters. The Zeroes blasted numerous holes in the hull, put a hole in a gas tank, wounded the port waist gunner, Gene Gillis, and finally shot away a rudder cable.

Flying a PBY with no rudder control is not a job for an amateur. Flying a PBY with no rudder control on instruments while trying to avoid enemy aircraft takes a truly professional touch. Campbell's many hours of flying as an enlisted pilot before being commissioned made the difference between success and failure. For two hours after being shot up by the enemy he nursed his aircraft through the clouds, gradually climbing and on course for Scotch Cap. His gas ran out when he was over Unimak Pass. At 1500 in the afternoon he made a dead-stick landing and prepared to abandon ship

---

[4]Fuchida and Okumiya, *Midway*, 126.
[5]Brian Garfield, *The Thousand-Mile War* (Toronto: Bantam Books, 1982), 32.

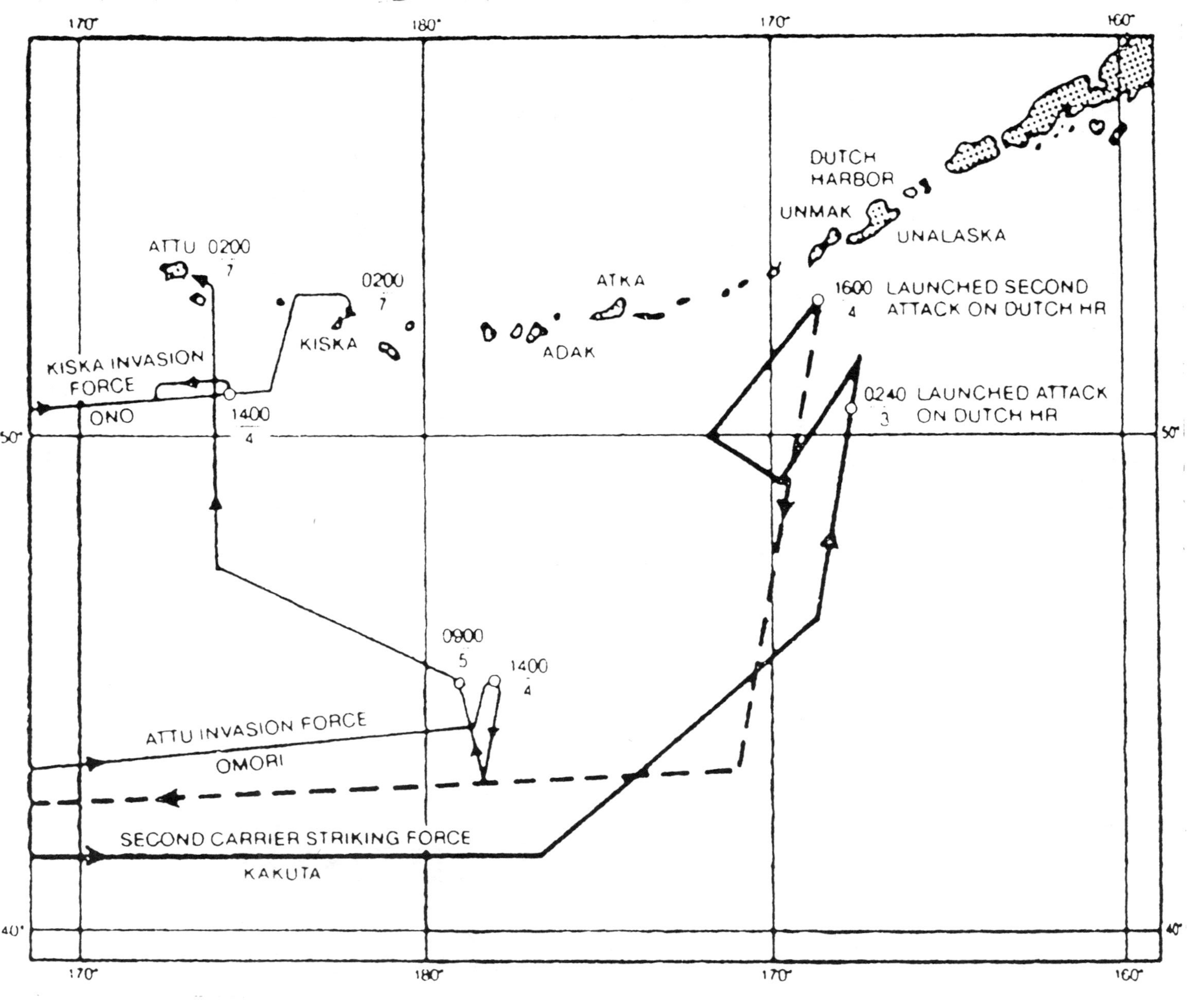

Movements of Japanese Carrier and Invasion Forces, 3-7 June 1942

(Naval Institute Press)

in the rubber boats. But the riddled PBY refused to sink so the crew decided to stay aboard. By using smoke signals they managed to get the attention of another PBY flying in the vicinity and the other plane relayed the downed plane's position to USCGS *Nemaha*. At 2140 the *Nemaha* arrived and commenced rescue operations. Futile attempts were made to tow the damaged and sinking plane; it was finally sunk by .50 caliber machine gun fire at 2340. As their heroic PBY finally disappeared beneath the waves, Lt.(jg) Campbell and his crew reflected that it had been a long day.[6]

Since *Nemaha* was under strict orders for radio silence, no message could be sent to reconfirm the contact. It was almost two full days before Campbell's crew was put ashore and could tell their story. They were on the "missing" list for a full forty-eight hours. (Our squadron planes saw so little of each other during those few days that we were usually not sure who was actually missing.) Meanwhile, the search went on until another contact report located the Japanese fleet in the early morning hours of 4 June.

From then on it was our mission to keep radar contact with the fleet and send in position reports so the Army bombers could carry out an attack. The fog was our best friend for the kind of mission we had. With the radar we could keep in contact, but they couldn't find us in the soup. At least that was the way it worked most of the time.

We lost two more planes during our desperate round-the-clock surveillance. Lt.(jg) Eugene W. Stockstill and his crew, flying in plane 42-P-11, were dispatched to relieve a search plane tracking the task force at 0820 in the morning of June 4. First reports from Stockstill indicated that he located the Japanese fleet and then came under attack, but the last radio contact with Stockstill's crew was shortly before noon. That night, as already noted, Ensign James T. Hildebrand and his crew were also lost while trailing the Japanese fleet.

Another contact was made during the morning of 4 June. Lieutenant C. E. Perkins, our Executive Officer, flying in plane 42-P-5, was carrying a torpedo and two 500-pounders when he found the Japanese fleet. He shadowed the task force from the shelter of the overcast for a time and then lined up by radar for a torpedo attack. When he dropped below the overcast he was headed right for the carrier. The only problem was that there was a cruiser between him and the carrier. The cruiser opened up with every gun she could bring to bear, and before Lt. Perkins was past her he had caught a slug in the port engine oil system. The resulting stream of oil not only signalled the finish of the engine but put an end to the torpedo run.

With the co-pilot, Ens. M. E. Johnson, hauling back on the yoke to get the plane back up into the soup, Lt. Perkins proceeded to jettison his torpedo and bombs. The PBY couldn't stay in the air on one engine with that ton-and-a-half load. Then began the retreat toward Dutch Harbor with one engine and on instruments. Flying on instruments was pretty normal operation in the Aleutians. The single-engine situation was only a small additional burden.

When Perkins' crew arrived at Dutch Harbor, they made their landing, put their landing gear down and with the judicious use of a sea anchor managed to taxi to the ramp on their single engine. At that point a tractor was hooked to the bow pennant and the plane was towed out of the water. Al Birchman and Boyd Peer, Plane Captain and Second Mech in Lieutenant Perkins' crew, dutifully turned in the Yellow Sheet,

---

[6]*War Diary: Patrol Squadron Forty-Two (28 May 1942-31 July 1942)*, prepared by Officers of Patrol Squadron Forty-Two (Washington D.C.: Naval Historical Center), 43-44.

Crashed PBY on sand spit near N.A.S. Dutch Harbor

(National Archives)

Aviation planning chart of western Aleutians

Bull. Biogeogr. Soc Jap., Vol. 5.

Plate III

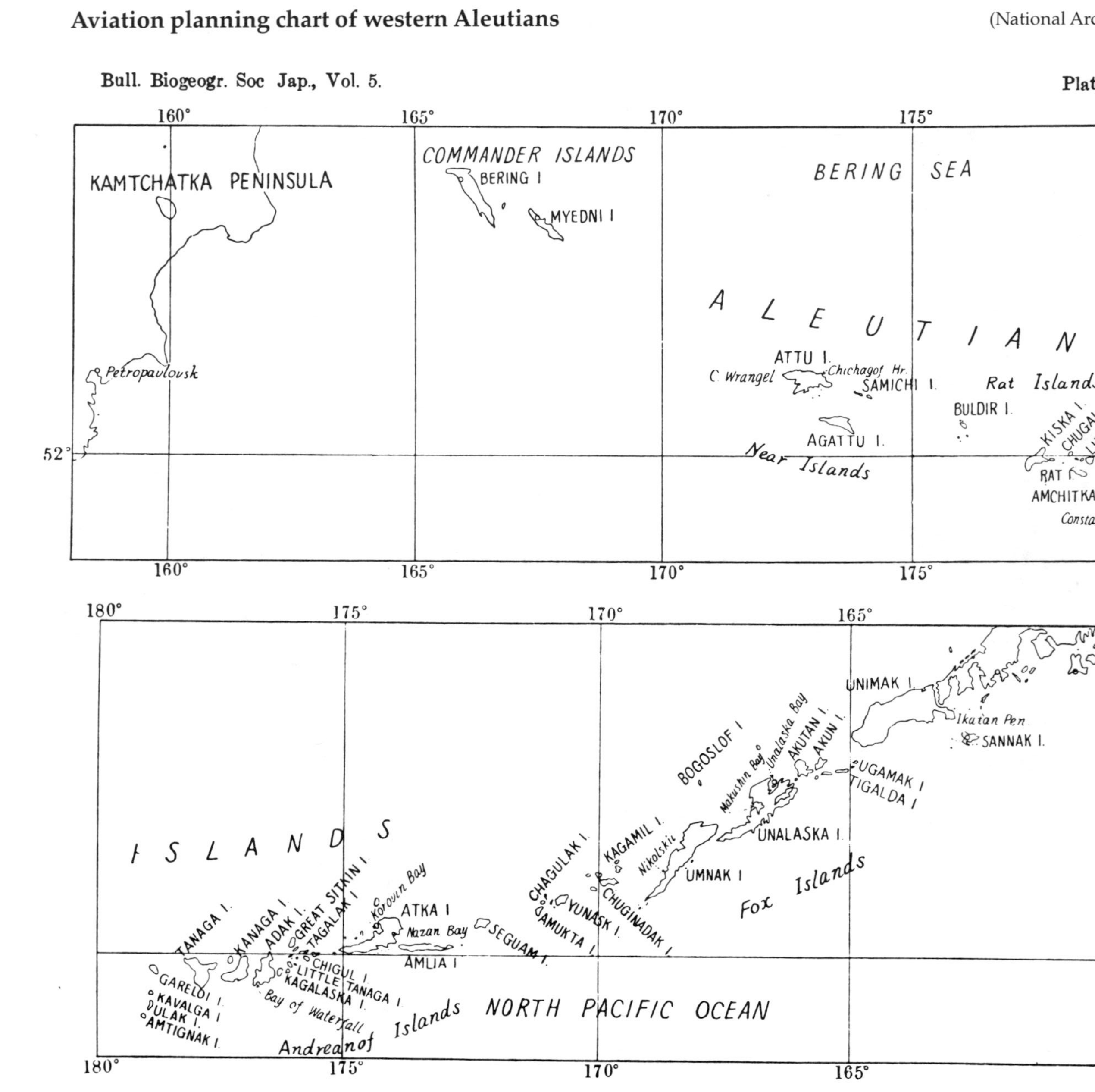

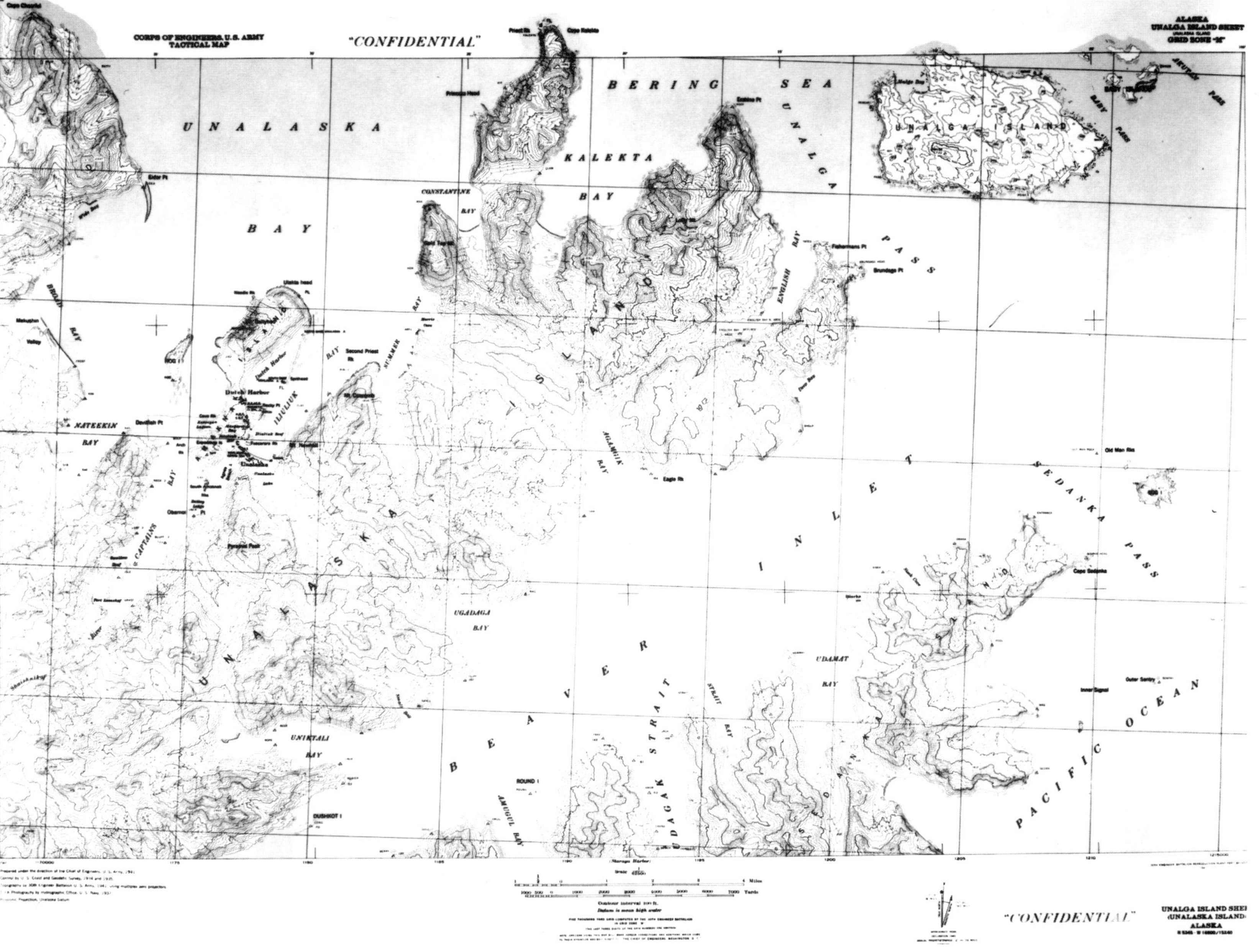

Chart of section of Unalaska Island showing Beaver Inlet and Unalaska Bay

(National Archives)

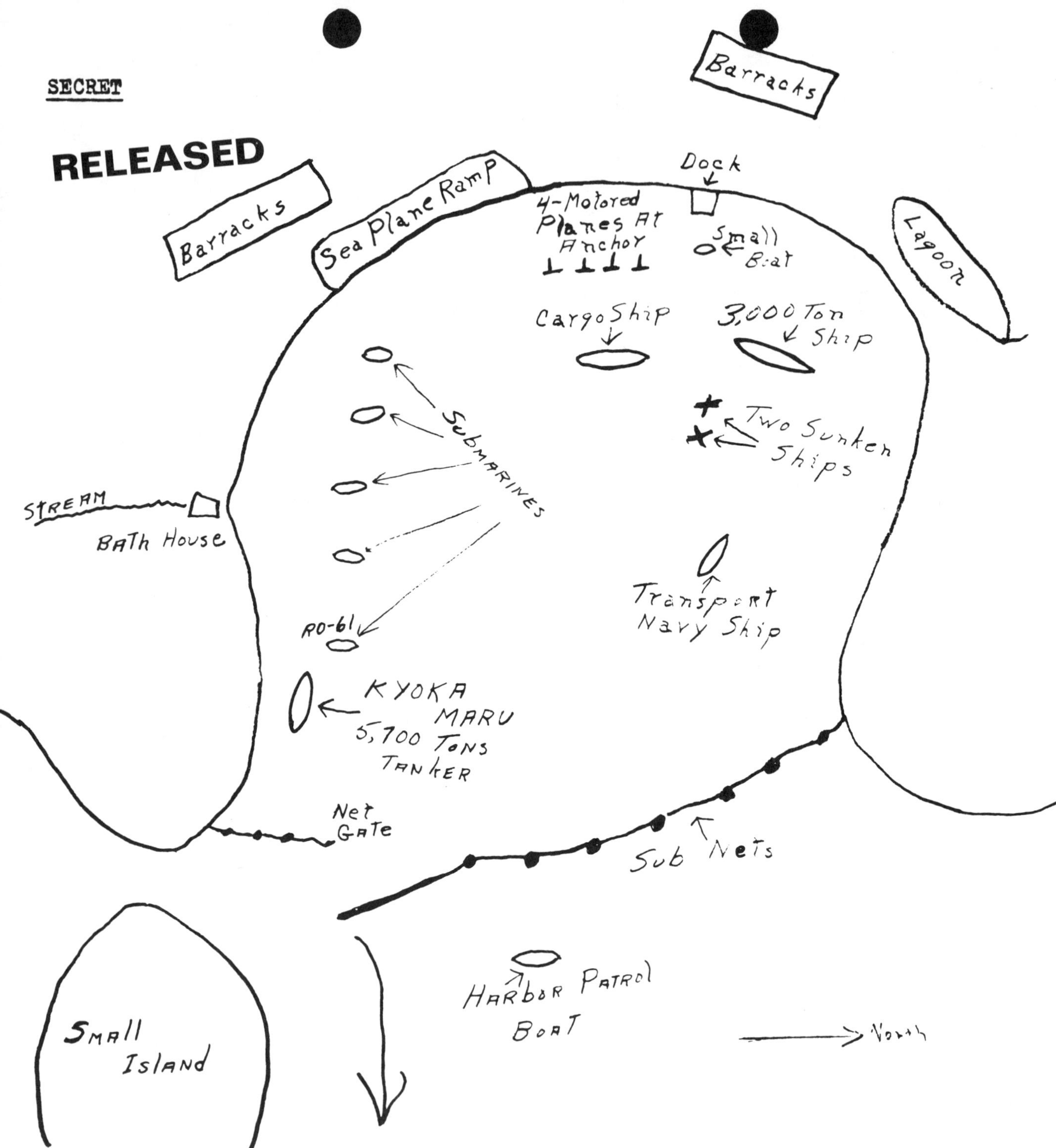

FACSIMILE OF CHART OF KISKA HARBOR WITH SHIPPING AND INSTALLATIONS AS SKETCHED BY YOSHIO USHIKADO, TORPEDOMAN – 2ND CLASS, JAPANESE NAVY. SKETCHED AT DUTCH HARBOR, ALASKA, SEPTEMBER 8, 1942.

Chart of Kiska Harbor hand-drawn by Japanese prisoner saved from submarine sunk near Nazan Bay in September 1942

(National Archives)

noting that an engine change was needed and at least one bullet hole needed repairs. Birchman and Peer experienced mixed emotions when they heard Lieutenant Perkins declare his intentions to get back in the air and make another attempt at attacking the carrier.

The first hangar to be built at Dutch Harbor was about half completed. It had all the steel framework up and a roof in place; it also had a VP-41 plane parked in it, the only plane under cover west of Kodiak. The maintenance guys were preparing to move the VP-41 plane out of the hangar and to move 42-P-5 in to get set up for an engine change. While they waited for the tractor to pull the plane out of the hangar the air-raid alarm went off and the Japanese dive bombers came roaring out of the clouds for their second raid on Dutch Harbor. They got a direct hit on the hangar roof.

All the maintenance people had gotten clear before the bomb hit, but the hangar and plane were demolished. That ended any thoughts of moving the airplane. When the smoke and dust cleared the PBY had become a mass of spare parts.

The VP-42 engine-change crew had thought they were going to have the opportunity of working under cover, which would have been a rare treat. But with the hangar in a shambles it was back to the usual routine of working outdoors. The crew turned to immediately after the air-raid and had a new engine installed on 42-P-5 in a few hours. In the diary he kept at the time "Hoot" Smith, navigator in Lieutenant Perkins' crew, has a notation that they took off in 42-P-5 the next morning at 1000.

The weather caused endless trouble for the Army bombers. These B-26's, flying out of Cold Bay without radar installed, had to depend on dead-reckoning navigation. They made a valiant effort to carry out torpedo attacks, but were defeated by the Aleutian weather. A couple of their planes actually found the carrier group but couldn't attack effectively in the low overcast conditions. One B-26, piloted by Capt. Thornborough, could not get lined up for a torpedo attack so he attempted to arm his torpedo in the air by executing a high-speed dive and dropping the torpedo in a dive-bombing run. He reported a hit on one of the carriers, but the torpedo did not arm before he released it and it did no damage. He came back to Cold Bay, loaded up with bombs and headed out for a second attack. Heavy fog prevented his landing when he returned to his base and he eventually was assumed lost at sea.

The weird part of these operations was that there were times when our planes and enemy planes passed each other, probably within a mile or so, and never saw each other. But after their second attack on Dutch Harbor the Japanese met some unexpected opposition. When they headed back toward their ships, they were met by P-40's coming from the west. That was a rude surprise because they were not aware of any base west of Dutch Harbor. In fact, the same thing should have happened on 3 June, but the patchwork radio set-up failed to get the message through to the P-40 outfit at Umnak that there was an attack in progress.

At that time the Navy had a policy allowing brothers to be assigned together aboard a ship or in some other unit. VP-42 had several sets of brothers: Dan and Orrie Reed, Steve and Stan Brozich, Uther and Foy Taylor and one set of three brothers named Hanson. Noel, the oldest, was Plane Captain in Ensign Mitchell's crew. Melvin and Ray were in the maintenance crew at Kodiak.[7]

---

[7]Later, in November 1942, five Sullivan brothers were lost in the sinking of USS *Juneau* near Guadalcanal. Because of that tragedy, Navy policy was changed to forbid brothers from serving together for the remainder of the war.

On 4 June Noel had gotten a blast of 100-Octane gas in the face while working with the fuel system on his plane at Cold Bay. The plane had been having recurring problems with bad fuel for several days and had even gone clear to Kodiak trying to obtain a good decontamination job on its gas tanks. The fuel problems on the trip back to Cold Bay were evidence that there was still trouble with the fuel system. Although Noel's accident in the afternoon of 4 June wasn't very serious, the Plane Commander decided to have the medics keep him under observation for a few hours. When the crew was called to fly to Dutch Harbor, Noel was left behind and Wheeler "Rebel" Rawls replaced him as Plane Captain in Ensign Mitchell's crew on 42-P-4. As the PBY approached Dutch Harbor a message was received saying that the base was expecting an attack and to stay clear. The plane reversed course and was in the vicinity of Egg Island, to the east of Dutch Harbor, when several Japanese fighters caught it and attacked. In a matter of minutes the PBY went down in flames. A day later "Rebel" Rawls' body was found floating in the water with his hands still clutching the grab line on a riddled life raft. His body had over thirty holes from machine gun fire, indicating that he had survived the crash and gotten out of the plane with a life raft, only to be strafed mercilessly while in the water.

However, during the attack one of the PBY gunners had gotten a burst of .50 caliber rounds into a Zero. When the Zero started to fly back to his carrier the pilot found his oil system had been damaged and his engine would probably quit in a short time. He attempted to make a forced landing on Akutan Island, which the Japanese had designated as a submarine pickup point if a plane couldn't make it back to the carrier. When the plane touched down on what looked like a level, grassy area, the wheels sank into soft mud and came to a sudden stop, nosing over violently.

At Dutch Harbor Ensign Mitchell's message that he was under attack, afire and going down was received, and in a short time Melvin and Ray Hanson, in Kodiak, were aware that Noel's crew had been shot down in flames. A couple of days later they were stunned but delighted when another PBY came flying into Kodiak and Noel climbed down the ladder to turn in his Yellow Sheet to the maintenance crew. Noel, who was not aware that he had been considered lost, was overwhelmed by the boisterous greeting he received from his two brothers.

It was a month later when a PBY spotted the crashed Zero on Akutan Island. A crew was immediately dispatched from Dutch Harbor to attempt a salvage operation. Their attempt was not successful but they did locate and examine the plane. They reported that it could probably be salvaged and made flyable again if the proper equipment were taken to the site. Another party was dispatched with better equipment; they loaded the Zero on a barge and returned to Dutch Harbor with it. The plane had not sustained a great deal of damage, but we were told that the pilot's neck had been broken in the crash landing and that he had probably died instantly. When we examined the vaunted Japanese fighter we could not help but note that the propeller was an exact duplicate of the Hamilton Standard props which were on our own PBY's. The Zero was solid evidence that the low, slow guys could get in a few licks sometimes too.

That Zero proved to be one of the great prizes of the war for our aircraft design people. When it reached the States it was repaired at the Assembly and Repair shops at the Naval Air Station, San Diego and flown to reveal design weaknesses. U.S. aircraft design and flight tactics would take deadly advantage of those weaknesses after that.

The urgency of our searches took on a new dimension after 3 June. Previous to

Damaged Zero Japanese fighter found on Akutan Island—July 1942

(National Archives)

Damaged Zero on barge being taken to N.A.S. Dutch Harbor

(National Archives)

Hoisting damaged Zero from barge to dock at Dutch Harbor—17 July 1942

(National Archives)

that date we *thought* the Japanese were heading our way. Now we *knew* they had arrived and were dead set on giving us a hard time. We flew a lot of hours with the blisters open and the guns rigged and ready because when we made a contact there would be some shooting going on.

I wondered how it would feel to bang away at a Japanese plane. Were their gunners better than we were? I had heard of guys freezing at their guns the first time they came under fire. I decided to let time answer the questions. I felt a meeting with the enemy was pretty sure to happen before very long and I would know the answers then.

It turned out that Admiral Kakuta's carriers were as intent on trying to evade us as we were on trying to find them. Every contact report put them in a different location, and we adjusted our searches accordingly. We had a dispersal system with planes flying from Sand Point in the Shumagin Islands, King Cove near the end of the Alaska Peninsula, and Dolgoi and Akutan—a couple of islands east of Dutch Harbor. This was in addition to Cold Bay, Dutch Harbor and Umnak. Umnak and Cold Bay had steel matting runways. Dutch Harbor had a ramp for beaching. All the other places were strictly water operations. Most of the time there was a tender at Sand Point. We flew a layout of sector searches from each of these locations and hoped one of the sectors would cover the latest reported location of the Japanese ships.

During the first ten days of June our search force was made up of VP-41 and VP-42 PBY's. Lieutenant Commander Russell ran things out of Cold Bay, and Lieutenant Commander Foley, skipper of VP-41, ran operations out of Dutch Harbor. PBY's from both squadrons were operating out of all locations, trying to get maximum search coverage wherever it was needed. We seldom gassed up at the same place twice in a row. And we never gassed up without using our old reliable strainers. Some of our fuel stops were just some steel drums of gas on a beach with a hose and hand pump, and we didn't dare take a chance on loading up with bad fuel. I never used the strainer without thinking of the time I dumped gas all over the chief back in Seattle.

When we checked out a likely-looking bay for a possible dispersal location, we used a very simple system of gauging the water depth. We made a low pass a few feet above the water and tossed our "VP-42 Depth-Finder Device" over the side. This device was a six-foot length of line with a rock at one end and a block of wood at the other. When we came around for a second pass we checked to see whether the block was floating or had been submerged by the weight of the rock. If the block was floating we knew there was less than six feet of water. If it had been pulled down out of sight, we knew there was a safe depth.

Experience had taught everyone how important it was to test the water's depth. In one instance a PBY crew landed in what seemed to be an ideal little lake. They immediately found that the water was shallower than it had appeared to be from the air. They were stuck in the mud. Fortunately they could lighten ship by offloading enough equipment to refloat their aircraft and get out of there. There was an embarrassing series of messages exchanged with their base during their sojourn in the mud.

Cold Bay, located near the end of the Alaska Peninsula, was used by the Army for flying P-40's and B-26's. It also offered a haven for the Navy's vagabond PBY's. On 4 June we landed there, coming in from a ten-hour search. As usual we topped off the gas tanks and checked the plane over for departure on short notice. At Cold Bay our communication procedure was unique. The Operations/Communications center was in a dug-out hole in the ground about a half mile away from our parking area, across

U.S. Army Air Corps P-40

(National Archives)

Martin B-26—U.S. Army Air Corps Medium Bomber

(National Archives)

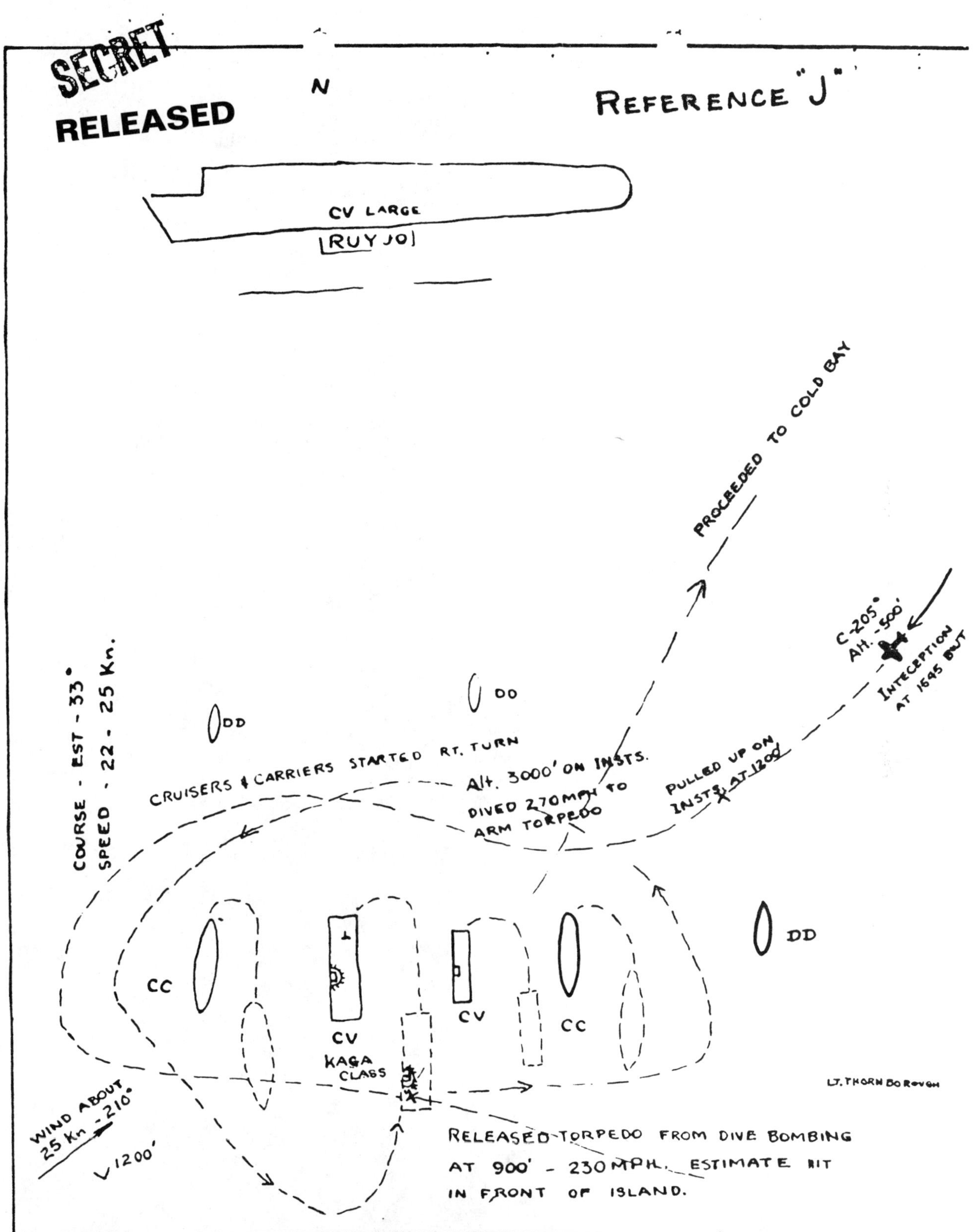

Drawing of Capt. Thornborough's torpedo attack on Japanese carrier, 4 June 1942 (VP-42 War Diary)

Setting up VP-42 Encampment at Cold Bay, Alaska—June 1942

Setting up VP-42 Encampment at Cold Bay, Alaska—June 1942

(National Archives)

PBY-5A parked near nose-hangar at Cold Bay, Alaska—June 1942

VP-42 Operations Mound at Cold Bay—June 1942 (they did laundry too)

(National Archives)

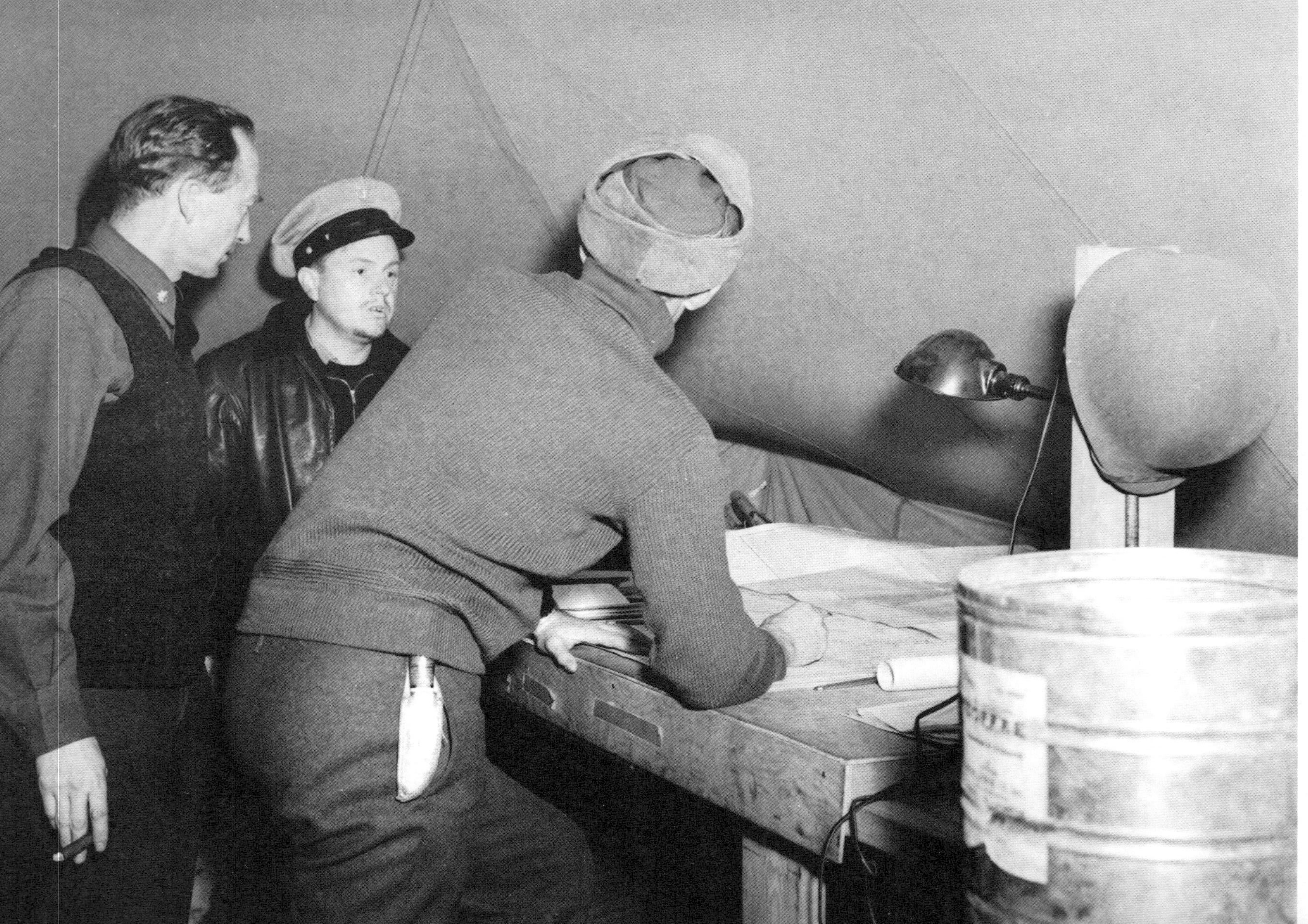

Lt.Comdr. Russell and Consultants plan another day's operations at Cold Bay

(National Archives)

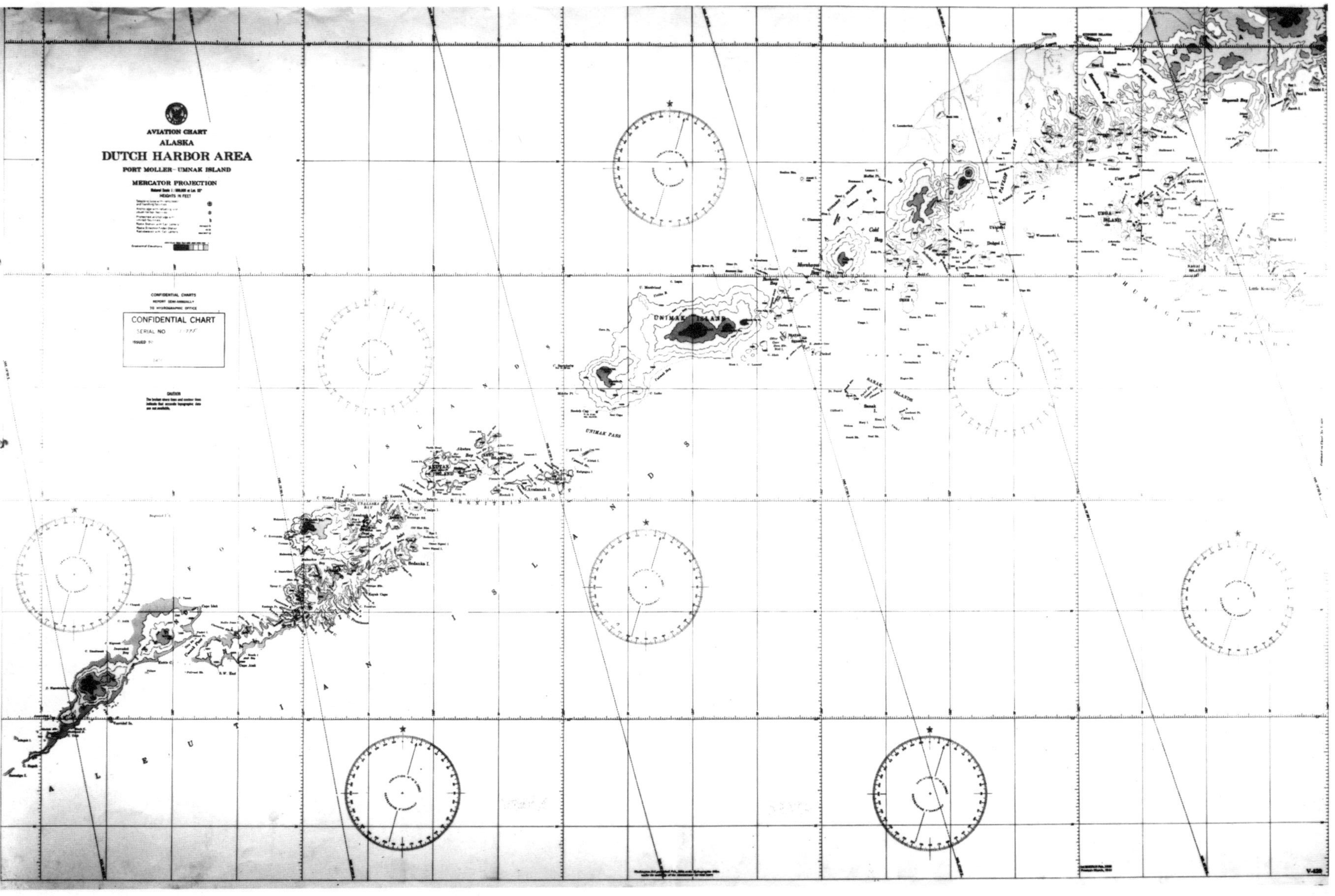

Aviation Chart showing Dutch Harbor area

(National Archives)

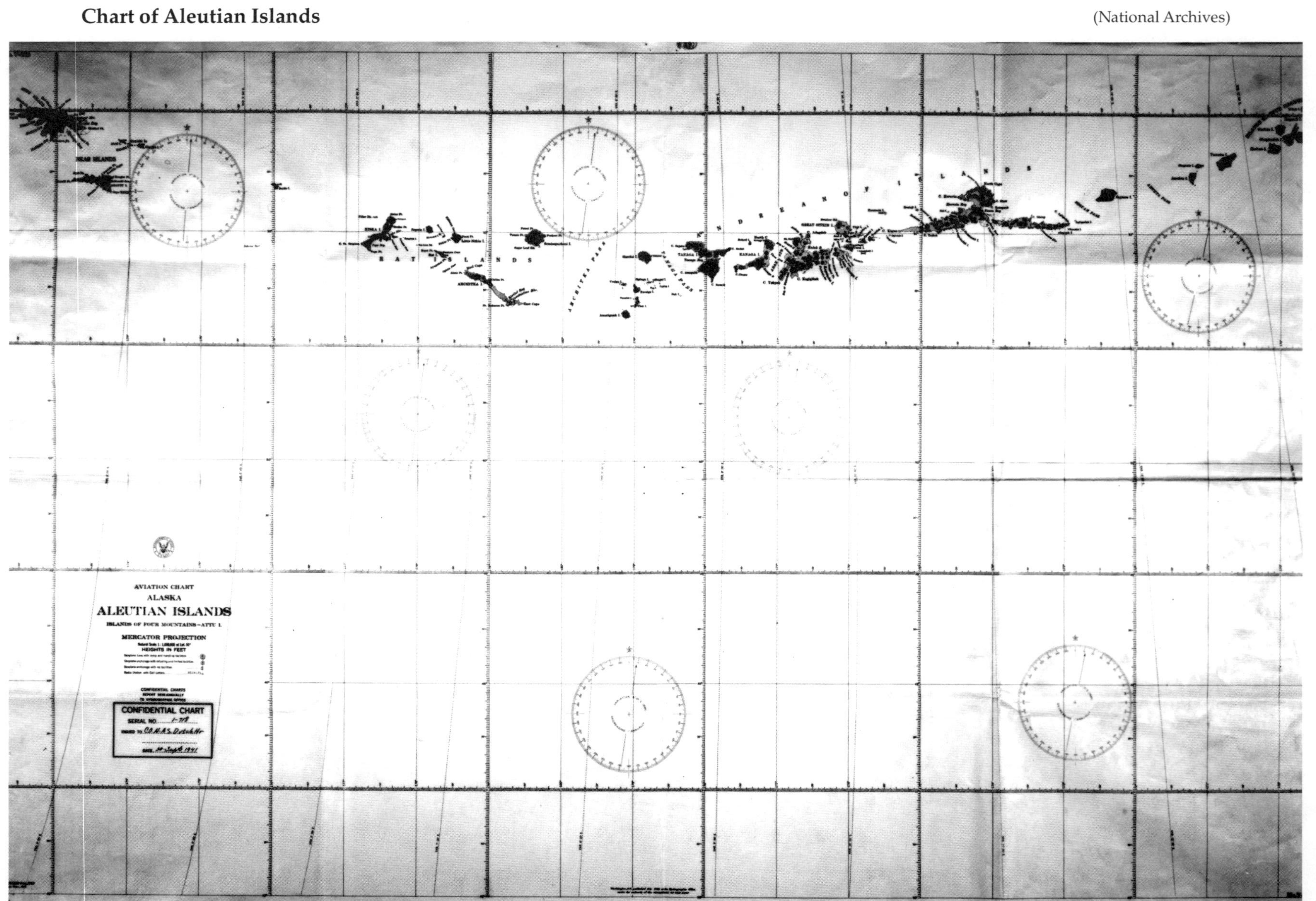

AVIATION CHART
ALASKA
ALEUTIAN ISLANDS
ISLANDS OF FOUR MOUNTAINS—ATTU I.
MERCATOR PROJECTION
HEIGHTS IN FEET
CONFIDENTIAL CHARTS
CONFIDENTIAL CHART
SERIAL NO.

the runway. Once we were gassed up and ready we watched a mound of dirt right outside Operations. Gabriel, our Leading Chief, appeared on the mound every so often and started sending semaphore. He didn't use flags as signalmen did. He just used his arms. During our training in the Beach Crew and as Third Class we were all required to learn semaphore, so he expected us to be able to read his signals. He would send "Dickey stand by" or "Russell stand by" using the name of the plane commander to designate the crew to let us know who had to be ready to go. One of us sent back "ready" so he knew we were ready to go and had received his message.

As we were standing by the airplane on 4 June waiting for our signalman, Gabriel, to show up on the mound, the air-raid signal went off. All of the residents of the base headed for their foxholes or gun stations, and those of us who were transients headed out across the tundra looking for a place to hide. Our crew found a series of shallow trenches a couple of hundred yards from the runway, and we all dived in and then started searching the sky for enemy planes. After a few minutes of waiting with no attack we began a closer examination of our surroundings. I noticed what appeared to be some metal showing through the turf next to me and pulled the grass apart to get a closer look. It turned out to be a steel drum of gasoline. A little bit more frantic examination revealed that we had picked a gasoline storage area as our "safe" haven. There never was an attack that day, and the all-clear sounded as we madly bailed out of our trenches. If a bomb or strafing attack had hit anywhere near where we had been, a whole acre of tundra would have gone sky high with us right in the middle of it. When we arrived back at our plane Gabriel was signaling us from his mound: "Dickey stand by." Eventually the Army furnished us with some tents and we set up an encampment not far from the runway there at Cold Bay, our first experience at living with the Army. We even had our own foxholes.

On 5 June we took off from Sand Point to relieve the crew on duty following the Japanese fleet. They hadn't reported in for the previous two hours and things didn't look good for them. We were loaded with four 500-pound bombs and were trying to anticipate what we were going to tangle with as we headed out. "Their last report gave the fleet location as 165 miles southeast of Umnak," Lt. Dickey was saying. "We'll be in the area pretty soon, so stand by to man all the guns and keep a sharp lookout. Looks like there is plenty of overcast, so we'll try to spot them on radar but keep out of sight while doing it."

Although I was in the port waist I could visualize Townsend working at fine tuning his radar. Summers was on lookout up in the bow and Stallings had the starboard waist. We had a new man in the crew, Cola. He was back aft getting ready to man the tunnel gun. Babbitt was in the tower. Ensign E. A. Arnold was Lt. Dickey's co-pilot at this time. He was new to VP-42. New pilots checking into the squadron were not immediately assigned to a crew permanently. Ensign Arnold had flown with a few other crews as an extra pilot on some flights to gain experience but was now flying with us as a regular crew member.

About an hour out Lt. Dickey asked, "What does the radar look like?"

"Seems to be working fine but I'm not picking up anything yet." Townsend sounded pretty sure of his equipment. That was reassuring. Sometimes the radar was kind of balky. Considering the fact that we had only been operating with radar for about three weeks, it was reassuring to me that our radiomen had done so well with the new equipment.

"We should be picking them up within the next hour. Open the blisters and get all the guns manned. They could have some scouts out and we don't want to be surprised. We don't expect any friendly aircraft out here so the orders are to shoot on sight." Lt. Dickey was just verifying what we all knew, so that there wouldn't be any misunderstanding.

He knew the second the blisters were opened. The slipstream passing the open waist compartment increases the noise level inside the plane, even up in the cockpit. "Starboard gun rigged and ready." "Port gun rigged and ready." "Bow gun rigged and ready," and finally, "Tunnel gun rigged and ready." We had done this enough times that the reports seemed automatic. But today I wanted a little extra assurance.

"Request permission to fire a test burst on all the guns." As Plane Captain I made that request whenever we rigged out the guns if Lt. Dickey didn't tell us to fire. I always wanted to make sure nobody had a jam. It happened to me once on a target run and I never forgot it.

"Good idea. Everybody fire a burst."

Immediately all guns opened up, firing four or five rounds, and all stations reported guns ok.

Now came the looking and waiting. We hadn't picked up any targets on the radar and we should have been getting within radar range of the last known location of the Japanese ships. We had been flying underneath a thousand-foot ceiling with pretty fair visibility. Gradually we pulled up into the soup and went on instruments. "Townsend, we're blind now. Let me know the second you see anything. The radar is our eyes from here on in." Being on instruments was nothing new for us, and Lt. Dickey was a good instrument pilot.

Pierson finally broke the silence. "We've passed the spot."

"I'm coming around to starboard. We'll change course ninety degrees and I'll hold this heading for fifteen minutes and see if we can come up with anything." Lt. Dickey apparently was going into some sort of square search pattern.

Two hours later we had changed course several more times and it seemed we were completely alone on the whole planet. I kept leaning on my 50-caliber, slowly swinging it back and forth as I tried to see through the soup along the gun barrel. If I pulled down my goggles they fogged up. If I didn't cover my eyes the wind made them water.

"Possible target on the port side," said Townsend, "Might be a plane. Something like five miles."

There was no way I could see five miles—five yards was more like it. But I stared into the soup, waiting to hear another report. Finally I reached for the intercom mike without moving my eyes and asked, "Is he getting any closer?"

"If it is a plane, he's on the same course we are and holding the same position. Must be making about the same speed."

The last remark was reassuring. It didn't sound like a Zero. A Zero would be making at least double our speed. If we were going to tangle with something, we were a better match for the cruiser observation planes the Japanese were using. And it was very likely that if their ships were around here they would have scouts out tooling around trying to spot us.

Suddenly I realized that the soup wasn't solid anymore. There were some broken places in it. "He's moved in to about two miles. Sure looks like a plane." Townsend put us all on edge with that report.

I kept my eye right at the gunsight, trying to look down the barrel. It's hard to keep from being sort of hypnotized from staring into the fog. It took an effort to keep moving my eyes to continue sweeping fore and aft.

When he first showed up he was just a dark grey blob. "I think I see him." I grabbed the mike without looking. If it was a plane he was a bit lower than we were, probably just under the overcast. Assuming he didn't have radar he would have to stay clear of the overcast to be able to see anything.

"He's in pretty close," was Townsend's reply.

"Fire if you have a shot. Bow gun did you see anything?" Lt. Dickey wanted as many guns in on this as possible.

When that dark blob in the soup showed up again I got it in the gunsight. It almost faded out but then there was a break in the overcast and I was looking right at a single-float biplane flying on the same course as we were.

The gun kicked in my arms as I let go with the first burst and the tracers tracked right at his engine. Normally I tried to fire four rounds to the burst, but I was aware that at least six rounds were away before I let up on the trigger. For a split-second I considered moving my aim back a bit, but decided not to risk spoiling what seemed to be an ideal shot. The adrenalin was pounding through me as I had never before experienced. The second burst tracked the same as the first, and it seemed to me I saw a tiny wisp of smoke streak back from his engine. The tracers from my third burst were lost in the fog as the enemy was again swallowed up by the overcast. I guessed I had gotten off at least fifteen and possibly eighteen rounds. And I finally breathed again.

I had noticed the Japanese rear-seat gunner out of the corner of my eye and he seemed to be looking away from us all during the brief encounter. His gun was rigged and ready but he just got caught looking the other way.

"He's moving away pretty fast," called Townsend.

"I never did see him," said Lt. Dickey. "Do you think you got him?"

I was still peering into the soup along the barrel of my gun as I reported. "He was pretty far away, but it was a no-lead shot and I aimed a little high. The tracers seemed to track right into him. He was only in the clear for a couple of seconds so I never got to see any results. It was one of those biplanes they have on cruisers. Townsend did you see anything on the radar?"

"He's gone now. Went off the screen right after you fired."

"Pierson, mark that position on your chart and we'll report a possible. Babbitt, how does the fuel look? If we don't make a contact in the next hour or so, we'll have to head for home." Lt. Dickey sounded a little discouraged. "They must have hightailed it right out of our territory. Wish we knew what direction that cruiser plane came from."

"Maybe somebody told them we were coming out here to get them." That anonymous observation was met by silence, but we could envision the Japanese trembling on their ships when they got the word that 42-P-12 was on their trail.

When we reported back to Cold Bay that we were heading for home we knew there would be as much frustration there as we were feeling. It didn't seem possible for the Japanese fleet to elude us. First we had them spotted and then we didn't. Each search plane went out with high hopes. Some were able to make contact and some didn't. Some who did make contact got off a couple of contact reports and were never heard from again.

It was good to know for sure that I could do what needed to be done when the chips were down. It seemed to boil down to one simple fact. If I didn't shoot him, he was going to try to blow me and my shipmates out of the air. Better he got blown out of the air first. Other encounters with the enemy would require the same skills, but this first one was the crucial one I was glad to have behind me.

The Japanese managed to use the Aleutian weather to keep their task force pretty well hidden. When we were able to give the Army bombers a fix on any Japanese ships, the soup was so bad that any decent bombing attempt was out of the question. All we could do was keep trying.

An interesting aspect in all of our searches was that we never were alerted to any movements of U.S. ships. The question was bound to come up sooner or later: Don't we have any U.S. ships in the area? It seems that there was a small cruiser task force working out of Kodiak, but the Commander, Rear Admiral Robert Theobald, was never convinced that the Japanese would be satisfied with attacking only Dutch Harbor. Admiral Theobald positioned his ships to protect Kodiak and points to the east of Kodiak and never did change his mind. Thus, the two surface forces were separated by at least six hundred miles at all times.

In addition to keeping track of the Japanese carrier force near Dutch Harbor, we continued searching farther west, and on 10 June one of our planes reported a group of ships in Kiska harbor, assumed to be Japanese. The next day Lt. Bergstrom's, Ens. Leo Nuss's and Lt.(jg) Campbell's planes were assigned on VP-42's first bombing missions at Kiska.

Although the weather was nearly solid overcast over Kiska, two of the planes found enough breaks to make bombing runs. Upon returning to base Ensign Nuss made a detailed report of his bombing attack on Kiska, including a drawing of ships' types and positions. His crew told us that there were a fair number of anti-aircraft guns already in place and operating. Although they had not been attacked by fighter aircraft, they were pretty sure that they had seen fighter-type seaplanes on the water in the harbor. The Japanese had come prepared to defend their position, evidently bringing aircraft with them and getting their guns ready to go immediately after setting foot ashore.

While Admiral Kakuta's carrier task force had been prowling about the Dutch Harbor area, Vice Admiral Hosogaya had steamed into western Aleutian waters with an invasion force. His forces made their landings on Kiska and Attu in the middle of the night of 7 June. They captured a small group of Aleut people and an American couple, named Jones, who were school teachers on Attu. At Kiska they captured the weather team. The first nine men were captured within a day or two, but William House managed to evade the Japanese and survive in the hills for fifty days. He finally was starved into surrendering.[8]

The 11 June Kiska bombing missions departed from Dutch Harbor, and the continued surveillance of the Japanese fleet was set up out of Cold Bay and Sand Point, in the Shumagin Islands. As soon as *Gillis* got set up out at Nazan Bay, Atka, most of the bombing flights originated from there. After their initial landing, the Japanese managed to get ships into Kiska and reinforce the original landing party well enough so that they offered plenty of fireworks for any of our planes making bombing runs.

It must have been a stunning revelation to our officials in Washington, D.C. to receive battle reports from the remote areas of the north. They had studiously ignored this part of the world and only now were becoming aware that their laxity was the source of considerable danger to the northwest coast of America. There was a mad

---

[8]Fuchida and Okumiya, *Midway*, 126.

scramble to try to correct the errors of years past. But they weren't quite sure what to do or where to do it—and worst of all, they might even have to spend some money.

How long could the fate of the west coast of America be left in the hands of a bunch of Navy guys and their PBY's?

Japanese Imperial Navy landing party coming ashore on Kiska — June 1942

(Adm. James S. Russell Collection)

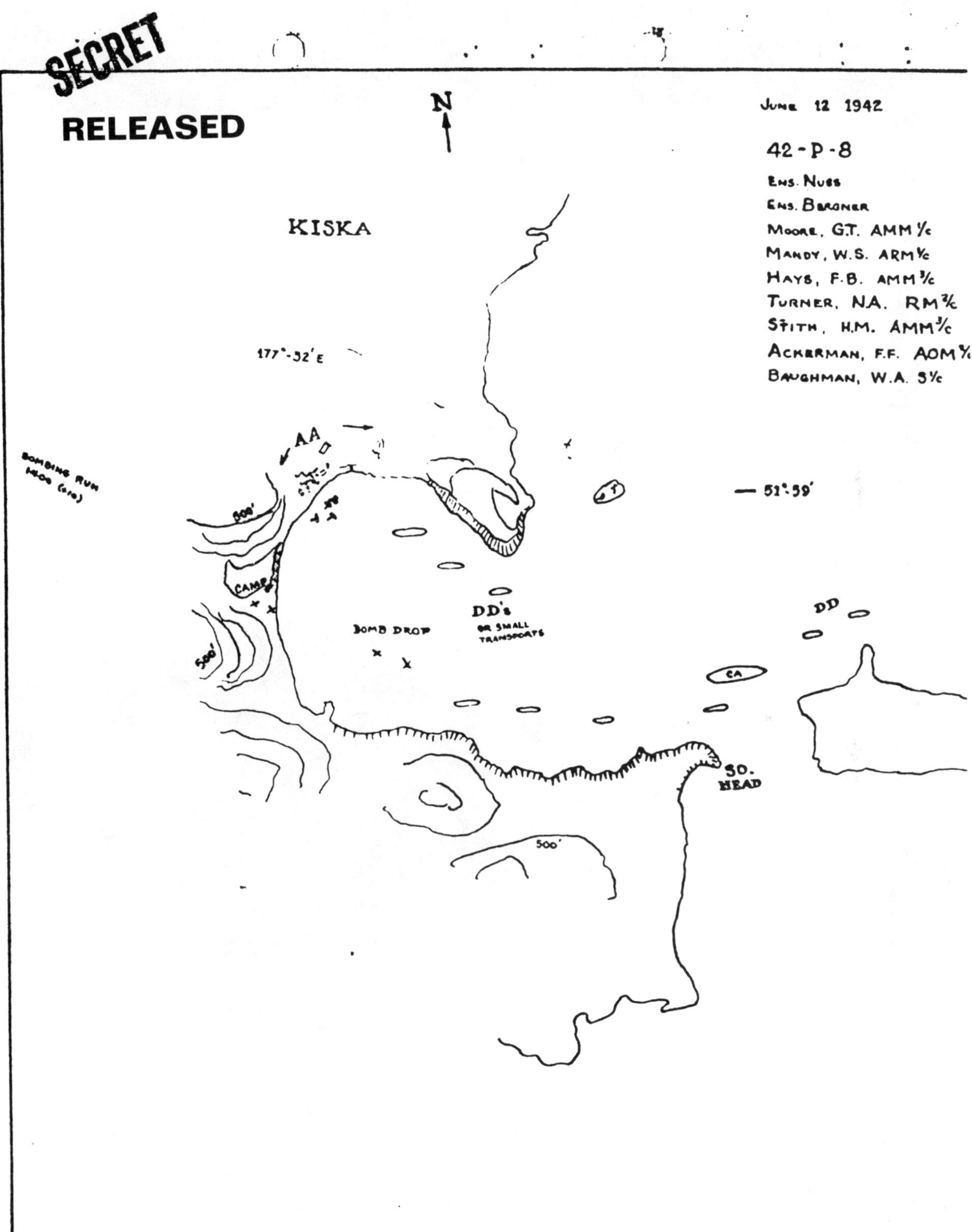

Drawing of Ens. Leo Nuss' bombing run on Kiska—12 June 1942

(VP-42 War Diary)

Bomb blast in Kiska harbor—June 1942

(Adm. James S. Russell Collection)

U.S. bombing attack on Kiska harbor—18 June 1942

(National Archives)

View of Kiska harbor with Japanese planes and installations

Chapter **6**

Moving West through Umnak,
Atka and Adak

ANYONE LOOKING AT A CHART of the north Pacific area can see the possibilities for an invasion route from Japan through the Aleutians to Canada and the United States. General Billy Mitchell had called attention to this problem twenty years earlier, in the 1920s, but his ideas were pretty well suppressed when he was chastised for bucking conventional military wisdom of the time. So the present problem was that, aside from the PBY's and a few B-26's and P-40's, the United States had absolutely no defenses in the Aleutian Islands. Not only that but the powers in Washington would not break loose with any funds to build anything in that area. Finally General Buckner, the Commander of the whole area, managed a bit of high-handed maneuvering and a new base was built at Cold Bay, on the end of the Alaska Peninsula. General Buckner sent Colonel Benjamin Talley of the Army Corps of Engineers out to engineer the building of the base at Cold Bay. From there he was to move ever further west, laying down millions of feet of Marsten Matting for runways. Marsten Matting was the name given to the interlocking, perforated steel strips which were laid down on a flat dirt surface to transform it into a runway. A Marsten Matting runway may not have been the smoothest runway in the world, but the air war in the Pacific would have been slowed down many months without these "quickie" air facilities.

Finally there was some movement in Washington and the start of a plan emerged. My own theory of how the defense plan was set up is that the Army and Navy appointed a committee of desk jockeys in Washington, D.C. When they finally found a chart of the Aleutian Islands, they couldn't pronounce anything on it, so they came to a profound and far-reaching decision. "We won't build a base on any island unless at least two of us can pronounce the name."

Semisopochnoi, Chuginadak, Vsevidof, Khvostof, Anagaksik. Names from a Russian novel? No. Names of some of the Aleutian Islands. Since the Russians were the first white explorers in this chain of islands, it is not surprising to find a number of Russian-sounding names.

Can you imagine some headquarters picking up a radio transmission: "This is Navy Flight 305, enroute to Semisopochnoi, passing Chuginadak. Our next checkpoint is Vsevidof, estimating at 1305 Zebra. Do you wish us to check out Khvostof or Anagaksik on the way?" Headquarters would immediately stick a pin in the middle of their Siberian map, report Navy Flight 305 to be 2700 miles off course, and prepare to notify the next of kin.

Kodiak and Dutch Harbor, with the small base at Cold Bay in between, were too

119

far away from Kiska and Attu to allow for the kind of surveillance and attacks needed on those islands. Bases to the west were needed, and until they were built, Seaplane Tenders were used in several spots to set up and take care of the PBY's and flight crews. The survey and exploration voyage of *Williamson* the previous summer provided our planners with some likely locations for Seaplane Tender operations. Once we had such operations in place the entire Aleutian chain clear past Attu, the westernmost island, could be patrolled. So the truth of the matter was that when the President of the United States asked his military planners what kind of defense the country had in the Aleutians the answer must have been, "We've got a bunch of Navy guys with their PBY's out there. Nobody knows exactly what they are doing, but we do ship some gas and bombs and food out there once in a while so they must be doing something."

Umnak was a pronounceable name, so that was where the first base was built west of Dutch Harbor. When the Japanese carrier planes were surprised by the fighter planes from the west during their 4 June attack on Dutch Harbor, they figured there was a secret base out there. Top secret? Well, the same terrible weather that prevented us from finding the Japanese task force before they attacked also hid our base-building activities. You could have built New York City out there, and nobody would have known it. Actually, because there were some unusual sources of financing for building Umnak, all construction materials being shipped were sent to a fictitious "canning company." The U.S. government didn't even know there was such a place as Umnak.

The base at Umnak consisted of a stretch of steel matting laid out on a flat part of the island, and numerous tents. Our planes had retractable wheels, so we could operate from either water or land. Landing at Umnak we never knew which we were doing. There was a time when I thought the rollercoaster on the Pike in Long Beach was the wildest ride in the world. One take-off from Umnak convinced me I was wrong.

"Advance Base Operations" is a term used to describe flight operations where crews leave their permanent base behind and give up the comforts and amenities for the sake of battling the elements twenty-four hours a day—air, land and sea—and, with any luck, become more adept at their job under adverse conditions. When we first started flying out of Umnak and later, Atka, it didn't take long for us to realize what an advance base really was.

The names Atka and Adak aren't too tough to pronounce, so they turned out to be our next advance bases. Atka was about 300 miles west of Umnak, and Adak was about another 100 miles out. That put us within 300 or 400 miles of Kiska. Attu was a couple of hundred miles further to the west than Kiska. Cold Bay was the base right at the tip of the Alaska Peninsula, but it was so far from Kiska that it was not practical to run regular bombing missions from there once we began making Kiska the prime focus of attack operations. In July VP-42 used Cold Bay as a sort of home base from which we sent detachments to operate from Atka. After a couple of weeks of operations from one of our tenders, a detachment was relieved by fresh crews and planes, and the original detachment returned to Cold Bay for ground maintenance and search operations further up the chain.

By 27 June there was some indication that the Japanese might be moving northward toward the Bering Strait. Our skipper's plane and three others moved to Nome for the purpose of convoying shipping and patrol duty in the area. No contact was made with any Japanese forces, but it turned out to be the second time VP-42 personnel came in contact with Russian aviators. Since the day a year earlier when we had serviced the Russian PBY's at Kodiak, a great deal had changed in the world

VP-42 PBY-5A's on Umnak Island

(National Archives)

PBY-5A's in revetment on Umnak Island

(National Archives)

View of Ship Rock offshore from Umnak Island

(National Archives)

Apparently nobody could decide where to build the roads at Otter Point, Umnak

P-40 takes off from mat at Umnak Island—June 1942

(National Archives)

Living quarters at Umnak Island in 1942

High level conference to consider beer procurement at Umnak: Rear—Freeman, Townsend, Stallings; front—Brady, McGrath, Pierson (Freeman Collection)

Butcher, Babbitt, Olubych (Freeman Collection)

situation. Fairbanks, Alaska was the exchange point for Lend-Lease aircraft going to Russia. American pilots flew the planes to Fairbanks and from there Russian pilots flew them on into Russia via Nome.

VP-41, commanded by Lieutenant Commander Paul Foley, had a rotation operation similar to ours going out of Dutch Harbor, sending a couple of planes to Nazan Bay for two weeks and then relieving them with fresh crews. VP-43, with Lieutenant Commander Carroll B. Jones commanding, was operating mostly from Nazan Bay at Atka.

In mid-June 1942 USS *Gillis*, another Seaplane Tender just like the *Williamson*, set up a seadrome in Nazan Bay at the island of Atka. *Gillis* was commanded by Lieutenant Commander Norman Garton, with whom I had flown during VP-42's operations at Tongue Point. We started operating from Nazan Bay shortly after the Japanese attacks on Dutch Harbor. Eventually a couple of other tenders took their turns taking care of our needs at Nazan Bay. *Hulbert* was another converted four-piper and arrived from the States after the middle of June. *Casco* had actually been built as a Seaplane Tender and was used as a communications station while at anchor at Cold Bay in early June. Later she moved out to Nazan Bay to service our PBY's. *Casco* was better equipped to handle itinerant flight crew personnel, with better messing facilities and bunk spaces. Our patrols extended clear out past Attu from Nazan Bay and we began hearing warnings about getting too close to the Russian islands west of Attu. We were told that if we were forced down in that territory the Soviets would intern us for the rest of the war. It seemed kind of unfriendly for an ally to do that, but that was the way the politics worked.

Adak was to be a shore base, and it became operational a short time later. It was another of those steel matting and tent type of bases, built by Army Engineers.

VP-43 arrived in the Aleutians at about the time the *Gillis* set up shop at Atka, about 11 June 1942. They had been operating out of San Diego and suddenly received orders to head for the Aleutians. It must have been a shock to go from great flying weather to some of the worst in the world in a matter of a few days. The weather would have been enough shock, but the Wing Commander had ordered continuous bombing of Kiska by his PBY's, and VP-43 led the way, shuttling back and forth between Nazan Bay and Kiska. A couple of the VP-43 guys told us they loaded their bombs in San Diego, hauled them all the way to the Aleutians and dropped them on Kiska on their first bombing run. There had been a lot of bombing training before the war started, but nobody had thought of training in dive-bombing in PBY's. Due to the constant low ceilings over Kiska, it became common practice to come diving out of the clouds, drop the bombs and then have both pilots haul back on the yoke to get back up into the safety of the overcast. It was very difficult to catch the Japanese by surprise. No matter what method of attack was used they always seemed to be ready to bang away at us with their anti-aircraft batteries.

Now and then someone would recall the hours of training with the Norden bombsight. It was truly a wonderful tool for bombing from high altitude in clear weather, conditions which were rare or non-existent in our operations. We seldom bothered to have a bombsight installed for our missions. The only crewman stationed in the nose position was the guy firing the bow machine gun.

VP-41 and VP-42 had had several months of Aleutian seasoning before the Japanese occupied Kiska and Attu, so we were as familiar with the territory as it was possible to be, given the restricted visibility of the whole area. We had standing orders to stop by and drop our bombs on Kiska whenever we passed reasonably close while on patrol to the west. VP-43 must have found their first month or so of operation pretty tough. VP-51 had some PBY's operating with us after the middle of June too. Altogether we must have had about forty PBY's flying around.

But after a couple of weeks of shuttle-bombing, losing two or three airplanes and crews and not seeing the Japanese preparing to depart, the order came through during the last few days of June to cease the constant pounding. The enemy had gotten well dug in and it was going to take more than aerial bombing to jar them loose. Besides that, the Army had started flying their B-17's and B-24's from Umnak, making the long haul to Kiska. The heavy bombers did a better job than the PBY's could do. We were pretty happy to turn most of the bombing duties over to the "heavies." One of our pilots, Lt. Clark Hood, went along on one of the early B-24 bombing missions out of Umnak to help with the navigation and as an observer. Sadly, the B-24 was shot down over Kiska and all hands were lost. Bombing Kiska was dangerous business, no matter what kind of plane we were flying.

Eventually the Navy got some ships out in the Kiska area and did some bombardment with their big guns, but that didn't chase the Japanese out of Kiska either. They just went into their caves until the shooting stopped.

Whenever we were on patrol in the vicinity of Kiska, we were on the alert for reports of Army Air Corps pilots being shot down. Sometimes we circled around just outside Kiska harbor when we knew the Army guys were making an attack. That way we could visually monitor the area and help out if somebody got in trouble. The Japanese had some fighter planes on floats at Kiska; if we saw one of them taking off, we high-tailed it for the nearest overcast, which was never far away. Nobody could survive for very long in the icy waters but several times our planes managed to get there in time to set down and rescue downed pilots. One of the Army pilots was so impressed with this service that he wrote a poem about it. Our Wing Commander issued a letter with the poem and had copies distributed to all hands in the PBY squadrons.

UNITED STATES PACIFIC FLEET
FLEET AIR WING FOUR

P15
Serial 1293
Subject: Letter from Commanding Officer, ELEVENTH Fighter command.

"APPRECIATION"

by
Jacob W. Dixon
1st Lieut., Air Corps

I don't have much use for the Navy,
    being an Army man.
But I must take off my hat to some pilots
    of this sea-faring clan.

These boys didn't give a damn for the weather,
   and Jap lead meant even less.
I've seen 'em fly thru storms a-plenty,
   their planes a riddled mess.

I'll always remember the way they informed us,
   of the Jap's position at sea.
And how they told us almost to the minute,
   the time an attack would be.

Then when we went on the offensive,
   and flew with no land in sight.
We knew that in the clouds above us,
   a rescue plane watched the flight.

They even patrolled where we were fighting,
   to save us if we fell.
They hid in the clouds from the "Zeroes,"
   and the ack-ack could go to hell.

So here's to those boys of the Navy,
   a bunch of damn good guys.
And especially to those great pilots,
   who fly the P B Y's.

(Signed) L. E. Gehres

With no bases west of Umnak our Aleutian operations depended entirely on our tenders. Our movement west was not exactly unopposed. Since there was no fighter protection for the ships playing mother hen for our PBY's, the tenders were pretty vulnerable. While serving as tender for VP-43 aircraft (and itinerant VP-41 and VP-42 planes) at Atka, *Gillis* survived a couple of bombing attacks from the Japanese flying out of Kiska. For a period of time they had a couple of their big four-engine flying boats making some bombing missions around Atka. But on 5 August the Army sent out some P-38's and caught the big flying boats near Atka and shot them down.

The converted WW-I destroyers such as *Gillis*, *Williamson* and *Hulbert* were sorely overtaxed trying to service ten or more planes and crews. At Atka the flight crews took over an abandoned shack ashore for berthing. The tender managed to furnish them and their planes with food, gas and bombs by continuous shuttling of boats, ship to shore to plane. During one period *Gillis* stayed on station at Nazan Bay until she was completely out of bombs and aviation fuel and running low on ship fuel, before being relieved to return to Kodiak for replenishment.

On 26 August 1942, when a VP-43 plane reported being down in heavy seas off Amlia Island and needing assistance, *Williamson* went to the rescue. They found the wallowing PBY, got a line on it and began the slow journey back into Nazan Bay. Towing a flying boat in the open sea is never easy, but at night when the sea is heavy it becomes pretty hazardous. When the wave action caused the plane to collide with the starboard screwguard of the ship, a wing broke off, releasing the depth charges being carried on the plane; they exploded right under the ship. There were casualties both on the ship and on the wrecked aircraft, even though the skipper made the decision to illuminate the area with searchlights to assist with the rescue of the aircrew from the sinking aircraft. Illuminating your ship when enemy submarines are suspected in the area can be awfully risky, but the action did allow some rescues which would not have been possible otherwise. *Williamson* sustained some serious damage to her bottom and had to go back to the States for repairs.

For the most part we were so occupied with our own operations that we didn't have time to worry about what was going on anyplace else. However there were a few times when we had the luxury of wondering how the rest of the Navy was fighting the war.

Now and then an Intelligence Officer briefed us on how the war was progressing in other parts of the world. The day he told us about the *Lexington* being sunk in the South Pacific was a pretty sobering time. I had seen the *Lexington* in San Diego and it was hard to imagine that huge carrier being sunk. We hoped that the Pacific war would soon take a turn for the better.

In fact a short time later we got the word that the Japanese had lost four carriers at the Battle of Midway. That was a lot better news. And we wished that we could have accounted for a couple more in our area. But it was not to be. The Japanese carrier task force disappeared from our area intact. They left an occupation force behind, and we were left with the problem of building primitive bases on barren islands so we could battle their troops.

Bases such as Umnak did have some improvements as time went on. There eventually got to be several buildings on the island, and quonset huts replaced most of the tents. A new bunch of Navy construction people, called CB's (Construction Battalion), showed up on the scene and took over building of the Navy installation on the island. They built a frame building for a mess hall and put up a few Quonset huts to replace the tents. With winter coming on we were pretty thankful to move into something more substantial than a tent. It got to be a pretty comfortable place to come back to after a couple of weeks of flying bombing missions and patrolling from Nazan Bay. We even got to fly to Dutch Harbor once in awhile and bring back a cargo of beer.

Not long after the buildings began going up on Umnak the Chaplains started visiting on a regular basis. Catholic and Protestant Chaplains alternated their visits. The Catholic Chaplain flew in one Saturday, and the Protestant Chaplain flew in the next Saturday. The Catholic Chaplain always held Mass on Sunday morning when he was there. The Protestant Chaplain always held services Sunday evening when he was there. It sounds like a normal and satisfactory arrangement, but a problem developed.

The problem stemmed from the fact that the Chaplain brought our weekly movie with him. The movie was always shown on Sunday evening. With Catholic services in the morning, everybody got a fair shot at the movie seats. But when the Protestant Chaplain held evening services, the movie followed immediately in the same building. So the Protestant guys always got all of the good movie seats.

I guess all of us Catholic guys had heard about the early Christians being thrown to the lions for their faith and wondered whether we could stand up to that. But being forced to have a lousy seat for the movies seemed to be more than even the martyrs had to endure. So we took our problem to Father Smith, the Catholic Chaplain.

I'm sure Father Smith had the finest in Catholic seminary training and knew all the rules and regulations concerning his religion. But when you have heard confessions in the Aleutian Islands and the guys are confessing mortal sins like, "I lost the starboard sea anchor out in Nazan Bay the other day," or, "I punched a 50-caliber machine gun through the glass in the port blister last week," or, "I dropped the tool box in the bilges and put a hole in the bottom of the plane," theology begins to take on new dimensions—or loses all of its dimensions. "These guys live by different rules. It's a different world."

The Pope couldn't have been more solemn than Father Smith. "I am granting you permission to attend Protestant Services." Then he smiled, "Everybody knows that Protestants sing lots better than Catholics. So you guys concentrate on learning how to sing. And I'll expect to hear real results the next time I come out here."

So at Umnak we had Catholic Mass with the beautiful old Protestant hymns. We could belt out "How Great Thou Art" as well as anybody. It would be thirty years before the Catholic Church finally did the same thing officially.

The Army Infantry had a base about three miles across the tundra from our base and they had a BX—which we didn't have. Occasionally some of us would make the trek over to the Army camp and load up on candy bars or other goodies which they might have. Tramping across the tundra on one of these excursions we began hearing sounds of a saxophone drifting along on the atmosphere. Since there was nothing and nobody in sight, we began a search of the area to determine whether there was actually a saxophone player in the neighborhood or if we had just been in the Aleutians too long. Finally the mystery was solved. We found a dual .50 caliber, water-cooled gun emplacement, consisting of two trenches coming out of opposite sides of a ten by twelve foot dug-out where the crew lived. It looked like a scene from World War One. Down in this hole in the ground sat a soldier blowing his heart out on his horn. Not surprisingly most of his music had a sad sound to it. We passed the time of day with the members of the gun crew and continued on our way, a little happier with our lot in life and glad we didn't have to live in a root cellar.

Church music and dug-out music weren't the only kinds of music we had at Umnak. We had one guy, Hoot Smith, who always carried a set of drum sticks with him and who could go like crazy on a couple of the cook's dishpans. Then there was Marcus with his guitar. And I hauled my clarinet with me wherever I went. I had the idea that if I practiced for the whole war, I might emerge as a latter-day Benny Goodman. Well, at least I ended up on the winning side in the war. You can't have everything.

We played together whenever we were at Umnak at the same time. We finally got to where we started and stopped together, and sometimes people even knew what we were playing. There were some who claimed our music helped to drive the Japanese out of the Aleutians. Could be.

Late in 1942 our skipper was Lieutenant Commander "Cy" Perkins. One evening in the mess hall we played "Beat Your Feet in the Mississippi Mud" for him. I was never sure whether he was punishing us or complimenting us, but he decided that we should put on a show, "You know—like they do in the movies."

Bill Brady, Lt.(jg) Campbell's navigator, was pretty fast with the one-liners; we got him to be Master of Ceremonies. Then we combed the squadron for talent. Any talent. We didn't come up with Hollywood calibre, but it was the best show on the island.

The skipper invited several Commanding Officers of different outfits on the island, and some of us invited the Army guys who lived in those dugout holes in the ground manning the water-cooled .50 caliber machine guns. It seemed to us that as lousy as our show might turn out to be, it had to be entertaining for those poor soldiers.

The title of this production was "From Craps to Reveille." It opened with some guys shooting craps. Pretty soon one guy lost all his money and decided to hit the sack. The band played "Goodnight, Sweetheart," he started snoring, and we swung into "Dream a Little Dream." A guy walked across the stage with a big sign that said, "HIS DREAM." The show was on!

Bill Brady ran out and did a ten-minute monologue and then introduced a tap-dance act. Two guys in GI shoes did a routine to "Tea for Two" and brought down the house—almost literally. We had to straighten out the planks we had rigged for a stage after their encore.

A guy did a recitation of the poem, "Hiawatha," and we played some Indian music like "Indian Love Call." Then one of the cooks, who really was a fine singer, sang "Chloe." With proper accompaniment he would have been tops on any stage. But he would never get a more enthusiastic ovation than he did that night on Umnak.

We had about eight acts and lots of Bill Brady's patter in between, and finally we worked our way to the grand finale. We had four of the beefiest guys in the squadron do a takeoff on the Rockettes. While one of our planes was in Kodiak the crew managed to get some girdles and bras and garters and anything else they could get hold of to outfit these guys. They were a smash. Their kicks weren't very high and they lacked something in precision, but the audience kept them coming back until they could hardly move any more. At a much later date I actually saw the Rockettes at Radio City Music Hall in New York. As pretty as those girls were and as wonderful as their dancing was I have to confess the vision was blurred by those beefy guys on Umnak.

Then the Master at Arms came on the stage and held reveille on the guy sleeping; the whole cast came on stage, and we closed with "Beat Your Feet in the Mississippi Mud." It's funny. In the movies they always end the big production with something real patriotic like "God Bless America." I guess we just weren't that patriotic.

That show would never make it in Peoria, but we were the toast of Umnak for one grand night. We did the show again for those of the crew who couldn't attend the first night, but it didn't come off quite as good the second time. Within about a day or so the cast was spread out all over the Aleutians and we never got up the nerve to impose that kind of treatment on our squadron-mates again.

He-e-e-re's Brady and the Sea Anchors appearing live at the Cafe de la Mess Hall, Umnak (they were a drag): L-R—Brady, Smith, Freeman, Marcus (Courtesy of Bill Brady)

Chapter 7

Boredom, Terror

I ONCE HEARD A PILOT SAY that flying is hours of boredom, broken up by moments of stark terror. That's a fair description of flying a ten or twelve hour patrol.

A typical patrol flight began with the pilot's being briefed in the evening for the flight we were to make the next day. The rest of the crew checked the plane over and got everything as ready as possible so that we would get off at the assigned time and stay flying for as long as we could. We always took off with full fuel tanks. In its original configuration the PBY held 1750 gallons of gas in what was called a "wet wing," the center section of the wing designed as the fuel tank. At about the time the war started we installed self-sealing cells in one half of the fuel tank; that cut our fuel capacity down by about 350 gallons. The self-sealing cells were a blessing when the enemy was shooting holes in your gas tank, but there were other times when it would have been nice to have the extra fuel. The ratio of time-in-the-air vs fuel capacity came out uncomfortably close sometimes.

On a typical day we got up at about 0400, ate breakfast and headed for the plane. If we were operating from land, we walked. If we were operating from a ship, we went by boat. Then we made out the "Yellow Sheet,"[1] checked the plane over again and climbed aboard, manned our assigned stations, and started the engines. Ordinarily, I was in the flight engineer's tower, the first radioman was at the radioman's station in the area behind the cockpit, the Plane Commander was in the pilot's seat, another pilot was in the co-pilot's seat, and the navigator was on the port side, across from the radioman. We had two people manning the waist lookout stations, and one more man standing by to assist wherever he might be needed. When we manned the guns he was assigned to take over the tunnel gun.

When the engines had been started and all stations had reported to the Plane Commander that everything was ready, we either launched from the ramp or cast off from the buoy and taxied out toward takeoff position. If we were lucky enough to be operating from a base with a runway, we taxied to the end of the runway for takeoff. When the engines came up to temperature, each was turned up to high power and checked for proper operation. When the Plane Commander was satisfied with all preparations, he asked all stations to report when ready for takeoff. When everyone had reported and we had reached the proper position, he went to full throttle and took off. Then we headed for our assigned search sector.

---

[1]As already noted in Chapter 4, the Yellow Sheet, the checklist for preflighting, also listed the crew and any aircraft problems which developed during the flight. Ordinarily the Yellow Sheet was handed to the ground crew before takeoff, but we often kept it with us when operating from an advance base.

A search sector was generally a pie-shaped piece of ocean marked out on the chart. It usually consisted of a 600-mile leg going out, a 100-mile cross leg, and a 600-mile leg coming back to the point of departure. Sometimes, if our base of operations was being moved, the assigned search took us from one point, such as Dutch Harbor, and ended at another point like Nazan Bay. Although we spent some time patrolling on the Bering Sea side of the Aleutians, most of our searches were on the Pacific Ocean side of the Aleutians, to the southwest, toward Japan, our mission being to intercept any Japanese ships which might be trying to bring supplies in to Kiska.

For the first four hours everybody stayed where they were at takeoff. If the ceiling permitted, we flew at about 900 feet altitude. Sometimes we had to fly quite a bit lower than that. All eyes were focused on the sea. If there were instruments to watch, they were checked every few seconds and the eyes again turned toward the sea. If it was dark we still looked at the sea simply because there wasn't anything else to look at. At about 0900 it was time to change watches.

Babbitt relieved me in the tower. Summers relieved Townsend at the radio gear and Townsend and I would take over the watches in the waist blisters. By this time Stallings was checking into whatever food rations we had received for the flight, and we might have a little discussion on who was going to cook. We generally had a pot of coffee going by this time too. The navigator took wind readings periodically, and he might give the pilots a few degrees change of course if we needed a bit more or less compensation for the wind. If we sighted anything which needed to be investigated, the navigator had to plot any deviations from our original course and then get us back on track after the side trip had been completed.

At about five or five and a half hours out, we reached the end of our out-bound leg and changed course. When we reached the end of the cross leg, everybody was beginning to get hungry, and the cook-for-the-day fired up the hotplate and dug out the pots and pans. Sometimes we just had soup and sandwiches. Now and then we lucked out and got some round steak, canned potatoes and canned vegetables. Such a gourmet meal really tested the chef's abilities, but hunger can compensate for a lot of less-than-great cooking. Whatever it was, it always tasted good and was a welcome break in the monotony. The cook always served everybody on station, and he did a good deal of running fore and aft getting everybody fed. There were a few occasions when the guy on the radar picked up a target during mealtime. Immediate manning of battle stations left half-finished meals all over the place and the cook muttering unkind things as he hurriedly secured his galley. Whenever the ship was identified as one of those "dumb Russians," it only added to our low opinion of them.

By this time we were about half-way back on our return leg, and we did some more changing of watches. There was never a change of scenery, but it was nice to look out of a different window once in awhile. One of my favorite pastimes while watching the sea go by was singing. There was something about the drone of PBY engines that added a whole lot to the quality of my voice. We were wearing headphones all the time, so nobody appreciated it but me. Somehow there was an operatic quality to my "Road to Mandalay" or "Ah, Sweet Mystery of Life." It was a little disappointing to get back on the ground and find that I still sounded like two cats fighting on the backyard fence.

When we were something like an hour from the end of our inbound leg, the Plane Commander quite often ordered the waist gunners to stand by for gunnery practice. The blisters were opened, the guns rigged out and the gunners reported ready to commence firing. It was a little drill to see how fast the gunners could be ready to

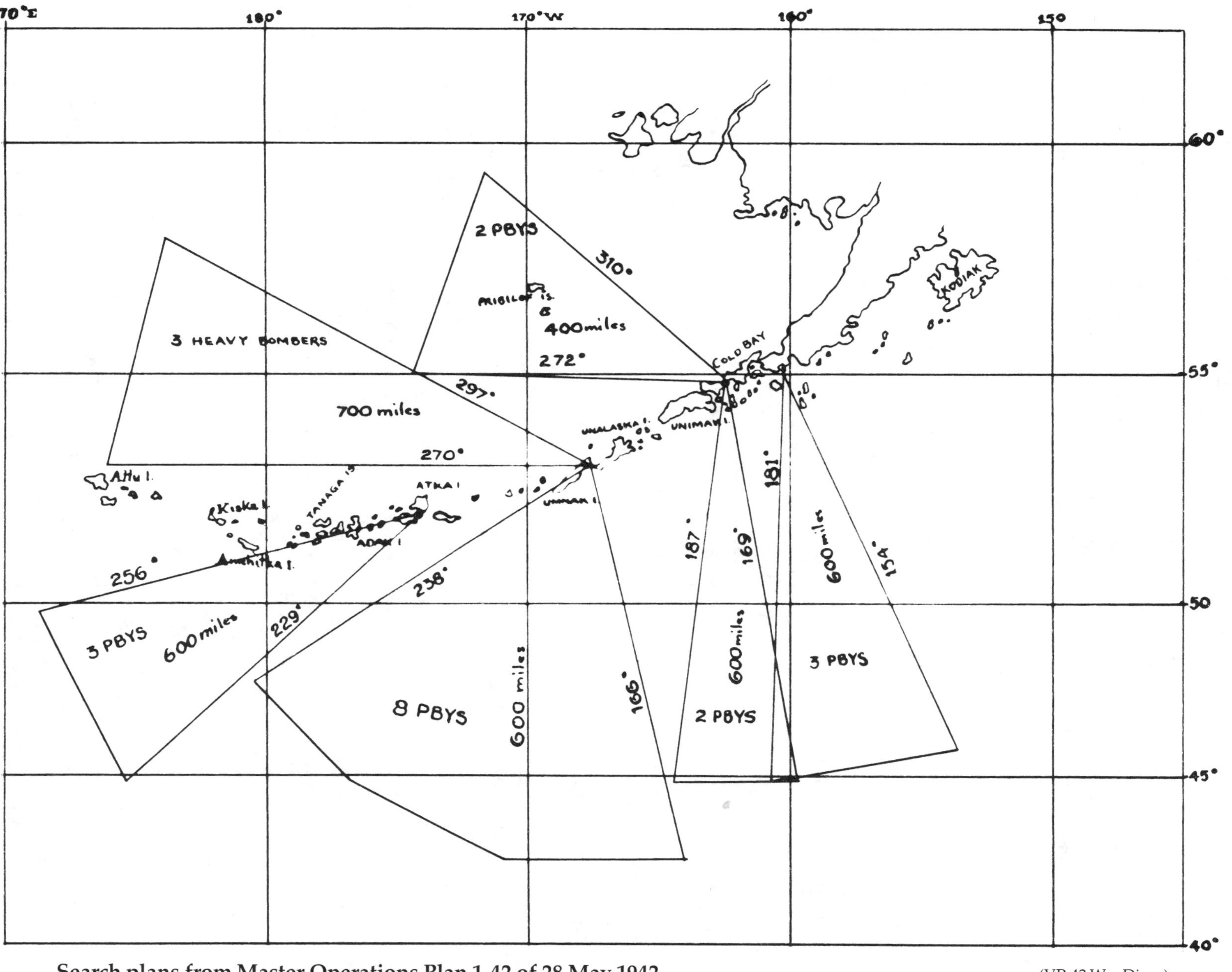

Search plans from Master Operations Plan 1-42 of 28 May 1942

(VP-42 War Diary)

137

shoot. When the order was given to fire a few bursts at a whitecap, the gunners started banging away at the ocean. There was no way to check the marksmanship, but the gunner generally knew pretty well what he was doing.

With the guns rigged back in, we started to prepare for landing. If our navigation was good, we would soon hit our departure point, which was generally a prominent rock or the end of an island. So, at the end of perhaps eleven hours we were right back where we started from. Most of the time it was hours of boredom, but there were some moments of terror, too. The following accounts highlight some episodes from my Aleutian flying experiences.

In late June 1942 we had to make a flight from Dutch Harbor to Kodiak to haul a patient who needed the more extensive medical facilities there. The patient was an old Chief (probably about 35) off a destroyer. There was no rush on the trip as he was not a bed patient and no medics were along to take any special care of him. So we made our usual search sweep offshore on the way to Kodiak and eventually made a landfall on an island just west of Kodiak. Somebody in the crew offered the information that there was a herd of wild cattle on the island. It was decided that it would not take us very far out of our way to verify this interesting report.

The island had a 3,000 foot mountain which dropped off to a flat plain toward the shoreline. The cattle were supposed to have been seen running around on the plain. The visibility was pretty good and we were flying at 2,000 feet over the plain with the lookouts trying to spot the herd of cattle. I was walking from the waist section forward to secure our leftover food items in preparation for our landing at Kodiak.

Suddenly the bottom dropped out of everything. It is really amazing how many things the human eye can see in a second or two. We had hit a super downdraft and I was suspended halfway between the bottom and the top of the hull. A bag of coffee and a sack of eggs were suspended right in front of me. Townsend had been at his radio table, strapped into his seat and typing. The seat broke its moorings and was suspended in midair with Townsend and his typewriter all in perfect place. Pierson was hanging in mid-air with his charts and navigation equipment right along with him. Lt. Dickey had his safety belt on, but there was a half foot of open space between him and the seat. This whole panorama of weightlessness lasted about two seconds.

When we bottomed out after dropping about 500 feet, all things in suspension immediately obeyed the laws of gravity. The coffee and eggs mixed themselves together in the bilges. Townsend, his typewriter and seat bounced under the radio table in a heap. Pierson caught the edge of the navigator's table on the way down and ended up under the table hanging on to the edge by his finger-tips. I was flattened in the bilges right alongside the coffee-and-egg omelet.

My first realization after the initial shock was that the engines were still running and we were apparently still flying. We hadn't crashed. After glancing forward and seeing that things were settling down, I went aft to the waist compartment. Our passenger had been sitting near one of the blisters sightseeing. He was now on his hands and knees with a terrorized look on his face, pale as a ghost. The two lookouts were on their feet looking at a hole in the port blister. A can of 50-caliber ammo had broken its hold-down strap and gone flying right out through the plexiglass blister.

I took over the phones from one of the lookouts and reported on the conditions in the waist compartment. Lt. Dickey grumbled that we should know better than to fly along the lee side of a mountain in williwaw country. "Dropping five hundred feet must be some kind of record. For a second there I thought we were going to join the wild cows. Did anybody ever see them?"

When I asked the Chief if he was feeling all right, he just grimaced and yelled back, "How much longer do I have to fly in this damned machine?" I got the impression that he definitely preferred his destroyer to our PBY. Trying to reassure him, I acted nonchalant about the whole thing, but I don't think he was convinced.

The thought of that mess of eggs and coffee to be cleaned out of the bilges didn't bother me at all. I was just glad we still had wings on the airplane.

The wingtip floats on a PBY are designed so that they can be lowered for use in landing on the water and raised to form the wing tips while the aircraft is in flight. They are powered by an electric motor located on the forward bulkhead of the flight engineer's station. The motor is just about between the flight engineer's knees when he is sitting up in the tower (the engineer's station).

When we operated from land we often lowered the wingtip floats in order to provide convenient tie-down points for securing the plane. Just before takeoff from the runway we would raise the floats. We had gone through this routine one morning in June 1942, getting ready for takeoff from Cold Bay with a full load of fuel and four 500-pound bombs hanging on the wing. The floats reached their upward run, and we blasted off down the runway. There is a limit switch on the float motor which is supposed to turn off the motor when the floats are at their up position. The limit switch failed and the motor was grinding itself to bits all during our takeoff run. Just as we got airborne I spotted smoke coming from the motor, and a second later sparks and small flames began spewing out of it. I called out, "Fire in the float motor."

In an instant Townsend and Babbitt were below me with CO_2 extinguishers spraying them on the fire. I was beating on my pants' legs to keep the sparks and flame from catching me on fire. We didn't need anybody in flames sitting right below the gas tanks full of 100-octane gas. The rest of the crew gets nervous about that.

Every time I put my head down between my legs I got a blast of CO_2 in the face. Lt. Dickey asked, "How are you guys doing back there?"

It took me a second to answer. "We've got it under control."

With the fire out we were still faced with a really tricky job of landing the plane with a full load aboard. We could have dropped our four 500-pound bombs and lightened the load by a ton, but wasting bombs needlessly was not what we were supposed to be doing. Lt. Dickey decided to try to get us down as gently as possible with the full load. He never made a smoother landing. He brought her in, slicked her down on the runway and taxied to a parking place. I didn't even get a chance to change pants. We cleaned up the mess, installed a new float motor and headed back out on our search.

The Flight Engineer's tower in a PBY could be pretty close quarters at any time, but during a night patrol the little compartment seemed even smaller. The small, oval windows on either side of one's head offered a mini-view of the outside world during the daytime, but at night the darkness made the windows seem like black-out curtains, and the normal six-inch space on either side of the Mech's head seemed to shrink to two inches. Anybody with claustrophobia problems would be in real trouble in the tower.

My routine in the tower was to look out the port window, look at the gauges—RPM, Manifold Pressure, Cylinder Head Temperature, Fuel Pressure and the Flow Meters—make sure the mixture controls were in "Auto Lean" (Automatic Lean fuel mixture), then have a look out the starboard window. I did that at night, even though both of the windows were black. Who knew? We might pass over a submarine with all his lights on.

We were about three hours out on a night patrol about the first of July 1942, and the cylinder-head temps were bugging me. The port one was running at about 220 and the starboard one at about 230. Nothing abnormal, but it was always more tidy when they ran the same. I had mulled over all of the possible reasons for the difference about ten times and was trying to ignore the whole thing when suddenly the starboard engine cut out.

There is nothing that will get a plane crew's attention faster than to have an engine cut out when they are three hundred miles from the nearest land and flying at 800 feet in the middle of the night. The steady drone of those engines provides a certain stability to a flight. A sudden cut-out causes immediate uncertainty. It was only for a second or two but it seemed like an eternity. My signal light from the Plane Commander went to "Auto Rich" and he said, "Tower, can you see any reason for that cut-out on your gauges back there?"

"Everything is normal and has been ever since we took off." He had "Auto Rich" even before the light went on. If the engine needed a richer mixture of fuel, it had it. We had about ten minutes to get our hearts out of our throats before we had the same kind of cut-out again. That time we went to "Full Rich."

When it happened a third time, Lt. Dickey said, "Pierson, give us a course back to Cold Bay." He had already sent them a message about the engine; now he followed it with notification that we were heading back to base. "Tower, unless you see some indication that the engine is going bad, we won't shut it down, but stand by for single engine operation on short notice."

We still had a pretty sizable load of gas and four 500-pound bombs, so single engine operation might be marginal. We wouldn't hesitate to get rid of the bomb load if the plane were in jeopardy, but we hoped that wouldn't be necessary.

"Aye aye, sir. The RPM jumps around a bit when it cuts out, but that's the only thing that is showing up. It is running cooler now with the richer mixture." I hoped my mental gyrations about the cylinder head temperatures hadn't put a curse on our starboard engine.

Once we went for a full fifteen minutes with no cut-out, but most of the time the cut-outs came at eight to ten minute intervals. A couple of times it seemed as if the engine might stop completely, but then it roared to life again. Everybody started breathing again and wondered what would happen the next time.

"What is our ETA, Pierson? Trying to get into Cold Bay in the dark might be out of the question." It was nice to know that Lt. Dickey planned on getting back, but nobody relished the thought of flying around in circles waiting for daylight.

"Zero-four-oh-five," answered Pierson. "Should be just about daylight when we get there."

I had been trying to keep track of how many times the engine had cut out. I thought I had counted twelve. It seemed to me if we got through six more times we should be pretty close to home. I happened to look below me and noticed the box of flight rations resting, untouched, on top of the hotplate. It was long past chow time, but nobody had brought up the subject. We had never had the experience of turning any flight rations back in. Maybe they wouldn't—and the damned engine cut out again.

Babbitt was tapping me on the leg, indicating it was time to change the watch. When I climbed down we just looked at each other and shook our heads and I went aft to take my station as port waist lookout. There wasn't much to see, but it was a relief to look at something besides those gauges.

The horizon became just visible in the east as day began to break and Lt. Dickey announced that land was in sight. If we could survive two more cut-outs we might be on the ground.

Finally the base was in sight and we went into the required recognition routine. We dipped a wing a couple of times and made a circle to port. No sense in having an anti-aircraft gunner spoil our grand entrance. Those guys sat there for days on end, just waiting for somebody to forget the recognition signals so they had an excuse to get off a few rounds. They knew friend from foe, but the friends had better tend to their recognition signals.

The engine cut out once on our final approach but ran normally near our touchdown and rollout. When we pulled up in a parking position and idled the engines it quit. We stuck around the aircraft long enough for the ground crew to get the engine started and run it up for a few minutes. Sure enough, it cut out. I had had three hours to explore all the possibilities and had concluded that a bad carburetor was the culprit. For what it was worth, that turned out to be right. But all of us agreed we could do without the necessity for such a brilliant diagnosis in the future.

On a day in September 1942 several members of our crew were assigned to fly with Ens. Leo Nuss's crew from Adak to Dutch Harbor to help pick up a new plane which had been delivered there. A runway had been built at Dutch Harbor by cutting out the side of Mount Ballyhoo and laying Marsten Matting. This was the first time our crew had been into Dutch Harbor since the runway was completed, and we were all looking out of windows, trying to view this new improvement to the base.

The approach was right over the seaplane ramp and the new runway appeared to be a long extension of the parking apron—not an ideal arrangement but it had to do. We settled to the ground right on the parking apron and immediately proceeded to turn sideways. There was ice on the runway. Ensign Nuss did a great job of keeping the plane on course down the runway, even though the nose was pointed every way but straight.

Viewing the scene from the starboard waist blister, I had the sensation of being on a merry-go-round, first seeing the runway ahead of us, then the side of the mountain, then the runway again and then the water alongside the runway. We never quite got to the point of sliding down the runway backwards, but that didn't make the landing less adventurous. We knew the runway was quite short and that it ended with a sheer drop into the water at the end. All hands expected to be swimming soon.

Finally we stopped fishtailing and just slid sideways, port side leading the way. We had gradually slowed down but were not quite stopped when we went off the end of the matting onto a short stretch of gravel between the matting and the drop-off to the water. That gravel saved us. The gravel was dry and gave us just enough traction

Blasting the runway out of the mountainside at Dutch Harbor in September 1942

(National Archives)

142

N.A.S. Dutch Harbor (SS *Northwestern* in foreground)

(National Archives)

to stop our sideways slide. We ended up with the port wingtip hanging out over the water.

Ensign Nuss cheerily called over the interphone, "Dammit, lads, this flying business is a thrill a minute."

He couldn't kid me. I was sure he had a few beads of sweat on his brow too. But his statement sort of summed up what most of us felt. We loved to fly and a few tense moments now and then didn't change that.

One day toward the end of August 1942, we changed our bomb loading. Normally we carried four 500-pounders, two under each wing. On this day we traded the two 500-pounders under the starboard wing for a torpedo. Not only were we changing the weight under the starboard wing from 1000 pounds to 1975 pounds, but that big cylinder meant a whole new method of attack if we found a target for it. On a torpedo run the pilot gets down about fifty feet above the water, holds a straight course toward the target and hopes her gunners are so bad that they let us get within about 800 yards so we can release our torpedo. Then we continue looking down all those gun barrels while we try to pull up and away. People who do torpedo runs for a living have trouble buying life insurance.

It seemed that intelligence had come up with the information that a group of ships was moving in the direction of Kiska; we were to intercept and attack the ships. We were sending six planes out on search, all carrying torpedoes. If contact were made, all planes were to converge on the point of contact while at the same time alerting the Army B-17's and B-24's to come out and join in on the attack.

The weather was unusual. There were broken clouds at about three thousand feet and the sun was shining through, casting shadows on the sea surface. Our lookouts were having a terrible time with those shadows. From a distance they looked for all the world like ships. We just weren't used to coping with bright sunshine.

Suddenly our radioman picked up a contact report sent out from a plane two sectors over from us. The position of the contact was about 110 miles from us and we immediately changed course, figuring that we would be sighting the enemy ships in about an hour. During the next few minutes the pilots reviewed the torpedo attack procedure. We figured that within about a half hour we would be charging right down the gun barrels of some ship. Now we picked up another report from the same plane setting the number of ships at twelve. We wondered why he hadn't included course and speed and whether he was attacking. By this time he should have been giving that information. Probably he was keeping a good distance away and waiting for reinforcements. He got reinforcements all right.

Within an hour or so we had six PBY's flying around the area trying to find these ships. All we could see were the shadows which had been giving us fits. The plane which had sent the original contact report wasn't saying anything now. Finally we exchanged a couple of messages with the base, giving our assessment of the situation—no ships anywhere around. The base was reporting a bunch of B-17's and B-24's on the way.

Finally we received a message to return to our original sector and continue our search. The rest of the day passed with no further reports of contacts and we returned to base somewhat later than we had planned. That poor guy who made the false contact report was from a different squadron so we didn't get immediate information on what happened to him. We felt sorry for him. He'd done his best and it turned terribly sour for him.

If those ships had been there I'm sure we would have made our torpedo run that day—we might even have survived. That business of "Sighted ship, sank same" makes for good newspaper stories, but doing it with a torpedo from a PBY would certainly be the ultimate adventure. Lt. Perkins and his crew could attest to that fact. After their aborted attempt at a torpedo attack on the Japanese carrier on 4 June, they told us all about the chills and thrills of that kind of flying. There were no cowards among us, but that doesn't mean we didn't get scared.

On night patrols we sometimes went out on a regular search. Sometimes we would take off and head straight for Kiska. We tried to sneak in under the overcast to get a look inside the harbor, but the visibility in the darkness was normally pretty poor. So our next move was to see what we could do from above the overcast. There was always a heavy cloud cover over the island, and our main purpose was to climb above the soup and fly back and forth, searching for a hole that might give us a view of the harbor. Once in awhile we got a break and saw a ship or two, but most of the time we couldn't see a thing. We were always conscious of the fact that the Japanese had some fighter aircraft to send after us and we stayed alert. But they had not sent their planes aloft at night in the past and we assumed that we would not be bothered with them. If they did come after us, we could always use our standard defense—dive for cover in the overcast.

Ordinarily when we had spent an hour or so searching for a hole and found none, we flew over the Kiska volcano sticking out above the soup. From this point we took departure and flew a certain number of minutes on a predetermined course. According to our calculations that would put us right over the Japanese camp. At that point we dropped a bomb. There wasn't much precision to it, but it must have kept somebody awake and could possibly have hit a worthwhile target. Then we continued to cruise back and forth looking for a hole. Every couple of hours we repeated the bombing routine.

One night in September 1942 we spotted a hole. Whenever we flew over one of these holes, we had about a second to see it and whatever might be underneath it. That night it looked like there was a ship down there, possibly some sort of transport. Or it might have been a rock. We still had three 500-pound bombs left, so Lt. McFarland decided to make a dive-bombing run. "Now remember, we both haul back on the yoke when we pull out. Double check to make sure the bombs are armed." The pilots were reviewing the usual struggle of pulling a PBY out of a power dive.

Of course, there were two problems. First of all, we weren't flying in a dive bomber. Second, the Japanese guys on the ground were looking for the same hole we were. When those guys landed on Kiska they brought plenty of firepower with them. They had had their anti-aircraft batteries operating within hours of their initial landing. If they saw one of the same holes we were searching for, they aimed every gun they had at it and waited. We always assumed they were sick and tired of being kept awake all night, and they would be in a foul mood.

Ignoring both of these logical reasons for caution that night, we lined up for a dive-bombing attack—making sure the bombs were armed and the fuel mixture was changed to "Full Rich." We assumed we might need full power before we finished this little trip. We were sure it would be more exciting than flying back and forth all night. I hope to tell you it was. When a PBY flies at 150 knots, the wings start making creaking sounds and the hull begins vibrating. The hull may have been vibrating that night, or maybe it was me. We hit the hole and started down through it. Bad plan. Any idea that we might catch the Japanese by surprise was lost in those neat red arcs which greeted us the second we entered the hole. When tracers start heading your way at night, it looks like every one of them is going to tag you right between the eyes. I heard the .30-caliber up in the bow start popping away, but I had to wait a second or two before I could get an angle to start shooting. Coming down at such a steep angle as we were, the waist guns were both trained at an extreme forward angle and we had to take care not to shoot pieces off our own airplane. The metalsmiths got mad about that.

As I banged away at one of those places where tracers were coming from, I saw the two bombs on my side of the plane drop off the wing, and we started our pull-out. Trying to stand when you are coming out of a dive is like playing hop-scotch with an anchor on your back: you fall down. The G-forces from the pullout caused my knees to buckle. I didn't stop shooting quickly enough, and the last few rounds I fired went in the general direction of the moon. We never did get all the way down through the hole, and the pull-out got us hidden in the soup immediately. We felt a sort of thunk beneath us as our bombs exploded, and all stations were reporting in with no damage as we climbed back out on top of the clouds. The whole thing took about thirty seconds.

As we settled back to our normal cruising speed of 105 knots somebody said, "Who's cooking tonight?" Now, there's a real chow hound.

Chapter 8

On to Adak, Hauling a VIP, Lost but Found

DURING THE LAST FEW DAYS of August 1942 we were assigned to do some anti-submarine convoy flying. When we reached the position of the ships we were supposed to convoy, we wondered if they could remain afloat even without any submarines attacking them. They were a rusty-looking lot: transports, cargo ships and destroyer escorts. We took turns flying cover for them until they finally reached their destination, the island of Adak.

The Army troops started their landing operation in the middle of the night in a typical Aleutian storm. An advance scouting party had determined that there were no enemy troops on the island, so our troops didn't have that to worry about. As in so many Aleutian operations on land, sea or air, the weather was the toughest enemy of all. One of our PBY's was supposed to land some command people in the bay the next morning, but the seas were running too high to risk a landing. Finally they went back and landed in Nazan Bay, Atka, where *Casco* was at anchor. Our Wing Commander, Captain Gehres, happened to be visiting aboard the *Casco* and he arranged for the passengers to go aboard *Reid*, a destroyer guarding the mouth of the bay, to make the final leg of their journey to Adak.

As soon as *Reid* got out of sight a Japanese submarine, which had been prowling around outside the bay, fired two torpedoes at *Casco*. One missed but the other one blasted a hole in *Casco's* side, causing so much damage that she had to be run aground to prevent sinking and to allow the damage-control people to make emergency repairs. Although the torpedo damage was very serious, it could have been much worse. The torpedo exploded in a mess deck compartment which was nearly empty of personnel at the time. Two people were killed and three people were wounded. If it had hit further forward it could have exploded an ammunition magazine; if it had hit further aft it could have set off the aviation gas storage tanks.

Lt. Amme's crew (VP-43) and Ens. Coleman's crew (VP-42) headed out to search in the vicinity of Nazan Bay. In a matter of a few hours they found the Japanese submarine. They spotted her on the surface, close in by an island and sort of hidden against a cliff. She was evidently recharging her batteries after having been submerged for an extremely long time, waiting for the chance to attack *Casco*. They unloaded their depth charges on her as she tried to submerge and were pleased to see signs that considerable damage had been done. By the time the submarine was forced to surface, *Reid* had hurried back to Atka and joined in the attack, picking up five survivors after finishing off sinking the enemy submarine. The rest of the submarine crew went down

Aerial view of Nazan Bay, Atka Island

(National Archives)

USS *Casco* (AVP-12) servicing PBY in the Aleutians during 1942

(National Archives)

USS *Casco* beached in Nazan Bay after being torpedoed—30 August 1942

with their ship, choosing to die for the Emperor.[1]

Following the emergency repairs on the beach at Nazan Bay, *Casco* limped back to Dutch Harbor for more repairs. Damage was found to be more serious than had originally been thought. Some of the steel beams from the wrecked hangar were dragged to the pier and welded around the bottom of the ship to beef up the wrinkled keel. *Casco* then steamed on to Kodiak where a more permanent repair job could be done before heading for Bremerton and extensive repairs in the shipyard.

Colonel Talley was again on the scene, this time at Adak. His crew of Army Engineers located a likely-looking tide flat, waited until low tide, bulldozed a dam to prevent flooding at high tide and with a bit of levelling and several acres of Marsten Matting, produced a landing strip. Ten days after the Engineers landed, the first airplane landed. Of course, our PBY's were among the earliest arrivals.

During the initial stages of operations from a new shore base such as Adak, we lived with the Army between flights. They fed us and provided tents for us. We all carried the regular GI mess kits with us and lined up with the soldiers when chow was served at the mess tent. It always amazed me how those Army cooks put together the meals they did. All they had to work with were their crazy-looking GI field stoves, but they were tops in their trade.

As good as the Army chow was, I never got used to trying to get everything in its proper place in the mess kit. I always seemed to run out of places to put things before I got to the end of the serving line. When we were served the better meals such as meat, potatoes, gravy and vegetables and bread and butter, the really fancy part of the meal would be a half a peach. By the time I got to the guy serving the peaches, I had always run out of space. And I always ended up with a peach half perched on top of my potatoes and gravy. I guess all of the nourishment was there, but the combination of potatoes, gravy and peaches took quite a bit of getting used to.

When we first started operating from Adak in the middle of September 1942, it was more or less a secret base as far as the Japanese were concerned. They hadn't spotted the ships bringing the Army Engineers to the island, and during the construction the weather had been so bad that they hadn't seen it from the air. For the first ten days there was no air cover over the runway workers, but once they got some of the strip finished the fighters began coming in. From then on the Army fighters kept the Japanese far enough away so that they couldn't find out the exact location, even though they did figure out that there was a base somewhere on Adak.

The tide flat had provided a convenient location and the dams keeping the tide out were very effective. But the dams did no good when it began raining. Sometimes the airstrip looked like a lake from the air. When a PBY-5A took off from the runway it threw up almost as much spray as it did taking off from the water. An Army squadron of P-39 fighters was assigned to Adak and they had particular problems when the runway was covered with water. Their landing gear was sort of spindly looking— plenty strong enough for normal operation—but when they blasted off down the runway in about six inches of water they could barely get up to takeoff speed. In a few instances the landing gear collapsed from the strain of water resistance, and the planes ended up skidding along like speed boats until they came to rest in huge sprays of

---

[1]Post-war interrogations revealed that the submarine was the *RO-61*. United States Strategic Bombing Survey (Pacific), Naval Analysis Division, *Interrogations of Japanese Officials* (Washington, D.C.: United States Government Printing Office, 1946).

"Navy Town" at Adak Island — November 1942

(National Archives)

"Navy Town" at Adak Island — November 1942

(National Archives)

Navy Mess Hall Quonset at Adak—November 1942

(National Archives)

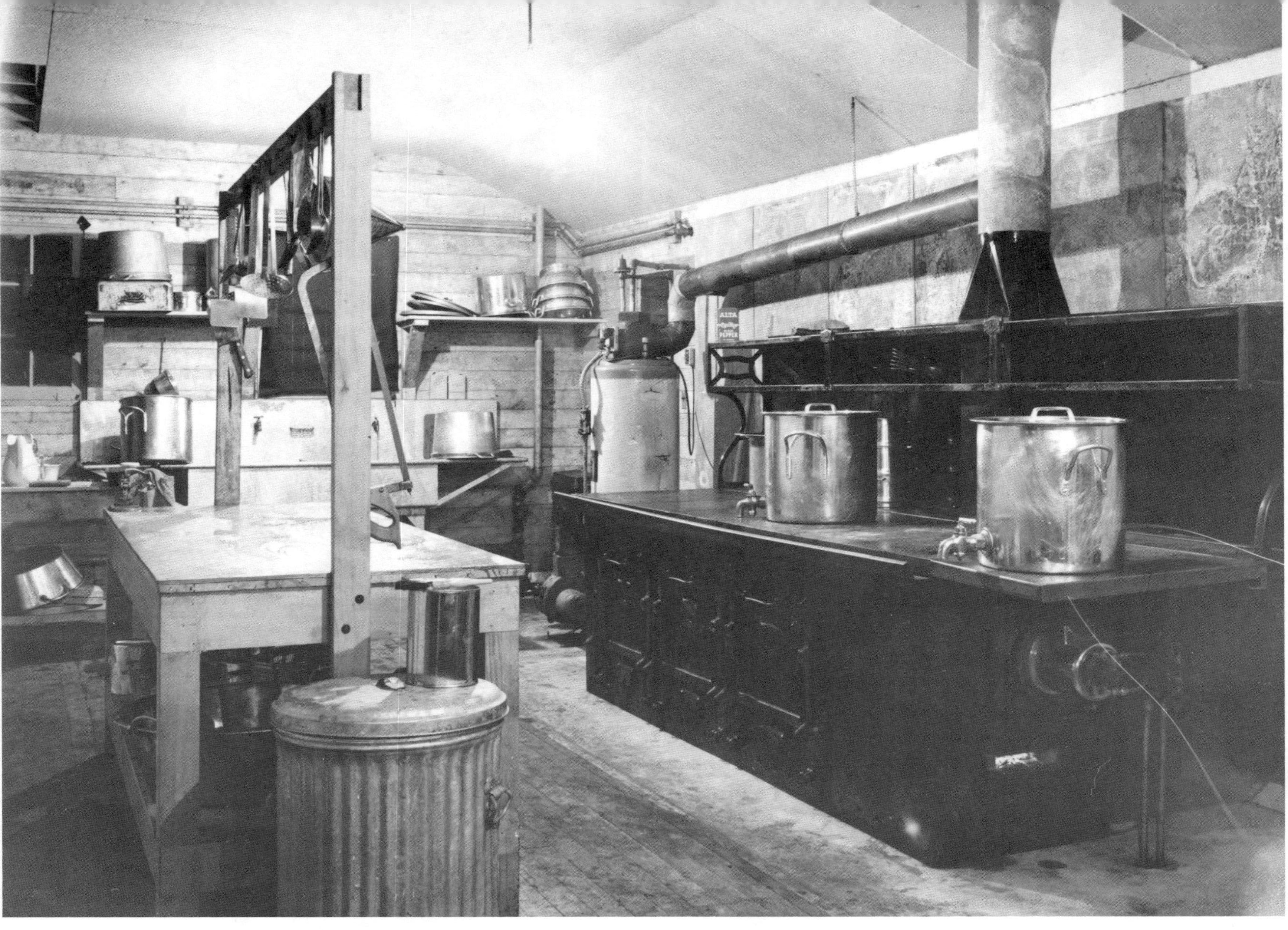

The Galley in the Navy Mess Hall at Adak

(National Archives)

155

Navy Docks at Sweepers Cove, Adak

(National Archives)

water. One could hardly call them crashes. The pilots just climbed out of the cockpits and waded toward higher ground while the runway crew feverishly cleared the plane away so the runway was back in commission again.

There was complete radio silence from Adak so that the Japanese couldn't get a radio fix on that location. The first PBY to come in from patrol in the afternoon landed and picked up all the radio traffic to be transmitted from the base. Then he took off and flew out to sea a hundred miles, and the radioman in the flight crew sent all the messages.

By the process of eliminating areas they did get to see on the island, the Japanese got an idea of where the base might be. Just to keep us from getting too smug about our secret base they sent a plane over our way almost every morning at just about daylight. He made one pass and headed for home. He dropped a couple of bombs through the overcast strictly by guess and by gosh. He never did hit the base. Sometimes the bombs hit five miles away, and a few times they came within a half mile. But they did let us know the Japanese were thinking of us.

The Navy SeaBees (CB's) moved in right behind the Army Engineers, and every day a new building or quonset hut or shack would blossom around the runway. The wind blew the buildings down a few times, but the SeaBees rebuilt them until they stayed put.

Depending on the primary mission of our flight, we carried either bombs or depth charges, and on some rare occasions we carried a torpedo. The word was passed to the Ordnance shop about what was to be loaded on each plane for the next day's operations. Sometimes the existing load on the planes was correct. Sometimes certain planes required a change in loading. Some Ordnancemen became very casual in the way they handled this job.

One day after we had landed and parked our plane on our flight line, a couple of Ordnancemen showed up and notified us that our loading had to be changed from depth charges to bombs. They were towing a couple of loaded bomb trailers behind their tractor and they went right to work. One Ordnanceman climbed into the plane and went up forward while a couple of us in the flight crew were getting our tie-down lines out. I had just picked up a tie-down line and glanced up toward the wing-tip float where I intended to put it through a ring when, from the corner of my eye, I saw the two depth charges drop from the wing.

Knowing the construction and arrangement of the fuse of a depth charge, I suppose I should not have been alarmed. But I had not seen depth charges unloaded in this fashion, and during the split second that it took for those things to reach the ground I died a thousand deaths. As the Ordnanceman was climbing out of the plane I said, "You scared hell out of me. Do you always unload those things that way?"

"Oh yeah. It saves a lot of time. We figure it works fine as long as the plane is parked on sand this way."

In the pre-war days we had strict specifications on how many hours PBY engines could be operated before being sent to an overhaul shop. Our planes had R-1830, Pratt and Whitney engines, which were to be sent to overhaul after 500 hours of operation. There were circumstances when this could be extended to 550 or 600 hours, but this was the absolute maximum.

During the first months of the war we were accumulating hours on our engines at a rate that was unheard of in the past. At the same time, the availability of new or overhauled engines couldn't begin to keep up with the demand. We just had to forget the 500 or 600-hour limitations and keep churning around in the fog out towards Kiska and Attu. By the time the engines have about 800 hours on them, there's very little compression left, and they are using three times more oil than normal. The engines run on gas, oil and imagination.

During one ten-day period at Adak in October 1942, our starboard booster coil quit working, and there was no replacement available. It was impossible to start an engine without the booster coil, so I used the port booster coil to get the starboard engine going. The starter electrical system was set up so that the starter was energized (wound up) by pushing a toggle switch to the up position. In about a minute, the starter was turning up at the proper speed and the toggle switch was moved to the down position. This engaged the starter to turn the engine over and at the same time send electrical power through the booster coil to develop the hot spark needed for starting. Once the engine had started, the toggle switch was returned to center position, cutting all power to the starter and booster coil. There was also a standby system with which we could crank up the starter with a hand crank, as well as a steel cable with which to engage the starter manually.

When we got ready to start up, I would be up on top of the wing between the engines. I had a fifteen-foot length of wire, which I had attached to the port booster coil and run across to the starboard booster coil. Babbitt was in the tower, and he energized the starboard starter; then, instead of engaging the starboard starter, he moved the *port* toggle switch to the down position to send the juice from the *port* booster coil to the *starboard* engine. At the same time, I pulled the manual engaging cable for the starboard engine to get it turning over. Once we had the starboard engine running, I unrigged my wire, secured all the cowling, and climbed back down inside the plane, and we were set to get the port engine running in the prescribed fashion. It was weird, but it worked. And it was typical of the things being done up and down the flight line to keep the engines running.

Finally some new engines started coming through to our part of the country. The engine changes were to be done in Kodiak, so we started a rotation system, in which we flew one plane at a time back to Kodiak to turn in for engine changes. The Kodiak crew would have a plane with new engines ready to go, and we would trade planes and head back out for Adak.

We had taken our plane back to Kodiak for engine changes, and there was a plane waiting for us with new engines, ready to fly back out. We were also supposed to haul a large cast iron pump and a bunch of four-inch hose out to Dutch Harbor, where some ship was waiting for it. After much heaving and grunting we finally muscled all of that stuff through a waist hatch and into a center compartment, approximately at the center of gravity. In that position it was just extra weight. Positioned back aft it was sure to make us so tail-heavy we would never get off.

Although I was regular plane captain on the crew, Gabriel, our Leading Chief, had made the trip with us. As senior man in the crew, he was sort of ramrodding and generally observing to see if the rest of us knew what we were doing.

Lt. Dickey, Gabriel and I discussed the gas loading the night before our departure, and it was decided that, due to the extra weight we would be carrying, we would not top off the tanks, which would have taken about 800 gallons. We decided to put in 400 gallons, which would give us plenty of gas to reach Dutch Harbor, but still not be so heavy for takeoff. I proceeded to call the gas truck and put in 400 gallons without telling Gabriel. A little later, not having heard from me, Gabriel called the gas truck and put in another 400 gallons. During the fueling operations word had been passed to Lt. Dickey that the Wing Commander, Captain Gehres, was to ride with us to Dutch Harbor. Now, besides the load of cargo, we would have a VIP aboard to worry about.

The crew was alerted to the latest development, and we arrived at the launching ramp earlier than we normally would have to make sure we were ready when the Captain showed up. The pump and hose made a pretty cumbersome load, and it was spread all over the walkways and bunks. The plane was not all that shipshape for the VIP, but there wasn't much we could do about it. While Gabriel and Lt. Dickey stood by to pipe the Wing Commander aboard, I was making our routine prelaunch check and suddenly realized that our gas tanks were all but topped off. About the time I hustled out to tell Lt. Dickey, Captain Gehres showed up and we became occupied with getting him into a Mae West and up the ladder into the waist hatch. Finally Lt. Dickey took a moment to verify with me that we indeed had a full load of gas. He commented that it would be a good test of the new engines getting us off the water. There was nothing else we could do at that point.

Meanwhile, Townsend was preflighting the radio gear and radar. Sitting at the head of the ramp, all he could check on the radar was that something showed up dead ahead and something showed up to port and starboard. All seemed in proper order, and he so reported. What he couldn't tell was that the radar had been hooked up backwards and his indications on port and starboard were reversed.

The water conditions were good, and we became airborne after a few extra hundred yards of takeoff run; at an altitude of fifty feet we were swallowed up in the usual fog. After we set course for Dutch Harbor, the radioman reported land on the starboard side. The navigator said the land should be on the port side. Most of the time when we climbed through the fog and came out on top, we could spot a mountain and take our bearings from there. When we finally broke out at 9,000 feet all the mountains were covered, and all we could see was white fluff. The big argument continued.

Listening to the conversation I visualized us flying along some unknown valley with land on either side. Lt. Dickey had faith in the radar and wanted to believe it, but he had no reason to doubt the navigator either. Finally he said, "Does anything show up on radar dead ahead?"

Townsend answered, "All clear dead ahead, sir."

"Navigator, does your chart show anything dead ahead?"

"All clear dead ahead, sir."

Lt. Dickey sounded a little grim. "Very well. I'm going to hold this course and let down to a thousand feet and try to get under this stuff and try to get our bearings."

But at a thousand feet we were still in the soup. So we gradually let down more until we found the ceiling at just over a hundred feet. At this point the radar and the navigator were no more in agreement than they had been before.

Captain Gehres began clambering back and forth from the cockpit to the waist to the cockpit, trying to get a better view of the nothingness outside. After four hours, Gabriel relieved me in the tower, and I joined Summers on watch in the waist. About every twenty minutes Captain Gehres would show up in the waist and stand between the blisters, looking out. About six hours out on our flight, which should have taken five hours, I was betting Summers a dollar that we would spend the night at sea. The Captain showed up during this loud conversation, looked at us as if we were some kind of nuts, and scurried back forward again. He wouldn't even offer to hold the stakes for us.

Eventually Townsend announced that he had a ship dead ahead at about ten miles. We went to battle stations and approached the target, ready to pull up into the soup if she began firing at us. Finally, the ship came into view through the fog—it was one of our old four-pipers.

We circled her a few times and Summers, working from a blister, tried to blink out a request for our position. Due either to the lousy weather conditions or the fact that they didn't know where they were either, we got nowhere with that effort. (A month later Lt. Dickey told us he had heard a couple of destroyer officers telling a wild story about "this crazy, damned PBY that came out of the fog, flew around us a couple of times looking for submarines and then roared off into the fog again!")

I guess we began some sort of square search pattern after that, and picked up a landfall when we were about eleven hours out. Townsend was trying to work a new radio directional aid which was supposed to be beaming out of Cold Bay and seemed to be picking up something as we skirted the coastline cautiously, trying to recognize a landmark.

Finally Lt. Dickey recognized a rock or bay or something and judged that we were in the vicinity of Cold Bay. It turned out that he was right on the money. The next hour was a little scary, dodging hither and yon, but eventually Cold Bay came into view and we dropped in at just about dark. The gas was so low I expected the engines to quit while we were taxiing to a parking place. I never did hear any further word about the foulup in gassing the plane at Kodiak.

After we got the plane tied down and secured, we headed for the mess tent to beg something to eat. The officers had left earlier for the officers' mess. For some reason their mess was secured for the night. Our crew had just gotten seated at a table in the enlisted mess tent when Lt. Dickey stuck his head in the door and asked if they could feed four more vagabonds.

It's not often that a regular old flight crew shares a table with the Wing Commander for dinner. Captain Gehres was all smiles and seemed happy with his lot. But the next morning he contacted a destroyer in the harbor and caught a surface ride the rest of the way to Dutch Harbor.

By nightfall the next day we had stopped in at Dutch Harbor, gotten our radar fixed, offloaded our cargo, and started to fly on to Umnak. Operations had us scheduled to take off an hour before daylight the following morning to go out and see what there was to see on Attu. The Japanese were always trying to sneak in more airplanes. Maybe we could head them off. But we received an in-flight message changing the plan for the next day.

Instead of returning to Umnak we were to make a search to the west and eventually land at Nazan Bay, Atka and proceed to operate from a tender. We did mostly night searches from Atka.

On night searches we took off about an hour before dark and got to our sector departure point. The navigator got his wind readings as we started out on our first leg. Once darkness set in, he couldn't get any more wind readings, and he had to use his last reading for the remaining ten hours of the flight. With no other navigational aids available, we were depending strictly on dead-reckoning navigation, which can become pretty inaccurate if you don't allow for wind changes. It was not unusual to find ourselves fifty miles off course at the end of a night search. But the rocks and islands had become familiar enough so that within a few minutes we knew where we were and could return to base with no great difficulty. We were never lost, just a little off course.

On the night of 27 July 1942 we took off from Nazan Bay on one of these night searches. We were to join two more of our planes in forming a submarine screen for our surface forces who were scheduled to shell Kiska. Trying to spot submarines during daylight hours was hard enough to do. Unless the submarine was on the surface we figured that night submarine hunting was not going to be too successful. This type of mission was a new experience for us. When the Japanese task force was steaming around south of Dutch Harbor in early June, we wondered if there were any Navy surface craft in our part of the Pacific. Wherever they had been then, they were now out here ready to do some bombardment. We figured that watching the night fire display from the air should be pretty spectacular. We were in for a disappointing night. We did make contact with the shadowy forms of our ships, but it was pretty stormy and nothing was happening.

After flying around Kiska all night only to find out that our ships couldn't do any shelling due to the foul weather, we finally got so low on fuel that we had to head back to Nazan Bay. But at the time when we should have been seeing something we recognized around the island of Atka, we realized that our usual landmarks were nowhere to be seen. At this time we were not observing 100% radio silence, but communication with the ship was kept to a minimum. We didn't call in and say we were lost. But the big question remained: which way were we off course? As we skirted along an island, we decided that we were looking at Amlia Island. We were a good hour's flight from the ship, but we didn't have an hour's fuel left. As the gas gauges showed lower and lower, we started looking for a decent bay where we could avoid being down in the open sea.

When I reported that we were showing empty fuel tanks, we were already in a landing attitude and headed for a small bay. The sea was fairly smooth, and Lt. Dickey made a nice landing right toward the little bay and then taxied on in. We had just cleared the mouth of the bay when the engines quit. We continued coasting for a short distance with Summers standing by the anchor. On Lt. Dickey's order, he let it go and we came to a stop about 100 yards from shore.

There was a small reserve supply of fuel to be used for running the Auxiliary Power Unit, so we could use the radio for a short time if we wanted to. With this in mind the Plane Commander and the navigator were poring over the chart of Amlia Island trying to identify our little bay. They finally arrived at a conclusion, and we fired up the APU. It was a little risky to broadcast our position because the Japanese might send out a search and destroy mission before our ship could get a search and rescue mission out our way. But Townsend got on the radio and sent out the message. He got a roger from the ship and that was all. It was their move next; it was a cinch we weren't going anywhere.

We always carried emergency rations aboard, but in addition to that we had started carrying a couple of cases of C-Rations. We were good for a number of days as far as food was concerned. Our fresh water supply might become a problem, so it was decided to send a party ashore not only to scout for water but also to look over the possibilities for mounting a machine gun or two ashore if we had to. We pumped up a rubber raft and our four-man invasion force hit the beach.

There was a nice clean, clear stream close to where we landed, and it was full of fish. When we began inspecting rocks for possible gun mounts, we flushed out four blue foxes. As we moved along, we spotted more blue foxes scurrying around. The place was alive with them. Toward the middle of the afternoon we heard a plane going over—one of our own from the sound of it—but the heavy overcast hid him from view. One of the guys on watch in our plane fired a couple of flares from the signal pistol but the other plane kept right on going.

We decided to have fresh fish for dinner, and one of the pilots got out his .45 and fired at a good-sized salmon in the stream. He didn't hit him, but the concussion in the water dazed the fish. Before he could recover, we had him out of the water and lying in the grass. The place was so quiet that we could call back and forth from shore to the plane with no effort at all. We told them to get out the C-Rations, and we set about gathering wood for a fire and cleaning the fish. There weren't any trees, but there were fair-sized bushes and some brush. Roast salmon and C-Rations aren't listed on many restaurant menus. That's too bad. They are very good.

We spent the night aboard the plane, taking turns sleeping and standing watches at the guns. That was an uneasy night. Everything had been going our way so far. The overcast had persisted, but the general weather conditions were good. We were pretty sure we would have visitors by the next day, but would they be friend or foe?

At noon the next day we had a party ashore and our usual watches posted on the plane. The weather was still good, but a little fog had settled in. Suddenly one of the guys on watch spotted a ship outside our bay. He let everybody know about it. The ship hove to a few hundred yards from the mouth of our bay. It was our tender, *Hulbert*, and they were lowering a couple of boats in the water.

All hands hurried to get back aboard the plane, and when Townsend and Stallings came aboard, each of them was carrying a blue fox. Three of us stayed on the plane to assist in the towing of the plane to the ship. The others boarded the other boat and headed back for the ship. As we moved slowly out toward the ship, we saw their boat unloading at the accommodation ladder. Before we got to the ship, we saw Townsend and Stallings getting back into the boat and heading toward the shore again. It seems that Lt. Dickey felt that war and weather were enough troubles to cope with. The smell of those foxes as shipmates in our crew was too much to have to endure. So back to the fox farm they went.

With the tanks full of gas, our food supply replenished, and our crew back in the plane, we blasted off for an assigned patrol sector and the ship turned around to go back to Atka. We were mighty thankful for the favors we'd had in those thirty hours. The Japanese hadn't found us, and the weather had been as good as it ever is in the Aleutians.

In spite of all efforts to keep track of each aircraft, our method of operating on individual patrol missions made it tough to know just where each plane was at any given time. The expression "overdue and assumed lost" was used on a number of occasions when planes were missing. We could have been one of those.

As winter approached we had an idea that we might be moving back to Kodiak for operations. But bombing the Japanese on Kiska and patrolling the western end of the Aleutian Islands had to continue and we couldn't do that from Kodiak. Late in the fall of 1942 it became apparent to us that the old idea that "PBY's can't operate from advance bases in Alaska in the winter" had been forgotten. As the weather grew colder we operated from the tenders less and less, using the base at Umnak for our winter headquarters, with detachments moving back and forth to Adak. After we had shoveled snow from around our planes and swept off the top of the wing a few times we got the idea that we had better get used to winter flight operations.

A few of our new planes had come equipped with heating systems for the crews' comfort, but the heaters were not very dependable and were considered somewhat dangerous by some of us. Since they burned raw 100-octane gas for their source of heat, we were always afraid of an explosion if there were a malfunction in the distribution system. Our fleece-lined flight suits worked just fine.

Actually there was better flying weather in the winter than during the summer. We saw much more clear weather in January than we did in June. It had to do with the differential in temperatures between the Bering Sea and the North Pacific Ocean. When the cold air over the Bering Sea met the warm air from the summer Pacific Ocean, it produced fog. During the winter the Pacific air cooled off and the differential temperatures were closer together and produced less fog.

Flying was great but ground handling was miserable. Working on aircraft on the flight line in the wind, snow and rain became an exercise in survival. It was a job of heroic proportions.

The maintenance guys had some sort of tent affairs to put up over the engines when they were working on them. But when the wind came up, the tents ended up flying off the workstands.

At Umnak the Navy finally furnished us with some heaters, equipped with large canvas ducts which were long enough to reach up inside the wing and heat it enough to melt off the snow. Many times getting the heater engine started was the toughest part of the whole flight operation. And we always had to be watchful that the thawing process didn't result in ice on the wing when the heater was removed. The heaters were troublesome, but they were nice in one respect. It was quite comfortable standing next to the hot ducts leading up to the wing on a cold winter day.

Living in a PBY at Nazan Bay was not too bad in the summer time but we hated it in the winter. The water was nearly at freezing temperature and when the wind kicked up, it had the feel of living in a deep freeze. Each member of a flight crew was given a down-filled sleeping bag which was supposed to keep one warm at forty below zero. They were lifesavers when living in the plane on the water. We also used them quite often at Adak, preferring to bed down in our plane rather than slog around in the mud looking for some lodging in the Army tents.

We spent more and more time at Adak and it gradually became the main base in the western Aleutians. As had happened at Umnak, we saw the tents slowly being replaced by Quonset huts and wooden frame buildings. Adak was within easy range of Kiska and far enough west so that we could patrol out past Attu. For the time being that was all we needed.

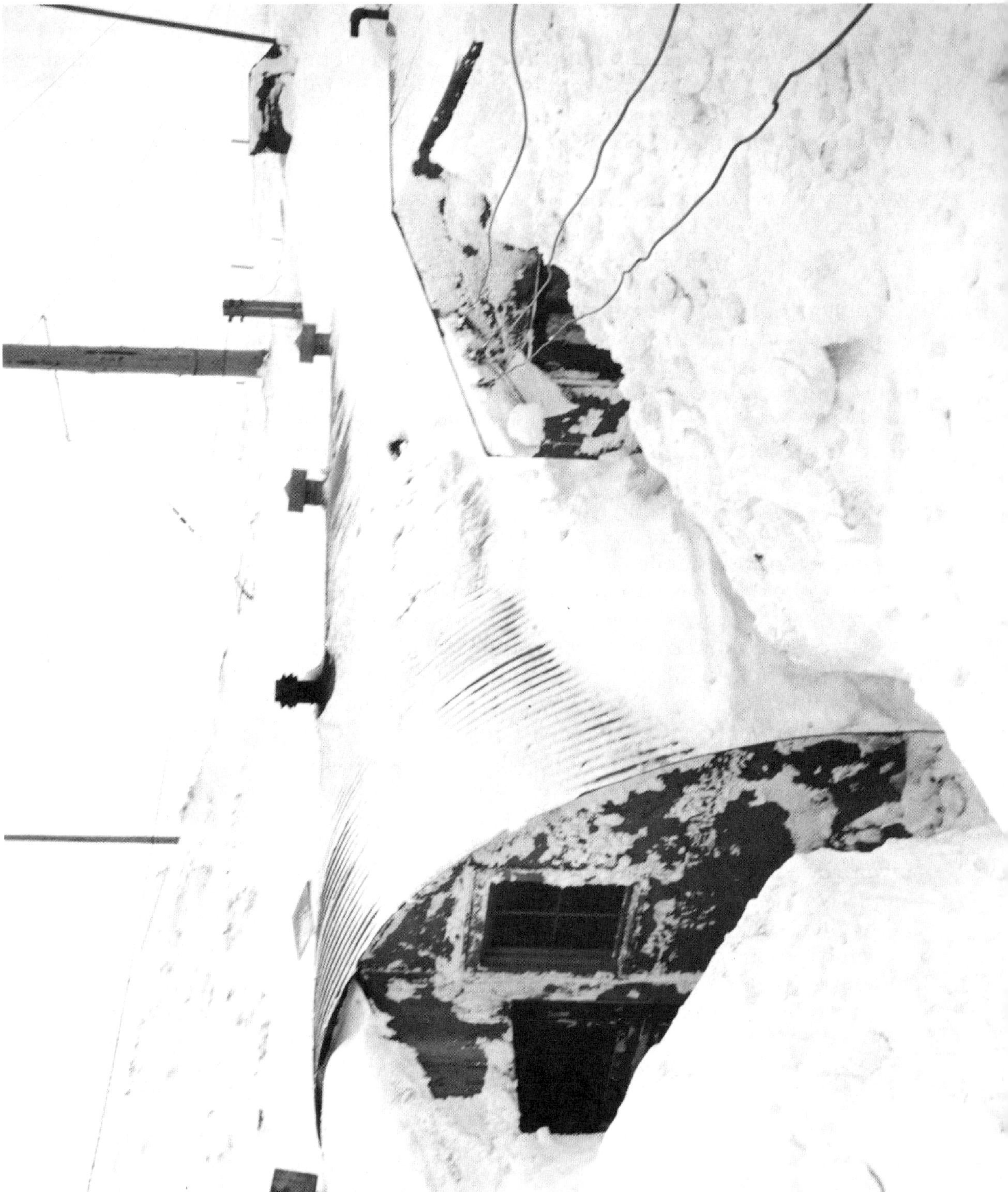

We had to dig our way out of our huts at Umnak in February 1943

Snow-covered PBY-5A at Umnak—January 1943

(National Archives)

Navy R4D transport plane arriving at Umnak in January 1943

Winter Operations at Adak — December 1942

PBY's in the snow at Adak

(National Archives)

Removing snow from PBY wing at Adak

(National Archives)

Chapter 9

The Aleutian Campaign:
Tactics, Losses and Awards

ALTHOUGH OUR PRE-WAR TRAINING was theoretically supposed to have been training for war operations, when the war really started we found that our training tactics did not quite fit the realities of war patrols in the Aleutian Islands.

Prior to the war the Navy used a standard system of marking planes so that a twelve-plane squadron was divided into four sections of three planes each. The first section was led by the skipper, the second by the executive officer, and the remaining two by the other senior officers of the squadron. The marking allowed identification of each section and the leader of the section. The system was a good device for identification when there were several aircraft getting into formation. But from the time the war started I don't believe our squadron ever had as many as two planes in any formation. The idea of the skipper leading a twelve-plane formation out on a search would have been ridiculous. We needed to cover as much ocean area as possible, and to do that every plane flew independently. Not only was the formation concept abandoned, but even the idea of all planes operating from the same base was forgotten. On any given day we had planes flying out of Dutch Harbor, Umnak, Atka and Adak. And there were times when we would be spread as far as Kodiak or even Nome. Besides those bases there were numerous bays where a tender might be anchored, taking care of a few of our planes.

Although our flying from so many diverse bases was demanded in order to maintain necessary patrol coverage, some of this dispersal was the result of caution. Our skipper, Lieutenant Commander Russell, took no chances of having a surprise bombing attack catch a bunch of our aircraft in one place. Numerous small bays on a number of islands in the vicinity of Dutch Harbor had been scouted out and were listed with standard navigation information as emergency dispersal anchorages. Coming in from an all-night patrol we often were ordered to spend the day at one of these spots. Late in the afternoon we took off and slipped into Dutch Harbor for gas and rations and then headed out on another night patrol. But for our dispersal tactics the Japanese bombing raids at Dutch Harbor could have wiped out a whole squadron in a minute. We had all seen pictures of the wreckage of the PBY's on Ford Island after the attack on Pearl Harbor.

VP-41 and VP-42 operations became so intermingled by the first few days of June 1942 that it was sometimes hard to know which squadron anyone belonged to. The inter-squadron rivalry was pretty much forgotten as we battled the common problems of lousy weather and tough maintenance, to say nothing of the Japanese.

170

If VP-41 lost a plane we considered the loss to be ours too.

After June the PBY's only got back to Kodiak for engine changes or other major maintenance. All VP operations had shifted to the west. The Wing managed to acquire VS (Scouting) squadrons to take over the patrol duties out of Kodiak. They were flying the OS2U single-float seaplanes ordinarily used on cruisers and battleships. They had a much shorter range than PBY's and didn't carry the PBY bomb load, but they did fulfill the scouting needs out of Kodiak. *Casco* sometimes carried one of these planes for short-range scouting while she was sitting at anchor, tending our PBY's. She did not have a catapult, as cruisers and battleships did, but used her crane to lower the plane over the side or retrieve it.

One result of all of our dispersed operations was that we lost track of friends for a month at a time. Then we might fly into Atka, Adak or Umnak to join a particular contingent for a few days, and there would be the friends still grinding out the hours over the ocean as always, ready to share the latest scuttlebutt about going back to the States.

The ordinary flight crew did not worry much about the overall plan of action. We just tried to keep our planes ready to go and went wherever and whenever we were told, hoping that doing our bit helped out in the grand strategy. After flying every day for a week or more we doggedly went about our business, wondering if there was ever going to be another day off.

The sad part of all of this was that sometimes a friend disappeared from the scene completely. Early in the morning of 3 June Lt. Cusick's plane got shot down: there were three survivors, who were dragged out of the water by the Japanese and taken prisoner. That same morning, Ensign Litsey's crew was caught in a strafing attack during takeoff while the Japanese were attacking Dutch Harbor. There were a couple of people killed, but the rest of the crew escaped. We lost Lt.(jg) Stockstill's plane and crew to enemy action before the end of the day on 3 June. While keeping contact with the Japanese carriers southwest of Dutch Harbor the next day, 4 June, Ensign Hildebrand's plane and crew disappeared and were never heard from again. We also lost Ens. Mitchell's crew in enemy action that same day. The body of Ens. Mitchell's plane captain, Rebel Rawls, was recovered; Rawls obviously had been machine-gunned in the water—that was hard to take.

Some planes shot up by Japanese Zeroes from the task force or over Kiska were able to limp back to one of our bases or tenders. Lt. Perkins' plane was one of those. Lt.(jg) Campbell managed to get his plane back toward home after being shot up by enemy fighters, having one gunner wounded and finally running out of gas and losing the plane after a forced landing, but saving the crew.

The weather caused some of our losses. On 30 July 1942 Lt. Brough's plane crashed on landing in heavy weather out at Nazan Bay, Atka. The plane hit the water and porpoised back up in the air, coming back down nose first. Lt. Brough, Ens. Mills, Ens. Love, Cameron and Small were killed, but Schreck, Chesnutt and Gebhart managed to kick a blister out of the wreckage and were saved. The crash boat did a super job that day saving the three crewmen. The plane had gone down so fast that it was a miracle anybody got out of it.

On 8 August a plane returning from a raid on Kiska ran into the side of a mountain in the fog. Makushin volcano is around 6600 feet high and is located on Unalaska Island directly west of Dutch Harbor. Coming in to Dutch Harbor in heavy fog, the crew evidently lost their bearings and crashed right into the mountain.

Crashed PBY on Mt. Makushin — August 1942

On 19 June we lost a plane which went out on a burial mission. Capt. Thornborough's B-26 had crashed at sea up on the north side of the Alaska Peninsula and a dead crewman had washed ashore. The PBY located the scene and landed on the beach. After burying the crewman, the pilot got his plane turned around and started to taxi back into the water but tangled with some heavy surf and got stuck in the mud. He went to full power trying to get free of the mud. At the same time, the surf kicked up and a solid wave hit the plane head-on. When the props hit the solid water, the props and nose sections of both engines took off without the rest of the airplane.

The stranded plane was wrecked by the surf in a matter of hours, but the crew was able to get back ashore after getting out a radio message reporting their predicament. Our skipper fired up another PBY and flew to the scene, made several passes to determine that the survivors were physically ok, and finally dropped instructions to the crew to walk some twenty miles along the shoreline to Port Moller, where they could be picked up and hauled back to Cold Bay. Hearing about this episode reminded me of our adventures when we taxied up on the beach near Mt. Pavlof. We had not considered the fact that we might get stuck in the mud. We lucked out—they didn't.

A couple of times our ten-plane complement was down to seven or eight. We received new replacement planes only at irregular intervals and were always glad to get them. The plane lost on the B-26 crew rescue mission was a brand new one. Some days our pilots were brilliant—other days they were less than perfect. The skipper was a bit disturbed when we had to scratch that one.

No doubt all of us had ways of coping with the tragedies we faced in the Aleutians. When I heard a report of a plane and crew gone, I sort of rationalized it as a transfer. I knew I wouldn't see any of those guys again and hoped they were enjoying a new tour of duty somewhere. I suppose that was my psychological defense against the realities of war. When we were scheduled to fly out to relieve another plane which had been declared missing, I invented a way to keep psyched up. There's an old Navy expression which is used to describe the passing of a shipmate: "He was transferred to the staff of the Supreme Commander." A couple of times we had the great joy of finding out that a "lost report" was wrong. A plane and crew were down and out of contact for a period of time but then were found and rejoined the rest of us in the thick of things.

Jumping back and forth between bases was pretty much routine for us. If a more concentrated search was needed in a certain area, a few extra planes would be dispatched to the nearest base or tender to join in the search efforts. So in early November it was no surprise when we were told to depart from Adak, fly a search along the south side of the Aleutian chain and end up in Umnak. It had become a sort of headquarters for our squadron. It was where most of us kept our seabags. When we flew into Umnak we would all get out our dress blues and reminisce about the good old days in Seattle, then pack them away and fly back out west. There was always the hope that maybe this time there would be orders to go back and fight the Battle of Seattle.

When we arrived at Umnak on this trip, we got the plane secured and headed for a quonset hut to get a bunk for the night. The Master-at-Arms notified us that we were to be in dress blues and fall out for inspection the next morning. Now this was something new! We had gotten used to doing without such mundane things as personnel inspections and could not figure out who cared what we looked like in dress

OS2U Vought "Kingfisher"

(National Archives)

Bert Miller's Tonsorial Parlor. McGrath is the victim, with Butcher standing by to stop the bleeding.   (Freeman Collection)

blues in the Aleutian Islands. Somebody came up with a possible reason. Of course they would want to inspect us before sending us back to the States! Get the shoes shined. Get the wrinkles out of the blues and get a clean hat. Every one of us needed a haircut. Every one of us got a haircut. But not everybody had his hair cut by a trained barber. The guy who cut my hair was a metalsmith, and I think he used his tinsnips. Not being a heavy tipper, I just thanked him and hoped he did a better job of patching bullet holes in airplanes. It was the first and only haircut I ever got standing up, outside, in a forty-knot wind.

The next morning we mustered outside the squadron office at 0800, the sharpest looking group ever to gather on Umnak. When muster had been completed, the Leading Chief reported to the Executive Officer that we were all present. The Exec went into the squadron office and came back out shortly with the skipper, and, of all people, the Wing Commander. They took up a position directly in front of the formation, and another officer ordered, "The following advance to front and center." Then he began to read off names. When he had finished his list, there were about thirty of us lined up facing the Wing Commander. The skipper began reading citations which accompanied the awarding of each medal. Most of the pilots were awarded the Distinguished Flying Cross, and the rest of us were awarded Air Medals.

UNITED STATES PACIFIC FLEET
Flagship of the Commander in Chief

In the name of the President of the United States, the Commander in Chief, United States Pacific Fleet, takes pleasure in presenting the AIR MEDAL to

ELMER AMBROSE FREEMAN, AVIATION MACHINIST'S MATE
SECOND CLASS, UNITED STATES NAVY

for service as set forth in the following

CITATION

"For meritorious achievement in aerial flight as a member of a patrol plane crew. Throughout the Aleutian Islands Campaign of June 1 to 15, 1942 he demonstrated courage, zeal and willingness to meet the enemy in combat in most severe weather conditions. He participated in numerous bombing attacks on the enemy concentration in Kiska Harbor, always in the face of heavy anti-aircraft fire. His conduct throughout was in keeping with the highest traditions of the naval service."

(Signed) C. W. NIMITZ
Admiral, U.S. Navy

THE SECRETARY OF THE NAVY
Washington

The President of the United States takes pleasure in presenting the AIR MEDAL to

ELMER A. FREEMAN
AVIATION MACHINIST'S MATE SECOND CLASS
UNITED STATES NAVY

for service as set forth in the following

CITATION:

"For meritorious achievement while participating in aerial flight during action against enemy Japanese forces throughout the Aleutian Islands Campaign, June 1 to 15, 1942. Under the most severe weather conditions of high winds, snow, rain and fog, and in the face of persistent anti-aircraft fire from enemy ship and shore batteries, FREEMAN, with conscientious devotion to duty, carried out the tasks assigned him during patrol missions and bombing attacks against Japanese ships in Kiska Harbor. His fine courage throughout was in keeping with the highest traditions of the United States Naval Service."

For the President,

(Signed) Frank Knox
Secretary of the Navy

I have to say that I was proud to be in that group, but the experience was a little bit unsettling for me. When they read the list of awards made posthumously, it took the excitement out of the occasion. When the formation broke up we quietly drifted back to our Quonset huts. As I thought about the awards, I could not help but remember that only twelve months earlier most of us were just getting started as aircrewmen. We had survived our trials and tribulations and managed to acquit ourselves honorably when the fortunes of war rushed us into responsible positions requiring a maturity none of us thought we had.

Lest we get to feeling too heroic, the Leading Chief growled at us to be sure and check the Flight Schedule. "Somebody has to get some flying done around here. You guys have goofed off long enough."

The squadron yeoman had informed us that Patrol Squadron Forty-Two had been recommended for the Navy Unit Commendation. Since none of us had much familiarity with medals and such, we really didn't know what all of this meant; however, it sounded like something good. At the time, nobody made the Navy Unit Commendation information official for us, and eventually it was forgotten. However, the Navy Department kept it in some sort of "Pending" file and it was finally awarded

177

in 1951. One is always glad his pay account didn't get mixed up in something like that.

THE SECRETARY OF THE NAVY
Washington

The Secretary of the Navy takes pleasure in commending

PATROL SQUADRON FORTY TWO

for service as follows:

"For meritorious service and outstanding heroism in action against enemy Japanese forces in the Northern Asiatic Pacific Area from 1 June to 1 August 1942. Undeterred by extremely inclement weather, the lack of navigational aids and the overwhelming numerical superiority of the advancing Japanese, Patrol Squadron FORTY TWO flew vulnerable PBY aircraft from Aleutian bases over treacherous terrain and icy waters to carry out their vital assignments. Operating with rudimentary electronic, weather and radio equipment, the gallant pilots and crews evolved new operational tactics and developed unprecedented dive bombing tactics to cope with the low ceilings encountered over enemy defense positions. With a minimum number of patrol squadrons deployed in this theater during the early defensive stages of the war, and the extraordinary tempo of operations required to cover a wide perimeter, this group ranged far from base to carry out day and night missions, reporting the position of enemy aircraft raider forces and maintaining contact with these forces despite vastly outnumbering fighter opposition and intense antiaircraft fire. Taxed to the limit of their endurance, they struck devastating blows against strongly defended enemy land and surface units, delivering brilliantly executed torpedo and dive bombing attacks in their determined efforts to delay and harass the enemy. The splendid record achieved by this combat group against tremendous odds is a tribute to the unyielding perseverance and courageous fighting spirit of its officers and men, and reflects the highest credit upon Patrol Squadron FORTY TWO and the United States Naval Service."

All personnel attached to and serving with Patrol Squadron FORTY TWO from 1 June to 1 August 1942, are hereby authorized to wear the NAVY UNIT COMMENDATION RIBBON.

(Signed) Dan A. Kimball
Secretary of the Navy

Possibly there were a couple of things overstated in the Commendation, but it was nice to know that the Secretary of the Navy recognized that we weren't up there on a picnic.

Were there heroes in the Aleutian Islands? Surely the men who gave their lives would have to be listed as heroes. But to me it boils down to "all or none at all." If flying was tough, it was no less tough to fight mud, rain, snow and wind as a member of the ground crew. And if it was tough ashore, it was no less tough for shipboard personnel fighting waves, wind and cold. The great battles of the war were not fought in the Aleutians. Indeed, the war reports from the Aleutians were so sparse that very few people knew there was anything happening there. Africa, Europe and the South Pacific got all the headlines. But we were trying to halt the enemy on the only front where they actually invaded the continent of North America, the first foreign invasion since the war of 1812. Had we not been able to stall the Japanese at Kiska they could have moved right on up the Aleutian chain to the mainland of Alaska and from there to Canada and Seattle. The "Battle of Seattle" would have been a completely different event than the fun thing we always thought about.[1]

The award from the Secretary of the Navy not only awarded the Air Medal but also included advancement to the next highest rating. I had flown into Umnak Second Class Aviation Machinist's Mate, and when we departed for Adak two mornings later, I was First Class Aviation Machinist's Mate. As we droned along the way, I couldn't help thinking that Seattle was getting farther away every minute. If I ever did get back there I would be First Class—maybe that would impress the girls along First Avenue.

Oddly enough, it never crossed my mind that there was a pay raise involved in the promotion to First Class. We had so little use for money that I had most of my pay going home where I had a joint savings account with my folks. When we operated from a tender we could patronize the ship's store to buy some toothpaste, shaving cream or soap and maybe a few candy bars—not a real expensive shopping trip. When we got into Dutch Harbor there was a beer hall in addition to the base exchange. There was no guarantee that they would have a supply of beer on hand, but most of the time we had the pleasure of hoisting a few. At Umnak the Navy didn't have any kind of base exchange, but we could tramp a couple of miles across the tundra to an Army base where they had a small exchange.

There was one unusual twist to the Air Medal award. During all of these months I was never allowed to mention anything in a letter home about where I was or what I was doing. The censor would cut it out. On *this* occasion the Navy sent the business to my home-town newspaper, Aleutian campaign and all. Of course, *I* still couldn't write home and tell anybody where I was; the censor would cut it out.

Writing letters home was always a hard task. We couldn't say where we were or what we were doing. We weren't even allowed to mention the weather. My letters usually consisted of saying I felt fine and that I had gotten their last letter. On some occasions I could say I had received a package from home. I think all packages had to be fired from a 16-inch gun on a battleship before they were delivered to us. Cookies

---

[1]There has always been speculation that, had the Japanese kept all of their carriers together instead of sending two up to the Aleutians, the Battle of Midway might have gone the other way. But they evidently thought the Aleutians were valuable enough to warrant the use of carriers, not only for the diversion, but also to support their invasion. If they had known that a bunch of PBY's was the first line of defense in the Aleutians, they might have sent only one carrrier to the north. But Admiral Yamamoto must have figured he had plenty of strength in both places to do what he wanted done. They had enough fire power in the Midway area to blow the whole American Navy out of the water. It just wasn't in the right place at the time it was needed. See Gordon W. Prange's account, *Miracle at Midway* (New York: McGraw-Hill, 1982), 376-78.

looked like brown flour. Fruit cakes got to us in packages that felt like beanbags, with the fruit in one end and the crumbs in the other. Sometimes we received only a few wads of paper with our names on them.

One break we did get from the Post Office Department was free mail. We just had to put our return address in the usual location on the envelope, showing our Fleet Post Office address, and then, instead of putting a stamp on the letter, we just wrote "Free" in that spot. We saved three cents per letter.

My parents had four sons in the Service, two in the Army and two in the Navy. Not knowing where we were or what we were doing must have caused them a lot of anguish. All of us were in the Pacific, but that fact was not known to any of us until late in the war.

My oldest brother, Aubrey (Aub), had been in the Service for about ten years. He was a Staff Sergeant in the Army Medics. He was at Clark Field in the Philippines when the war started and ended up being taken prisoner at Bataan. We found out later that he survived the Bataan Death March. He was listed as missing for a year, but then turned up in a prison camp. In 1944 he and several hundred other prisoners were being moved from Davao to Japan in an unmarked Japanese ship. One of our submarines sank the ship near the island of Mindanao. Although a few of the prisoners survived, Aub was caught below decks and went down with the ship. One of the survivors visited my folks and told them about the whole thing.

My second oldest brother, Claude, was a Second Class Storekeeper in the Navy. He was with a supply outfit on Guadalcanal with the Marines.

My third oldest brother, Kenneth, was a Master Sergeant in the Army Air Corps. He got shipped from New York to Australia a few days after Pearl Harbor aboard the *Queen Mary*, with 15,000 troops. He was moved up to New Guinea shortly after that and was in a B-24 outfit.

I guess my dad and mother watched for the stage (our term for the mail truck) every day and hoped for a letter. As sparse as the news was in the letters they got, it sure beat hearing nothing at all.

In the fall of 1942 promotions came through for some of our squadron officers, and some of the "old guard" were transferred to other duties. The skipper, Lieutenant Commander Russell, made Commander and left us, turning over the squadron to Lieutenant Commander Perkins. Lieutenant Dickey, our plane commander, was promoted to Lieutenant Commander and went back to the States to await further assignment. Our new plane commander was Lt.(jg) McFarland.

Due to the casualties our squadron had suffered,[2] new crews had to be formed to man replacement planes as we received them. Babbitt got promoted to plane captain and our new Second Mech was Uther Taylor. Summers was assigned to a different crew as First Radioman and Reeves became our Second Radioman.

Getting a new plane commander is sort of like getting a new quarterback on a football team. Both Lieutenant Dickey and Lt.(jg) McFarland knew their business, but each had his own way of going about it. The basics always remained the same, but Mr. Dickey's deliberate and thoughtful methods were now replaced by the instinctively faster pace of Mr. McFarland. Our crew didn't have much trouble adapting, and it didn't make any difference who was in the plane commander's seat—our PBY wasn't going to make more than 115 knots anyway.

---

[2]Please refer to Appendix for list of casualties suffered by Patrol Wing Four squadrons, as compiled from *History of Fleet Air Wing Four* (Naval Historical Center, Washington, D.C.).

Rear—N. W. Chaney, Lt. Comdr. C. E. Perkins, D. L. Jackson; front—J. B. Berdami, E. G. Matison, R. E. Strong   (National Archives)

Rear—C. J. Silva, Lt.(jg) Morrison, Lt.(jg) Bingham, Ens. Lindell, H. Bates; front—C. G. Brand, H. J. Katelinek, A. Alford, L. T. Tylor

(National Archives)

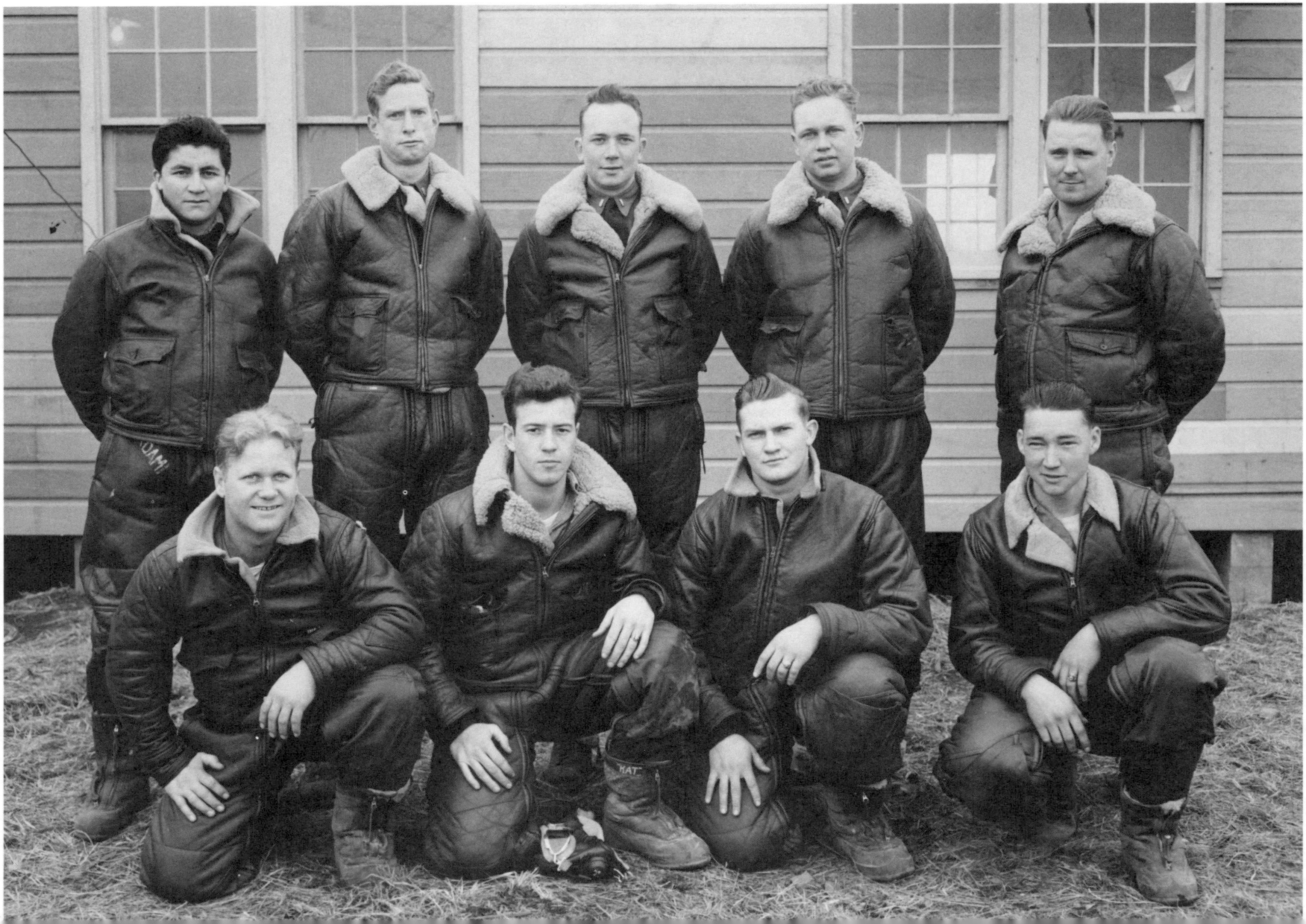

Rear—T. E. Dula, Lt.(jg) Thelan, Ens. Coonan, L. F. Flick; front—T. Krynitsky, W. T. Marquis, R. R. Shock, B. C. Rasche

(National Archives)

183

Rear—J. J. Yakich, Ens. Chaddick, Lt.(jg) Lindgren, Ens. Redwine, A. C. Merrill; front—M. J. Kulman, D. F. Butcher, V. E. Luther, F. L. Wentz

(National Archives)

Rear—N. G. Miller, D. M. Timlin, Lt. Woody, Lt.(jg) Conrad, W. W. Hopkins; front—W. W. Schreck, R. J. Keeney, F. J. Medved, A. K. Babbitt

(National Archives)

Rear—L. T. Tyler, Lt.(jg) Woody, Lt.(jg) Bingham, H. H. Bates; front—C. J. Silva, C. E. Katelinek, A. D. Alford   (National Archives)

Rear—H. Olubych, Lt. Dickey, W. J. McGrath; front—M. Y. Hanson, F. L. Rathburn

(National Archives)

Rear—J. Hollenbeck, J. E. Brunzell, Lt. (jg) Sullivan, W. S. Smith; front—M. R. Fitch, S. J. Strainer, E. O. Anderson, S. E. Hanks

(National Archives)

Rear—H. B. Peer, Lt.(jg) McFarland, Ens. Johnson, Ens. White; front—A. A. Birchman, D. W. Kirkes, H. S. Smith, E. S. Matison

(National Archives)

Rear—Bruce Haight, Bolton, Lt.(jg)Willie Mann, ? , Noel Hanson; front—Robert Brown, Albert Clement, Ray Hanson, Thomas Jefferys

(Courtesy of Robert Brown)

Rear—N. W. Chaney, A. M. Alberti, Lt.(jg) Erickson, Lt.(jg) Forbes, G. A. Dawn; front—H. G. Grabowski, A. J. Hassell, Jr., E. L. Summers, C. O. Grant

(National Archives)

Rear—J. F. O'Kula, W. B. Dever, Ens. W. S. Webster, Lt.(jg) McLemore; front—R. Wallenstien, D. M. McCullogh, W. D. Baker, L. Purnell
(Courtesy of Bob Wallenstien)

Rear—John "Jeep" Feher, "Fighter" Flick, Lt.(jg) Lucius Campbell, Lt. Brooks, Bill Brady; front—Bill Stallings, Stevenson, Flowers, Denning

(Courtesy of Bill Brady)

Rear—Ens. R. Cork, L. L. Dow, W. F. Wright, Ens. A. Glosecki; front—E. Mogasar, H. H. Young, Strickland, A. Lorang
(National Archives)

Rear—Lt.(jg) Conrad, A. K. Babbitt, W. W. Hopkins, N. G. Miller, Lt. Woody; front—W. W. Schreck, F. J. Medved, R. J. Keeney, D. M. Timlin

(National Archives)

Rear—H. S. Smith, H. B. Peer, Ens. Johnson, Ens. White, H. W. Baughman; front—A. A. Birchman, D. W. Kirkes, D. L. McKenley, W. A. Turner

(National Archives)

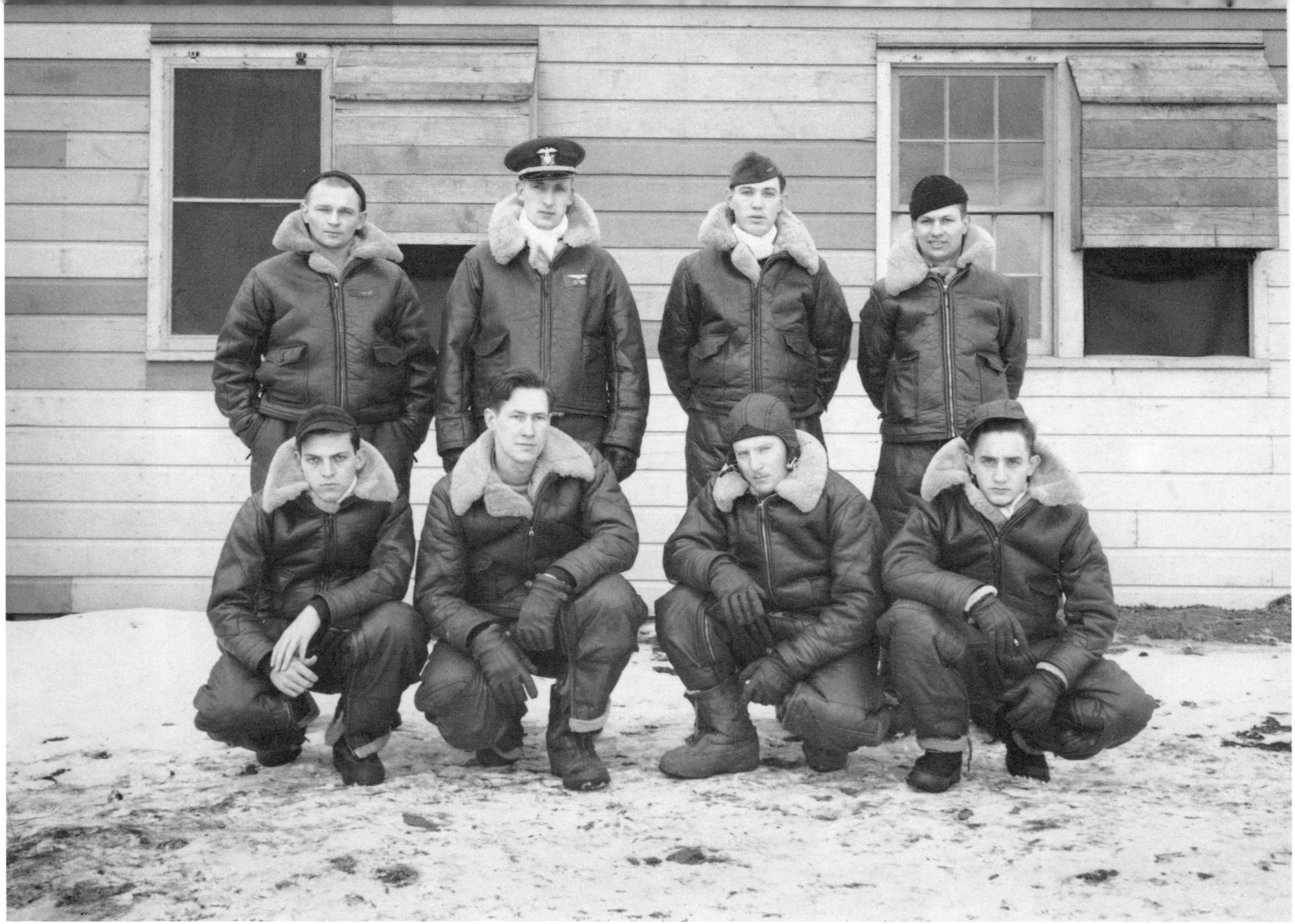

Rear—W. C. Underwood, Ens. W. P. Hagen, Ens. M. J. Noe, H. E. Moody; front—R. K. Mulligan, A. R. Anderson, W. W. Kessinger, J. H. Goode

Rear—Lt.(jg) W. Lindgren, D. F. Butcher, Ens. Redwine, A. C. Merrill, Ens. Chaddick; front— ? , J. J. Yakich, M. J. Kulman, V. E. Luther

(National Archives)

Lt. Lohse and VP-42 Flight Crew

(National Archives)

Non-flying personnel of VP-42. Rear—Lt.(jg) J. A. Brazelton, Chief A. A. Gabriel, Lt. F. S. Udall; front—S. S. Loft, J. Segar, C. R. Wilcox.

(National Archives)

"Russell's Rascals" — a group of VP-42 Aircrewmen who flew in the Aleutian Campaign in the summer of 1942

(Freeman Collection)

Chapter **10**

New Year, Visit Home

W HEN THE JAPANESE SENT THEIR NAVAL FORCES to the Aleutians in June 1942, they had two objectives: they wanted to create a diversion to draw attention away from their intended invasion of Midway, and they wanted to get some ground forces ashore in the Aleutians to gain a foothold there.

The diversion tactic was a complete failure because Admiral Nimitz' intelligence people had deciphered their code and knew the Japanese were trying to divert attention from the Midway invasion. The Japanese ended up losing four carriers at the battle of Midway. Admirals Yamamoto and Nagumo must have gone home talking to themselves after that one.

The Japanese proved largely unsuccessful in their second objective as well. Japanese submarines had been observing the Aleutians for some time. Although the U.S. efforts to fortify the chain were not really advancing very fast, the submarines could see that there was movement to the west, and that eventually the western islands would be defended by American troops. This seemed like a good time to move in and occupy several islands. The initial invasion force was to build bases at Kiska and Attu to be used for further expansion up the chain toward the mainland of Alaska. Once they got a base on the Alaska Peninsula they could begin making raids on the west coast of Canada and eventually hit Seattle with its Boeing plant.

The invasion tactic did succeed in that the Japanese forces managed to occupy Kiska and Attu.[1] However they dropped plans for any expansion past the two islands of Kiska and Attu because they exhausted all of their resources available for the Northern Operation trying to get supplies, planes and ships into those two bases. Also, we managed to establish bases on Adak and Amchitka, which they intended to occupy, before they got to them. The Japanese were known to have sent scouting parties ashore on Adak and Amchitka, but they never could muster the strength necessary for actual occupation of those islands.

We never did do much about the Japanese on Attu. Because Kiska was nearer to mainland Alaska, it got all of the attention. I don't believe our PBY's dropped a bomb or fired a shot over Attu during 1942. I imagine that the Japanese troops on Attu spent a lot of time on alert, though, since they were surely aware of the continual bombing

---

[1]It was interesting to us that they had chosen Kiska for occupation. In prewar days our planes had tried operating from Kiska several times as an advance base. The harbor was too open to the sea and was subject to very severe wind conditions. The official U.S. consensus was that it would be a poor location for an air base of any kind. As a matter of fact, after the Japanese finally evacuated their troops from Kiska in August 1943, the Army spent a couple of weeks making sure the place was really abandoned by the Japanese, then they moved out and left the place uninhabited. The U.S. never bothered to use Kiska again.

202

attacks being carried out on their buddies over on Kiska. After we started flying out of Adak, we flew regular patrols out past Attu with observation sweeps along the coast of the island, but we never did attack the place. Once in a while we hauled a photographer along with us and eased in close enough so he could snap some pictures for our intelligence folks to study. Although gun emplacements on Attu were observed on these photo runs, the Japanese seemed content to save their ammo as long as we didn't threaten to attack.

During the first nine months of the Japanese occupation of Attu we did not intercept any supply ships coming to the island, mainly because we didn't have the resources available to stop any shipping in that area. It was only in March, 1943, after we got a scouting force of ships out in those waters, that there was a definite effort made to blockade Japanese shipping.

Our small fleet of blockade ships roamed around about three hundred miles west of Attu in the vicinity of a group of islands called the Komandorskie Islands. As flyers, we were warned to stay clear of these islands because they belonged to Russia. We were unofficially given to understand that if we got in trouble and had to make a forced landing in the waters around the islands we would be picked up by the Russians and interned for the rest of the war. Even though Russia was our ally and their flight crews were treated as friends while they were ferrying Lend-Lease planes from Alaska on a regular basis, they promised to be very inhospitable to any of our people unfortunate enough to fall into their hands. The politicians in Washington had evidently cooked up some kind of deal which left us not only worrying about the Japanese but also keeping clear of the Russians too. The more I learned about the Russians the less I trusted them. Who needs enemies when you have friends like the Russians? Don't shoot at them—just be content to be captured.[2]

During the first year of the war in the Aleutian Islands we had managed to ward off Japan's initial thrust and now spent more time attacking than defending. During 1942 the United States and its allies had also gradually moved from the defense to the offense in other parts of the world. By the time New Year's Day 1943 rolled up on the calendar the Germans were being squeezed out of Africa and frozen out of Russia. And the Japanese were being shot out of the South Pacific. Admiral Halsey was storming

---

[2]The reason behind this strange policy was that Russia was afraid that Japan would take offense if Russia offered U.S. fliers any assistance. Russia didn't want Japan to declare war on her in the Pacific. As long as Russia used its Lend-Lease equipment to fight Germany, the Japanese were satisfied to live and let live in the Northern Pacific area.

The tragedy of this policy didn't emerge until 1944 and early 1945. During that time the Navy's PV's were flying regular bombing missions to targets in the Japanese Kurile Islands. At least a dozen PV's of VPB-131, 135 and 136 sustained enough battle damage so that they could not make it back to their bases on Attu or Shemya. Their only alternative was to land at a Russian air base on the Kamchatka Peninsula. Instead of being greeted like allies, they were met by armed soldiers and incarcerated in a manner only to be expected by prisoners of war.

In fact they were fed poorly and given practically no clothing. Kept under guard, they remained in the Russian camps until after VE-day in May 1945. Finally they were shipped by rail thousands of miles across Russia to the Iranian border, where they were loaded into trucks in the middle of the night and taken into Iran, eventually being turned over to U.S. authorities in Teheran.

U.S. authorities were still afraid to offend Russia by making any issue of the mistreatment of these men, so they became victims of their own government's politics. Eventually they were shipped back to the States and given leave with instructions to say nothing about what had happened to them. It was many years before any information concerning these "captives" began to filter out. Official acknowledgement is almost impossible to find forty years after their ordeal. (Please see "Casualty List" in the Appendix for the list of crews involved.)

around there with a couple of new battleships, *South Dakota* and *Washington*, and a few new carriers, as well as new cruisers and destroyers. Suddenly the Japanese found themselves retreating instead of advancing. Admiral Yamamoto wrote in his diary, "How splendid the first stage of our operation was! But how unsuccessfully we have fought since the defeat at Midway."[3] In 1940 he had told the Prime Minister that if Japan went to war with America, he could guarantee six months of success for the Japanese in the Pacific, but that if the war had not been won by that time, the industrial might of America would certainly seal Japan's doom.[4]

I don't know what Admiral Yamamoto did on New Year's Eve 1942, but I spent the evening at Blackie's Bar in Unalaska, near our base at Dutch Harbor. Blackie was pretty well stocked with beer, but there were about 200 guys trying to get into the place, which couldn't hold more than fifty. We ended up with a line in constant motion past the bar. The line formed outside and came in through the front door. As we inched past the bar, we were allowed to buy two bottles of beer. Then we moved along and out the back door. Once outside we fell in at the tail end of the entering line and drank our two bottles of beer while waiting to go in the front door again. It was a moving experience.

As if to celebrate the new year, the Aleutian weather kicked up a spectacular windstorm for us. In the South Pacific big winds are called typhoons. In the Caribbean Sea they are called hurricanes. In the Dakotas they are called cyclones. In Kansas they have tornadoes. But in the Aleutian Islands the wind just "blows like hell." No special name—just, "blows like hell."

The weather-guessers sit in a little shack with a pole sticking up through the roof. At the top of the pole is a little whirligig thing that is turned by the wind; at the bottom of the pole in the shack is a gauge which shows how fast the whirligig is turning. This tells the weather-guesser how fast the wind is blowing. The gauge shows readings up to 100 knots, and generally that is enough. When it gets above 100 knots, most of the time the pole, shack and all blow away. If they held a contest to find a name for the big wind in the Aleutians, I would suggest "Shackaway."

The wind on 6 January 1943 was threatening to blow the shack away. At Adak we put every available tie-down line on our planes. We had them tied down to oil drums filled with concrete and to concrete blocks. There was no flying activity that day, and the wind kept blowing right through the night. Our planes got bounced around, but the tie-downs held, and our squadron got through with very little damage. VP-43, equipped with PBY-5's, had some planes moored out in Kuluk Bay at Adak. When morning came they were just about out of business. Planes had broken their moorings and crashed into each other or run up on the rocks. They only had one or two good planes left. They had had the usual 3-man plane watches in the planes and those guys had spent a wild night. One of the guys told me that they had gotten their engines started when it began to appear that they were going adrift, but they still couldn't keep from crashing into one of the other planes. A couple of attempts were made to assist the doomed aircraft with boats, but the seas were running so high that the attempts had to be abandoned. Fortunately the planes were the only casualties. The guys inside the disintegrating planes managed to ride out the storm with no casualties.

---

[3]John Costello, *The Pacific War* (New York: Quill, 1981), 383.

[4]Hiroyuki Agawa, *The Reluctant Admiral: Yamamoto and the Imperial Navy*, trans. John Bester (Tokyo: Kodansha International, Ltd., 1979), 189.

In Dutch Harbor the wind had also gotten over 100 knots and had wrecked some more VP-43 planes. The howling wind caught one plane under the tail, lifted it up on its nose and flipped it over on its back. VP-43 went from twelve planes to three or four planes in about twenty-four hours.

The next day we took off on regular patrol and headed out past Attu, along the chain. As we neared Attu, we passed an island called Agattu and flew in to take a close look. The windstorm had caught the Japanese trying to bring some planes into Kiska for reinforcement. Evidently the planes had gotten into the bay at Agattu and tried to weather the storm. Five small seaplanes were scattered around on the beach. We sent a message back to Adak, telling them what we had found and eased in for a closer look. When we got within a half mile of the beach, a stream of tracers started coming at us from some bushes up beyond the beach. We moved out again and waited.

Our orders at this time were to radio in any contact and then let the Army guys carry out the attack. They sent out a half dozen P-38's. They flew about three times as fast as we did, so they weren't long getting there. They have all of their guns mounted right in the nose of the plane, and they look kind of like a blow torch when they make a strafing run. They got in line, one behind the other, and made a single run over that beach. When they headed for home, the job was completed. All the seaplanes were flaming wrecks. I don't know what those guys in the bushes did with their guns. They sure weren't going to fly out of there.

When we returned from our patrol, there were some P-38's getting in the traffic pattern as we circled to land. They buzzed us a couple of times and then pulled up alongside and were flying right with us. Lt. McFarland said, "OK, hotshots, you may be able to fly faster than we can, but try to match this." He started to throttle back slowly. A PBY will fly at 65 knots, but there is no way that a P-38 can stay in the air at that speed. In a few seconds, the P-38's started to stall out. They knew they had lost that contest, so they poured the coal on and waved good-bye as they swooped off away from us.

Just as we were turning for final approach to the runway there was a roar right above us and a B-17 dropped down and cut in front of us. We poured the coal on, made a low pass over the runway and went around for another approach. When we landed, we parked three planes down the line from the B-17 which had cut us out. Our pilots, followed by the whole crew, began walking over toward the bomber to demand an explanation for such a crazy maneuver. When we saw the ambulance parked near the plane we began to understand.

One look at that plane was all we needed. He had been out to Kiska and was badly shot up. The ball turret on the bottom of the B-17 had taken a hit from something pretty big; the gunner must have been killed instantly. Evidently the turret was jammed and nothing could be done for the gunner during flight so they had to wait until they got on the ground to try to help him. Thus, the rush to land. The medics were on their knees under the plane in a pool of blood trying to get the dead gunner out of the turret. Not a word was said among us. We silently turned around and went back to our plane.

Some guys from our ground crew were waiting for us when we got back to our plane and gave us the latest news. "We have orders to turn all of our planes over to VP-43 and go back to the States for new planes!" So the ill wind was not all bad. Rumor had it that we would be out of the flying boat business and would be getting some new land planes called PV's. While it might be exciting to fly in faster, higher powered planes, I had to confess I felt some mixed emotions about deserting our faithful old

PBY takes a beating in a storm at Dutch Harbor—21 November 1942

(National Archives)

VP-43 PBY wrecked by gale at Dutch Harbor—21 November 1942

(National Archives)

PBY's. I was not completely convinced that this was going to happen.

The next morning we loaded two crews apiece into two of our planes and the sixteen of us flew to Dutch Harbor, leaving our remaining two planes at Adak. We caught a ride on a destroyer from Dutch Harbor to Kodiak. They didn't have any spare bunks for passengers so we were berthed in the line locker. When we disembarked and checked into the barracks at Kodiak, everybody thought we were fugitives from a hemp factory. No matter. We were on our way to Seattle.

At Kodiak we loaded aboard the *Chaumont* for the rest of the trip. The *Chaumont* had been in the business of transporting military personnel for a long time and had the reputation for being the worst transport ship in the Navy. The horror tales of the treatment of passengers sounded like something out of the seventeenth century. Actually the stories were a bit stretched, but the truth of the matter was that the whole ship's company seemed to have an aversion to allowing any passenger to enjoy a trip aboard their ship. The Boatswain's Mates handed every passenger a paint scraper or chipping hammer as he checked aboard. They had the passengers chipping paint before they had even been assigned bunks. When an area had been scraped to the bare metal, the passengers painted the area. Before the paint was dry, the passengers started chipping and painting again. One would expect that, with all the painting, it would be a sharp looking ship. In reality it was a sort of rusty-looking hulk. Since our destination was Seattle, we figured that things could not get so bad that we couldn't put up with them.

It is cold in Kodiak in January; there's even a coating of ice on Woman's Bay. For most of the trip to Seattle we knew it would be cold. My friend R. M. Jones and I didn't relish the idea of scraping, chipping and painting frozen decks all the way to Seattle, so we sort of hung back as our group was checking aboard. Finally we spotted a Chief in dungarees coming up the deck. "We are experienced hands in the engine room, and we want to volunteer to stand watches for you on this trip." When the Boatswain's Mate moved towards us with his paint scrapers, the Chief grabbed each of us by the arm and ushered us past him. Over his shoulder he said, "These guys are mine." The trip to Seattle was warm and dry. We stood four-hour watches in the engine room, changing lube oil filters for the turbine every hour on the hour, and greasing the bearings in the shaft alley.

During the first two nights out of Kodiak it was pretty rough; the ice built up on the rigging and booms on the weather decks until a cable broke and a cargo boom was swinging around like a wild animal. All the passengers who worked for the deck force were rousted out of their bunks and chased up on deck to help get the wild boom secured. The language alone was enough to melt all the ice on deck and change the winter weather to summer. Finally we got far enough south to get out of the freezing weather.

On the *Chaumont* the Master-at-Arms, who theoretically was charged with enforcing the regulations, which included no gambling, ran a crap game in one of the heads every night. Some heavy betting went on sometimes. One of our group, Melvin Hanson, hit that crap game for nearly $2,000 the night before we got to Seattle. He was unconscious, making some of the craziest bets I had ever seen—and winning them.

It was great to stroll down the streets in Seattle again. Just being able to walk on a sidewalk was a treat. But somehow there had been a change. As Jonesy, Babbitt, Birchman and I walked along, we all felt it but couldn't identify it. When we turned down on First Avenue, it struck us. There were sailors, soldiers and Marines everywhere. Servicemen had been a definite minority group when we had last roamed the streets of Seattle in December 1941. Now, just a little over one year later, we were lost in the crowd of uniforms. We went to the Music Hall and couldn't even find a place to sit down. We visited a couple of our other old haunts and found them jammed the same way. Finally we abandoned First Avenue and went up to Fifth and found a place where we could get a table. Our spirits weren't dampened all that much, but it took a couple of beers to get back on the track again. We ordered the biggest steaks on their menu, went to a movie and came back and ordered another round of steaks. We were fighting the Battle of Seattle with all guns blazing.

Within a couple of days our records were all processed and we were given two weeks' leave, with orders to report to the new Naval Air Station at Whidbey Island at the end of our leave. As soon as I had my leave papers in my hand, I called home to let them know I'd be seeing them soon.

The Northern Pacific Railroad went through Dickinson, North Dakota, twenty-five miles north of my home town of New England. When I got off the train in Dickinson, I checked up and down Main Street for someone I knew to try to bum a ride home to New England. When I didn't find anybody to ride with, I went over to the Post Office and checked on the stage. They still called the mail-and-passenger vehicle to New England the stage even though it was now a pickup truck, instead of horsedrawn. They said he would be in pretty soon and would be heading for New England in about an hour.

My dad was there waiting when the stage pulled in. He'd seen that stage pull in a lot of times for over thirty-five years, but this was the first time the stage brought a son home from a war. We just shook hands and he said, "Guess they've been keeping you pretty busy." And, "Mama's waiting at home. Think she's baking an apple pie." As we walked up the street, we met a couple of ladies, and my dad tipped his hat, as he always did when he met ladies on the street.

Most of the houses along the street had a pennant hanging in a front window. These pennants were about a foot square and had a red star for each boy in the Service from that home. If a home had received the fateful word that a son wasn't coming back, they changed the red star to a gold star. We saw a couple of gold stars and my dad remembered the exact day when those folks received their telegrams.

Parents were always glad to get mail, but telegrams were frightening. The man at the telegraph station would notify people by telephone if he had an ordinary telegram for them. But if he had one notifying them of a son's death, he delivered it by hand. When he closed his station and started up the street with a telegram in his hand, everybody watched to see where he delivered it. Soon there would be a gold star replacing a red one.

Our home wasn't fancy, but it was well kept and always looked nice. When we got to our house, I saw it had a pennant with four red stars hanging in the front window. As we walked around to the back door a few memories drifted through my mind. Our house was right across the alley from the back door of the church. When I was an altar boy, I was always on Sister Ethel's "Minuteman" list. When she needed somebody on short notice, she could call across the alley and have me there in a minute.

We were never much for hugging in our family. It had been a long time since I had hugged my mother. But when I walked into the house that day, I wanted to hug my mother. We just hung onto each other, and she said, "It's good to have you home." Then she asked my dad, "Was there any mail?" He laughed a little bit and admitted,

"Forgot to check the mailbox."

We sat around the kitchen and talked for a long time. Mother asked if I was able to keep my clothes clean and did I have a good place to sleep, and I said, "Most of the time."

Dad told me how the crops had been. They had raised more wheat the previous year than he had ever heard of in that country. Farmers were talking about fifty bushels to the acre as if it was a normal thing. Dad and I both knew that three or four years earlier they were elated with a twenty-bushel crop. Dad and mother mentioned that quite a few things were rationed and they had to have government-issued coupons to buy those items in the store. But they assured me that this was only a minor inconvenience as long as we got what we needed out where the fighting was.

Then he told me about some of the other boys who had been home. It was interesting that regardless of the ages of the men in uniform they were all "boys" to the folks at home. Some of them were serving on ships in the South Pacific which were mentioned in the newspapers and on the radio newscasts. That was pretty exciting for the hometown folks.

There was so little news about the Aleutian Islands that very few people even knew where they were. My dad and mother thought I must have been on some kind of top secret mission because nobody knew anything about it.

My mother's apple pie turned out great, just like her apple pies always did. She had been saving up on their ration of sugar for months, waiting for the time she could bake a pie for one of her returning sons. There was a kind of reverence about the way she handled that pie. When we ate it for dinner that night it was like a religious experience.

Although it was a hard thing to bring up, I finally asked if there was any new word concerning my older brother, Aub, who had been stationed at Clark Field in the Philippines, north of Manila, since a year before the war started. Dad went and got a letter from the government along with a bunch of newspapers. The letter said that Aub was listed as missing in action. Some of the newspapers carried various accounts of the battle on Bataan and finally the capture of all the U. S. troops. I had heard that our troops had been forced on some kind of terrible march after they had been captured and that quite a few of them had died. I didn't see anything about that in the papers and didn't bother to ask if they had heard about that. One paper had an account of General MacArthur showing up in Australia and vowing to return to the Philippines. It always seemed kind of curious to me why he had left in the first place.

There were also several papers which had items telling of parents receiving word that a son who had been listed as missing had later received word that the son was in a prison camp. Those were the items which gave dad and mother some hope. They were sure that "one of these days" they would receive an official letter saying that Aub was a prisoner. I had to agree that there was cause for hope. And if anybody's prayers could bring about the miracle they were looking for, it would be my mother's.

They showed me the last letters they had received from my other two brothers in the service. They were getting along fine but there was no way to know where they were or what they were doing. That was no surprise. I was familiar with the ways of the censor.

When we went back down town to check the mailbox, dad took me over by the drug store. It had two large display windows in the front. One display window was completely filled with photographs of "Our Boys in Uniform." There was a special place for photographs of "Gold Star Boys." The only change they ever made in that window before the war was over was to add more photographs.

While we were looking at the photos, my younger brother, Ellis, came up the street on his way home from school. He was a junior at St. Mary's High. He was carrying a trumpet case and told me he had been playing trumpet for a couple of years. That was new to me. They had started some sort of boxing program at school, and he was participating in that. I hadn't heard about that either. He brought me up to date on which teachers were still there from my time at St. Mary's and said that they were looking forward to seeing me. Dad said I'd better plan to visit them in the next day or two. Ellis had quite a few questions about what I had been doing in the flying business. I told him about PBY's and pretty much what my duties were and that the job was kind of long on hours and short on excitement.

As we walked back home, we said hello to a few people, but nobody stopped us for very long. A couple of people mentioned the article in the paper about the awarding of the medal and said they were glad to see me home in one piece. There was a kind of unwritten law that when a serviceman came home he belonged to his family exclusively for the first couple of days. After that people would come to visit, and he would make the rounds downtown and say hello to everybody. It was a kind of humbling experience for me to hear the conversations and realize how patriotic these folks were. Another thing that surprised me was the universal hate that all of these people felt for the Japanese. People who had always been kind and gentle seemed to rank the Japanese right down there with Satan himself. I guess I just hadn't gotten around to really hating the Japanese. I was busy enough just wondering if they could shoot better than I could or could drop bombs better than we could.

At about nine o'clock in the evening dad looked at the clock and said, "Well, it's time to say our prayers and get to bed." We knelt down and prayed for "our boys and all the other boys in the war." I think parents suffer more than anybody during a war.

Although it was wonderful to be back among family and the hometown friends, I began feeling anxious to get back to the Navy again. At the end of a week I promised dad and mother I would do a better job of writing and headed for Dickinson to catch the train back to Seattle and then on to Whidbey Island to begin training in the new airplanes.

Chapter **11**

N.A.S. Whidbey, VPB-135,
Hedron at Amchitka

THE NEW NAVAL AIR STATION at Whidbey Island, about a hundred miles north of Seattle, could be reached by highway to Mount Vernon, Washington and west from there across the Deception Pass Bridge. Or there was a route via the Mukilteo Ferry, leaving from just west of Everett and landing on Whidbey about fifty miles from Oak Harbor, the small town near the base. Since we had been told that there was daily Navy bus service between N.A.S. Sand Point and the station on Whidbey Island, I checked in at Sand Point and caught the free bus. Several of us who had gone on leave at the same time were together on the bus; we swapped a few stories about our time on leave. We also speculated about the new base and what we would be doing there. Evidently the Navy had decided that expansion of the existing base at Sand Point was not feasible and had found a location where they could build the larger base facilities needed for expanded wartime operations.

In the Aleutians a new base meant steel matting on sand for a runway, tents and mess kits, mud and wind. But Whidbey turned out to be an honest-to-goodness Air Station with concrete runways, hangars, barracks, mess hall and even a club. There were actually two bases: the seaplane base where the PBY's operated and the landplane base, called Ault Field. So at the beginning of February 1943 all hands from VP-42 reported in at Ault Field for what was to be about a month's training.

VP-42 was being decommissioned. They were putting us out of business. What the Japanese bombs and bullets and the Aleutian weather hadn't been able to do was now done with the stroke of a pen. The pen is mightier than the sword.

The Navy was modifying its operational concepts. The squadron organization as we knew it was being phased out. Instead of having the flight crews and ground support shops and personnel all in one squadron unit, the new concept was to have the squadron made up of only flight crews. The new squadron was designated as VPB-135. VPB-135 was to have 12 or 15 PV's and after training would eventually be sent to the Aleutian Islands. Maintenance and other ground support were to be furnished by a new organization called a Headquarters Squadron (HedRon). The HedRon was to be semi-permanently located on one base and service whatever squadron happened to be operating from that base at any given time. The immediate problem for former VP-42 personnel was that there was confusion about just which organization we would ultimately belong to. For a week I was a member of VPB-135. Then one morning I was told to muster with a separate group—the beginning of HedRon.

It was only fitting that VP-42 have one last fling together. About mid-February

Ault Field, N.A.S. Whidbey Island, Washington—March 1943

(National Archives)

Seaplane Base, N.A.S. Whidbey Island, Washington—March 1943

(National Archives)

Seaplane Base, N.A.S. Whidbey Island, Washington

(National Archives)

we rented the Moose Hall in Anacortes, fifteen miles from the base at Whidbey Island, and held a VP-42 squadron party. It was a gorgeous affair with all the wives and girl friends, music and dancing; all hands were in dress blues and on their best behavior. What we had to do was remember that this was not an advance base operation in the Aleutians; acting like savages was not the thing to do. There were only a few times during the evening when the enthusiasm got a little noisy and the Shore Patrol came in the door to check on us. Lieutenant Commander Perkins, the skipper, went to meet them and assured them there was no need for their concern—he had things well in hand. He was a remarkable man: he really *could* ramrod a bunch of Aleutian crazies into a socially acceptable group. He had confidence that we could handle civilization, and we didn't want to disappoint him. At one point during the evening he introduced me to his wife and told her that I had played "Beat Your Feet in the Mississippi Mud" for him at Umnak. It was good that he didn't go into the details of our show at Umnak. I'm sure she would not have been impressed.[1]

The next day we continued our training operations in the new planes. Our new PV-1 Venturas were low-wing land planes built by Lockheed, with twin engines and twin fins and rudders.[2] The PV's had twin 50-calibers mounted in a top turret and twin 30-calibers in the tunnel. Bombs were carried in a bomb bay. Under each wing there was a streamlined drop tank. These fuel tanks extended the range of the aircraft a couple of hours and could be discarded in flight if desired. The unusual thing in the aircraft's design was that, instead of having a nose wheel, as all the newer medium bombers did, the PV's had tail wheels. They were tricky for takeoff and landing in a crosswind. They were fast, about 250 knots, and fairly long range when rigged with their drop-tanks. The engines were the biggest we'd ever seen. They were eighteen-cylinder Pratt and Whitney R-2800's.

We began a program of familiarization flights to learn how to operate the new equipment in flight, and we learned how to handle and maintain the airplane on the ground. But transfers and tragedy were breaking up our old flight crews. Babbitt and Townsend got orders to Flight School, Stallings got transferred to some other squadron, and Summers was killed in a PV while on a test flight at Alameda. The airplane blew up in mid-air. Lieutenant Commander Dickey rejoined us. While he was waiting at Whidbey for his new assignment he was acting as temporary skipper of VPB-135. We thought that when all the reorganization was complete he would be skipper of the squadron. However, that did not happen, and one day when I saw him he said he was leaving for a new assignment aboard a carrier.

As new people were transferred in, a trend developed toward forming new flight crews and assigning the more senior of us to ground maintenance. It was hard to get used to the fact that we had become "senior" to anybody, but by this time there were an awful lot of people around who were junior in time and rate to the old VP-42

---

[1]The VP-42 squadron party was supposed to mark the end of a great organization, but what really happened was that, although everyone recognized the Navy's decommissioning procedure, that bunch of guys would never forget the special association with each other and throughout their lives would remember the days of the Aleutian Campaign. It seemed as if the spirit of VP-42 would live forever. The VP-42 bunch set attendance records at N.A.S. Whidbey at both the 1973 and 1987 Patrol Wing Four reunions held there. The Aleutian campaign was fought and refought. The group even had one of the Japanese pilots who participated in the Dutch Harbor attack as a guest at the 1973 reunion.

[2]The PV-1 bore some resemblance to the Lockheed commercial plane called the "Lodestar," which had been modified into a military configuration and then called the "Hudson." The Hudson featured an open cockpit on top of the fuselage from which the gunner operated a couple of 30-caliber free machine guns.

bunch. A few of the original aircrewmen continued to be in flight crews, but most of us were assigned less and less to flying and more and more to ground maintenance. As my own situation pointed more and more toward being assigned to HedRon I was a bit uneasy with the prospect of very little flying and lots of ground maintenance duties. It seemed that my aircrewman days were, at least temporarily, to end.

The new flight crew people came in as Combat Aircrewmen; they had been through a special school and had an unending confidence in their ability to drive the Japanese out of the Aleutian Islands. Those of us who had tried and not quite succeeded in that venture, and who had become combat aircrewmen before there was any such official designation, were almost convinced they could do it. Almost.

There was considerable shifting around of personnel to get qualified people where they should be working. As a result of some of this reorganization two of us, Schreck and myself, were assigned to take care of two new planes until we were transferred back up north. The training unit had received two SNB's—Scout Trainers built by Beech—twin-engine, low-wing land planes, commonly called Twin Beeches. They were much smaller than the PV's, but they were designed to be used as bombing trainers for future bombardiers in PV's—and they needed a couple of plane captains to take care of them. The first thing Schreck and I had to do was order some tools so that we would have something to work with. Schreck came by and saw me with a pad of paper making up a list of tools for my order and suggested that I just double everything before I turned the requisition in to Supply. That way he would get his tools too. So I doubled the quantities on everything and turned the list in to Supply. The guy in supply knew we had two new planes. His reasoning was that this was my order and it should be doubled so Schreck would have his tools too. So he doubled everything. When the order went up the line, the Supply Officer saw only my name on the paperwork and reasoned the same way. He doubled everything again. At any rate, Schreck and I got transfer orders before anything on the order came in, so we were blissfully unaware of all this doubling until later when we were back up in the Aleutians.

When we finally got reorganized and headed for the Aleutians again, I was assigned to the HedRon. Each of us was issued a special seabag full of cold-weather clothing and given a briefing on weather conditions in the Aleutians. The guy who briefed us did his best to make it sound awful. There were those who thought he was exaggerating. But the rest of us needed no convincing.

The HedRon crew flew north by transport plane, touching down in Kodiak for a day and then moving out to Adak. From Adak we went by ship to a new base being built at Amchitka. When we went ashore at Amchitka, it had been snowing. I guess it was a beachmaster who met us as we floundered around in the snow. He pointed to what appeared to be several snowdrifts and said, "That snowdrift is a pile of tents, and the other one is a pile of poles and stakes. Just grab yourselves some tents, poles and stakes and set them up anywhere you want to. You can see where they are building the runway, so stay clear of that area." The new guys were in a state of shock. The rest of us knew we were home again—be it ever so humble. All we had to do now was set up a place to live, construct some sort of maintenance shacks and wait for the planes to arrive. If they ever got the runway built. And if the planes could ever find the place. And if the Japanese, over on Kiska, forty miles away, didn't insist on welcoming us with too much fireworks. They had wanted this island, but we got here first. We hoped they weren't too mad about it.

PV-1 Ventura built by Lockheed Aircraft Co.

SNB Twin-Beech built by Beechcraft

(Defense Audiovisual Agency)

Army-Navy Expeditionary Force lands on Amchitka—January 1943

(National Archives)

The Japanese were actually quite displeased with us. When we arrived at Amchitka, we were warned about the "Amchitka Express." Ever since the Army Engineers had started building the fighter strip, they had been harassed almost daily by one or two Japanese float planes making speed runs from Kiska, dropping a couple of bombs and running back to Kiska. Finally when the fighter landing strip was about finished, the Army moved in a squadron of P-40's. It was Major Jack Chennault's outfit with the tiger heads painted on their engine cowling. A few P-40's would blast off whenever the Japanese showed up and either shoot them down or chase them away. The "Amchitka Express" ceased shortly after the P-40's got there because Kiska was running out of airplanes.

Our squadron of PV's, VPB-135, had to wait until the bomber strip was finished. They had left Whidbey Island with twelve planes and stopped in Kodiak. One plane caught fire on the ground and was a total loss. Another plane cracked up on landing at Adak. The remaining ten planes finally headed for Amchitka, which was to be their permanent base. We had a pretty bad crosswind on the runway the day they came in, but they all managed to get down. One plane overshot the runway and cracked up in the mud 150 yards past the end. Nobody was hurt, but the plane was scratched for parts. VPB-135 was down to nine planes and hadn't even started to operate.

Lieutenant Commander Paul Williams was the skipper of VPB-135. C.L. (Frenchy) French was his Plane Captain and Bill Brady was his Navigator. Since Frenchy and Brady were old shipmates from VP-42, we had a powwow after the squadron planes were all on the ground and asked them about their trip from Whidbey Island. They had left Whidbey on 25 March and had finally made it to Amchitka on 1 May, fighting bad weather all the way. They had just about reached the conclusion that they would have been a lot better off in the old PBY's. With PBY's there was always the option of landing on the water. Lack of that option, along with the foggy Aleutian weather, made the PV's tough to handle.

Our engineering maintenance shack was a tent alongside the parking strip equipped with a workbench, a vise and a couple of ball peen hammers. We scrounged a few tools from the Army fighter outfit and traded them back and forth among ourselves trying to get some work done. It was a sad operation, and we complained to anyone who would listen. The SeaBees had pity on us and added a few more tools to our collection. Finally a new engineering officer showed up. He had left Whidbey Island about two weeks after the rest of us left. He listened to our sad tale of the tool shortage for awhile and then told the whole crew that most of the tools in the Navy were presently located at Whidbey Island, thanks to Freeman and Schreck and their super tool order. Then he told us about getting that monstrous order of tools for the SNB's. He had gone backwards through the supply channels and found out what really happened. It was interesting but didn't help our present predicament. We continued hoarding the few tools we had, and gradually all of us carried a personal bag of tools attached to our belts. They were our prized possessions and we never let them out of our sight. We slept with them.

Within a month a cluster of quonset huts had sprung up and had become the main living area for most of our people. There was a mess hall, as well as a shower hut with handy tables for scrubbing clothes. Most of the guys abandoned their tents and moved to quonset huts. Civilization was coming to Amchitka.

But a few of us had scrounged enough lumber to fix up the inside of our tent into a pretty classy home, and as long as it wasn't mandatory to move into the quonset

Navy area near Fighter strip at Amchitka — April 1943

(National Archives)

Navy Quonset hut near Fighter strip at Amchitka — April 1943

One of Major Jack Chennault's P-40's. Chennault's "Flying Tigers" of Alaska had a Bengal Tiger head painted on the nose cowling of their planes.

(National Archives)

P-40 parking area near Fighter strip at Amchitka — April 1943

(National Archives)

Building bomber strip at Amchitka—April 1943
(National Archives)

"Charlie" strip at Amchitka

(National Archives)

huts, we stayed at our original campsite, which even included a small pond right out in front of our door. We had built a two-by-four frame in our tent and then lined it with plywood. We had a plank deck and a door built from pine boards. We looked on it as a rustic masterpiece. Our paradise was soon threatened, however.

The main living area needed a sewer system, and the SeaBees routed their sewer line right by a corner of our tent. That wouldn't have caused a problem except that there was solid rock about a foot and a half underground, and they had to blast down through it to lay their pipe. They predicted destruction of our tent and warned us to move out. We rigged up a shield around the corner of the tent from pieces of armor plating taken out of wrecked airplanes and told them to blast to their hearts' content. Then we retreated to the other side of a little mound, and they set their dynamite charges.

The blast sent mud, rock and smoke a hundred feet high. After about a minute all that stuff quit falling out of the sky, and we were able to see how the battle had gone. Our tent was still standing! The canvas roof had suffered in a few spots, but our blast shield had taken most of the punishment and we still had a home. The only real casualty was the pond. It had a rock bottom, and the blast had cracked it. Within an hour the pond had drained like a sink with the plug pulled out.

Late in March one of the PBY crews operating out of Amchitka told us about an important sea battle which had taken place out west of Attu. After a few days we got some of the details. We had a force of cruisers and destroyers out there as a blockade against the Japanese shipping in reinforcements to their Aleutian bases. Sure enough, a Japanese task force of cruisers, destroyers and cargo ships tried to get through.

They shelled each other for three and a half hours and both sides sustained heavy damage. But the Japanese finally decided they couldn't make it through and turned around and went home. The battle became known as the "Battle of the Komandorskies," because it took place near those islands. The only U.S. aircraft in the area during the battle was a PBY armed with depth charges, so he wasn't able to give much assistance.

I was in a limited flight status, so I only made a few flights from Amchitka. A couple of times we headed out to Attu to help with air support for our troops who had invaded the island and were trying to finish off the Japanese forces. Those infantry guys had a tough time in the snow and mud. And the Japanese were holed up in caves. We tried to lob some bombs into the caves in a sort of torpedo/dive-bombing run. It didn't work very well. We were able to get some strafing done and hoped it helped our guys.

Every takeoff and landing in the PV's was scary. It seemed like the prevailing wind on Amchitka was straight across our runway. A steady crosswind is bad enough, but when the Aleutian williwaw is added, changing direction 180 degrees in a second, there is a fatal combination.

On the morning of 22 May 1943 we were getting a three-plane flight out. The first plane started his takeoff run, got halfway down the runway and got caught in a williwaw. He careened to the left on one wheel, tried to correct and went screeching off the right side of the runway. The landing gear carried away and a wing broke off, but he finally stopped right side up and the crew came spilling out to get clear of the wreckage. There was only a few minutes' delay to make sure the runway was clear before the other planes went ahead and took off, right past the wreck.

The next morning, 23 May, we were trying to get another three-plane flight out.

The first plane started his takeoff run, and we watched him get caught in the same kind of williwaw. The action was almost identical, and he ended up in the mud within a hundred feet of the previous day's wreck. Only this time the plane caught fire. Two members of the crew tumbled out the door dragging a third man. They made it a hundred feet and collapsed in the mud. There was a runway repair crew of soldiers standing clear of the runway while the planes were taking off. They were closer to the burning plane than anybody else. One of the soldiers ran to the flaming plane, went in the open door and came back out in a few seconds dragging a member of the crew. He just kept doing that over and over. By the time the crash crew got there, he had bodies lying all over the place. Some were moving and some were not. The crash crew took over and got everybody clear before the plane blew up. They cleared the runway of some debris from the exploding plane, and our other planes made it off. We never heard who the soldier was, but I hope nobody chewed him out for leaving his repair crew without orders. Crazy things like that happened too.

On 4 June 1943 we had just enough ceiling and visibility to get a flight of planes off the ground. They hadn't been gone fifteen minutes when we were enveloped in fog right down to the ground. The fog persisted all day and as the time approached when our planes were due back there was much concern about their getting back on the ground.

Finally we heard the engines of an approaching PV—we didn't see it, just heard it. We barely made out the dim form of the plane as he passed over the runway, too high to land. He made it down after three attempts. A few minutes later the same drama unfolded when the second plane made it in.

When we checked the time, we knew that the third plane had to be getting low on fuel. It was the plane Frenchy and Brady were in. Finally there was the familiar roar as the PV groped for the runway, only to miss the pass and go on around again. On his third attempt he touched down halfway down the runway but miraculously fishtailed, skidded and slid to a stop about two feet from the end of the runway.

As the crew was completing the flight report, noting that the remaining fuel was about thirty gallons, Brady became aware of the date. "Exactly one year ago today I was flying with Lt.(jg) Campbell's crew when we got shot up, had a man wounded, ran out of gas, made a dead stick landing in the open sea and ended up losing our PBY. I think next year on June 4, I'm going to stay on the ground."

It had taken until the end of May, but the Army had finally finished off the Japanese at Attu, and the next step was to get them out of Kiska. It was August before that operation started.

At Amchitka we were scheduled to assist with air support for the invasion. We didn't get a plane off the ground for three weeks. The fog was so bad that we never could see more than a couple of hundred feet down the runway. As it all turned out, there was no need for air support.

For several days late in July our crews had been reporting a strange lack of anti-aircraft fire on bombing missions and there was some curiosity about what was going on at Kiska. As it happened the Japanese had sent in some ships on a sneak speed run and evacuated all the troops. They hauled out over 5,000 people in that operation, and we didn't even know about it until the Army invasion force went ashore to retake Kiska. There was nobody there.[3]

---

[3]Brian Garfield, *The Thousand Mile War* (Toronto: Bantam Books, 1982), 290.

(National Archives)

PV-1 overshoots runway at Amchitka and into the mud—3 May 1943

Crash of PV-1 at Amchitka—June 1943

(National Archives)

PV-1's grounded by fog and rain at Amchitka — a common occurrence

(National Archives)

PV-1 taking off from snow-covered runway at Amchitka

(National Archives)

PV-1's fly over the initial U.S. landings on Kiska—15 August 1943

(National Archives)

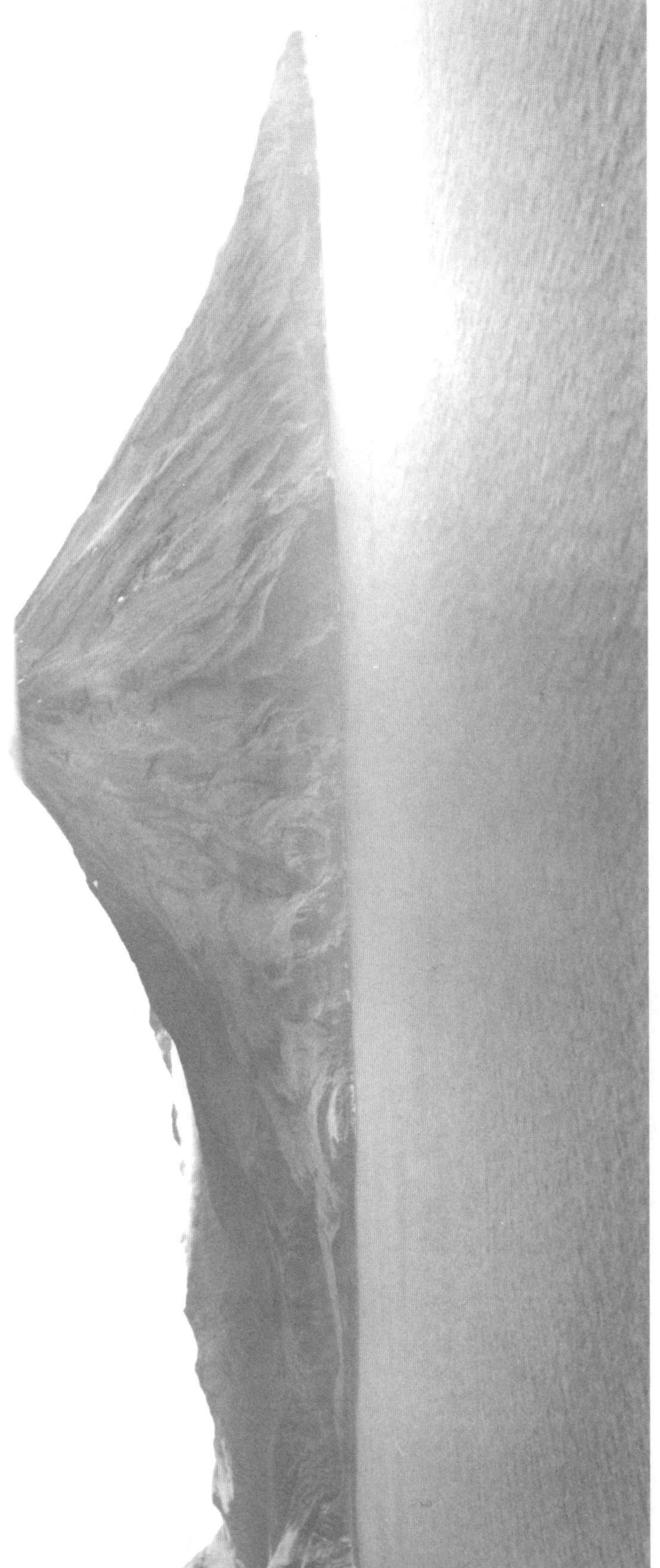

Striking photo of cloud-capped Kiska Volcano on 15 August 1943

(National Archives)

Japanese planes found wrecked in seaplane hangar at Kiska, apparently damaged by a direct American bomb hit prior to U.S. invasion in August 1943

(National Archives)

The PBY-5A's operated from Amchitka too.

(National Archives)

PBY-5A with one wheel off the taxi-way at Amchitka

(National Archives)

PBY-5A nosed off taxi strip at Amchitka—June 1943

(National Archives)

Interior of Messhall at Amchitka — April 1943

(National Archives)

240

Occasionally while at Amchitka I sat in my plane and turned on the radio. Once in awhile we could pick up Tokyo Rose. She always played pretty good music and gave us more up-to-date news than anybody else could. Granted, it was somewhat slanted toward the Japanese side. Although the Aleutians were mostly ignored on any news broadcast, U.S. or Japanese, on a couple of occasions she reported all of the U.S. planes in the Aleutian Islands wiped out. On one of these days she was reporting the heroic death of Admiral Yamamoto. All of Japan was in mourning for their revered admiral who had been killed in the South Pacific.

One day I happened to pick up the walkie-talkie conversation of the Army invading Kiska. One of those guys had a code name of "Terrific." Other people kept calling him, and he would answer, "This is Terrific." It was hard to know whether he was commenting on the progress of the invasion or not. But the Japanese were out of the Aleutians, and somebody began thinking about their base at Paramashiro and the Kurile Islands. Why not go over there and drop some bombs on them right in their own backyard? It would be maximum range for any of our planes in the Aleutians, so some of our planes made long-range scouting flights in that direction to prove that they actually could make it.

Lieutenant Commander Carl Amme, who had originally been with VP-43 when they came north in June 1942, had gone back to the States and formed a new squadron, VP-45. They were equipped with PBY-5's and came back to the Aleutians to operate from the seaplane base at Attu with Amme as skipper. On 10 July 1943 Amme led a flight of three VP-45 PBY's on their first bombing mission over the Kurile Islands of Japan. It was just one year after the date when our PBY's had made their first bombing raids on the Japanese at Kiska. Amme's planes found heavy overcast over the target, never could find a hole in the soup and finally dropped their bombs by radar. It surely lacked desired precision. But it was fitting that the first bombs dropped from Navy planes on the homeland of Japan should be from PBY's. They were also the first bombs dropped on the Japanese homeland since Doolittle's B-25's had raided Japan more than a year earlier. And now perhaps, the Japanese High Command remembered why they had thought it was important to occupy Kiska and Attu.

Not many days later a VP-45 plane had engine trouble and could not get back to Attu. The plane barely made it to the Komandorskie Islands, landing in a lake on one of the islands, and sent a detailed report of their location back to their base. Since this was Russian territory, and our relations with Russia in the Pacific were sensitive (though not sensible), the crew was in danger of being interned, and that is normally what would have happened.

But Lieutenant Commander Amme decided to send another PBY to the rescue. He declared radio silence for the duration of the rescue mission. The pilot of the rescue plane was instructed to send no radio transmissions until he had gotten the downed crew aboard, destroyed the crippled plane, taken off and gotten clear of the area. Amme then manned the radio shack at the base and in true Nelsonian "blind-eye-to-the-telescope" fashion instructed the duty radioman to listen but not send anything, not even a roger for incoming messages. If higher command people found out what was going on, they might interfere.

The rescue mission came off without a hitch and, as soon as the success message was received, the duty radioman was instructed to resume his normal sending-and-receiving watch. When the word got out about the rescue, VP-45's skipper was reminded about the existing directives in no uncertain terms, and withstood a barrage of unpleasant scoldings from above. That was offset by the wholesale approval of his squadron personnel, especially the crew which didn't spend the rest of the war in Russia.

The PV's of VPB-135 and 136 had opened a new chapter in Navy flying in the Aleutian Islands in 1943. Later VPB-131 and 139 shared in the bombing and photo missions to the Kurile Islands. The runways built at Adak, Amchitka, Attu and later at Shemya made the operation of landplanes in the Western Aleutians an option which was not there a year earlier. With the runways the attack missions could be taken over by the PV's.

By June 1943 a runway was laid down and a seaplane base built on Attu; a squadron of PV's and another of PBY's operated from there. The flatter terrain of Shemya, however, offered a much better location for the new large-bomber base to be constructed in 1944, and that finally became the main operating base in the western Aleutians.

In September 1943, several of us received orders back to the States for reassignment. Our first stop on the trip back to the States was at Adak. The Master-at-Arms came striding in the door of our quonset hut in the middle of the afternoon and called out the names of all of us from Amchitka. It seemed that the engineering officer had sent a message to Adak requesting that they detain us there until we gave up our tools. So paranoid about tools that we just couldn't leave them behind, we had departed Amchitka with our tool bags still attached to our belts. But when we were faced with the choice of keeping the tools or going back to the States, our paranoia left us in a hurry. The tools were on the next plane back to Amchitka.

Patrol Squadron Forty-Two had never made the headlines in any newspapers. Admiral Nimitz's people in Pearl Harbor knew what we were doing and the Navy Department in Washington, D.C. had a hazy idea of our operations, but for the most part our performance was pretty much in the same realm as the Aleutian weather—covered by fog and overcast.

In 1940 and 1941 we had been trained in the basics of fighting a war. During the critical days of June and July, 1942, we flew our PBY's out to meet a superior enemy carrier force, and we attacked the Japanese shore base at Kiska. We lost some good people in carrying out the missions assigned to us. Sometimes we exceeded the design capabilities of our aircraft, but the PBY's never let us down.

If any aircraft in the Navy's inventory was uniquely suited to a job, it had to be the PBY for duty in the Aleutian Islands. Designed in the mid-thirties, the PBY had evolved through several modifications by 1942. The PBY-5A offered the options of land operation or water operation, invaluable in the Aleutians, and had the range necessary for the long flights required in reconnaissance. It was rugged enough to stand the inevitable hard landings and rough weather, and could carry enough bombs, depth charges or torpedoes to damage enemy ships or shore installations. The engines were dependable, and armament and other equipment was adequate. On remote deployments the crew could live aboard if necessary. Considering the operating conditions and the jobs to be done, crews who had to fly in the Aleutian Islands in 1942 could not have asked for a better aircraft than the PBY-5A.

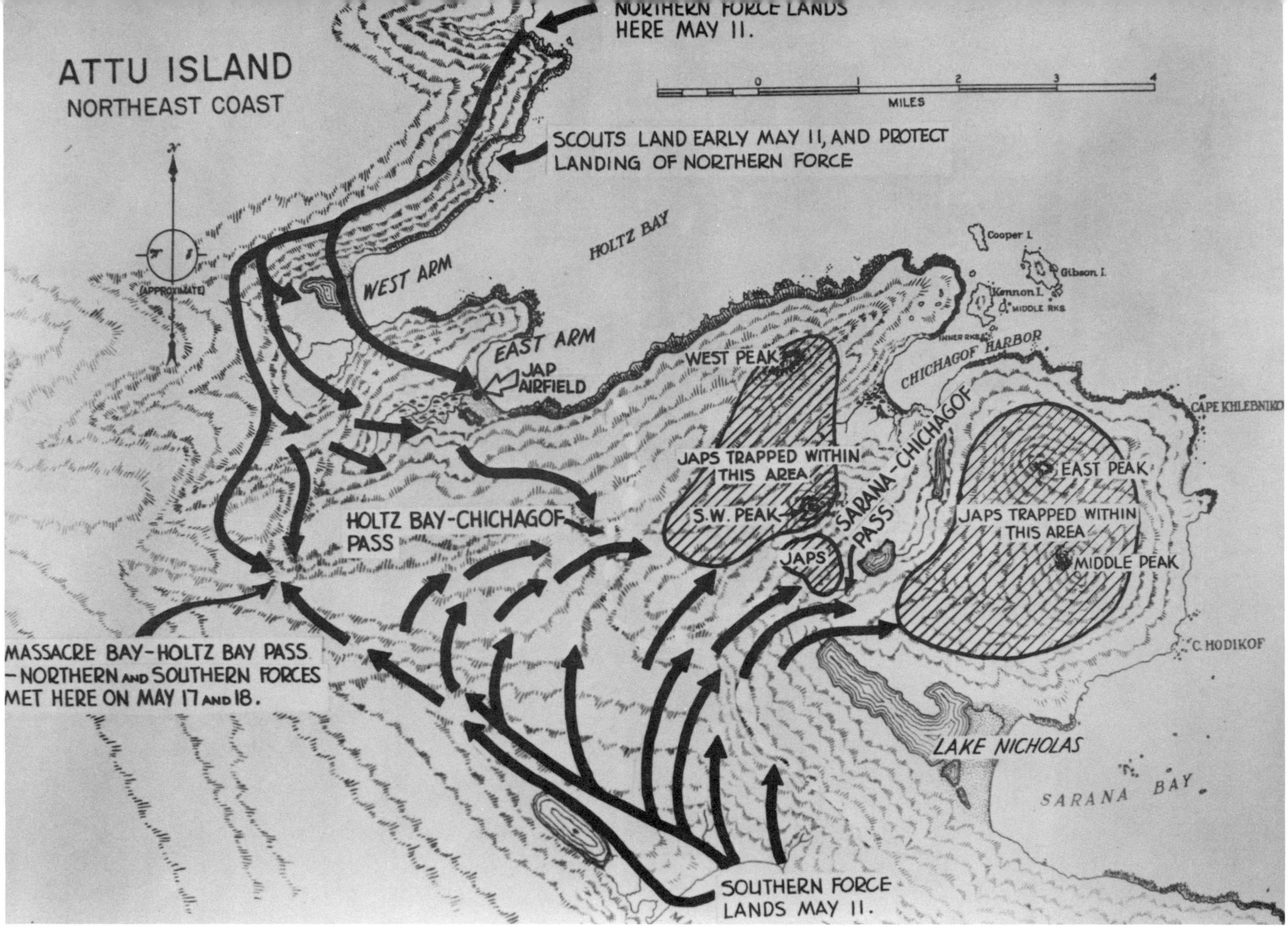

Map of northeast coast of Attu showing routes of northern and southern U.S. forces in retaking island from Japanese— May 1943

(National Archives)

Before the island was officially secured, the PBY's were operating from Attu. Refueling from USS *Avocet*. (National Archives)

Another view of PBY refueling from USS *Avocet* at Attu

(National Archives)

When the Navy sent PT boats to the Aleutians, the Seaplane Tenders were the natural candidates for servicing them. USS *Gillis* takes care of some PT boats alongside while fueling a PBY at the fantail. (National Archives)

Laying perforated steel planks—Marsten Matting—in Casco Bay, Attu, to make a ramp for the PBY's and OS2U aircraft.

(National Archives)

Beaching a VP-45 PBY-5 at Attu

(National Archives)

Beaching OS2U in high winds and rough water at Attu

(National Archives)

Beaching a PBY-5A with tractor at Attu

(National Archives)

Eventually there was a runway built at Attu, near Naval Air Facility

(National Archives)

When the core group of VP-42 pilots and aircrewmen who had struggled through the early training days came under fire, they performed as well as anybody in the Navy. That core group passed on its training and experience in Aleutian survival to new people who joined the squadron to replace our lost shipmates. VP-42 aircrews were ready to fly and the PBY's were ready to go.

The squadron maintenance crews worked under the most adverse conditions imaginable keeping the aircraft ready to fly. All of the maintenance work had to be done outside in weather that was pretty foul most of the time. It was always difficult to get parts, but the record turn-around time for regular checks kept our aircraft availability up with the world's best. In spite of the unprecedented scale of operations in June and July 1942, the VP-42 War Diary shows surprisingly few cases of aircraft down for mainte-nance.[4]

Throughout the war years there were always PBY's patrolling, scouting and doing air-sea rescue work in the Aleutians. VP-45, VP-61 and VP-62 continued to fly their PBY's in the world's worst weather conditions.

The PBY's of VP-41, VP-42 and VP-43 had not been able to stop the Japanese from occupying Kiska and Attu, but they made life miserable for the Japanese while they stayed, and finally convinced the survivors to go home. Americans won the Aleutian campaign. The Navy guys and their PBY's led all the way.

---

[4]*War Diary: Patrol Squadron Forty-Two (28 May 1942-31 July 1942)*, prepared by officers of Patrol Squadron Forty-Two (Washington, D.C.: Naval Historical Center).

"Patrol Squadron FORTY TWO flew vulnerable PBY aircraft from Aleutian bases over treacherous terrain and icy waters to carry out their vital assignments." (Excerpt from Navy Unit Commendation)

Photo from National Archives

APPENDIX

Casualties of VP-41, VP-42, VP-43, VP-61, VP-62,
VB-131, VB-135, VB-136, VB-139

As listed in History of Fleet Air Wing Four

23 April 1942	VP-42—	PBY-5A crashes on takeoff at Dutch Harbor in severe icing conditions. Ens. Smith and five members of crew killed
Mid-May 1942	VP-42—	PBY-5A missing on patrol from Dutch Harbor. Lt. Ed Winters and entire crew lost
3 June 1941	VP-41—	Killed in PBY-5A during Japanese attack on Dutch Harbor while Lt.(jg) Litsey was taxiing for takeoff: Martin H. Zeller, RM3c Merlyn B. Dawson, AP1c

VP-41— PBY-5A missing in patrol area where Japanese Carrier force was known to be operating:

    Lt.(jg) Jean C. Cusick
    Ens. Wylie M. Hunt
    Clark W. Morrison, AP1c
    John F. Collins, RM3c
    Carl E. Creamer, AOM3c
    Alton J. Davis, AMM2c
    Burdette B. Siler, AMM2c
    Louis E. Yurek, ARM2c
    Joseph R. Brown, S1c
(Ens. Hunt and two crewmen, Creamer and Brown were picked up by a Japanese cruiser and held prisoner until the end of the war.)

VP-42— PBY-5A missing in patrol area where Japanese Carrier force was known to be operating:

    Lt.(jg) Eugene W. Stockstill
    Henry M. Mitchell, AP1c
    Cyril A. Day, AMM1c
    Glen E. Ray, ARM3c
    Oscar J. Alford, ARM3c
    David D. Secord, S1c
    Frank E. Birks, S1c

4 June 1942	VP-42—	PBY-5A shot down by Japanese fighters:

4 June 1942   VP-42—   PBY-5A shot down by Japanese fighters:
    Ens. Albert E. Mitchell
    Ens. Joseph M. Tuttle
    Frank G. Schadl, AMM3c
    Wheeler H. Rawls, AMM2c
    Richard N. Sparks, ARM3c
    James B. Strom, ARM3c
    James D. Pollitt, S2c

4 June 1942   VP-41—   PBY-5A missing in patrol area where Japanese Carrier force was known to be operating:
    Ens. James T. Hildebrand, Jr.
    Ens. Leonard J. Hurley
    William B. Laing, AP1c
    Frank D. Geiger, Jr., AP1c
    William J. Glover, ARM2c
    Lester W. Dietrich, AMM1c
    Anthony H. Duesing, AMM3c
    Thomas W. Lowery, RM3c
    Willis H. Sweeny, S2c

11 June 1942   VP-43—   Killed in PBY-5 during bombing attack on Kiska:
    W. H. Lansing, AMM1c
    Ellis J. Keith, S2c

    VP-42—   Killed over Kiska while flying as observer in B-24:
    Lt. Clark A. Hood, Jr.

14 June 1942   VP-43—   Killed in PBY-5 during bombing attack on Kiska:
    Machinist Leland L. Davis
    Ens. Keller
    A. L. Gyorfi, AP1c
    R. A. Smith, ARM3c
    E. Alford, ARM3c
    J. H. Hathaway, AMM2c

25 June 1942   VP-41—   Killed in PBY-5A during photo mission over Kiska, in Lt.(jg) Litsey's crew:
    Austin W. Crosby, AMM2c

20 July 1942   VP-43—   Killed in PBY-5 in crash during take-off:
    Lt. Roy Green and all hands in crew

30 July 1942   VP-42—   Killed in PBY-5A in crash on landing in Nazan Bay:
    Lt.(jg) D. A. Brough
    Ens. L. J. Mills
    Ens. L. M. Love
    A. L. Cameron, AMM1c
    W. Small, ARM1c

8 August 1942	VP-41—	Missing in PBY-5A during search for Ens. Herrin plane SW of Umnak:

8 August 1942   VP-41—   Missing in PBY-5A during search for Ens. Herrin plane SW of Umnak:

     Lt.(jg) Julius A. Raven
     Ens. Thomas D. Moore
     Ens. Reuben M. Smith
     John L. Riley, Jr., AMM2c
     Steve Cuvar, AMM2c
     Delburt F. Cox, ARM1c
     Erven F. Falquist, ARM2c
     David C. Wren, AMM3c

8 August 1942   VP-62—   Killed in PBY-5 in crash into Makushin Mt. while returning from mission over Kiska:

     Ens. F. F. Kelly
     Ens. Leroy H. Dougherty
     Ens. Julius O. Hodges
     Harold A. Spencer, ACMM
     Paul H. Witham, AP1c
     Nathan Silver, ARM3c
     Comdr. Malcolm P. Hanson (BuAer rep.)

30 August 1942   USS *Casco*—Killed when ship torpedoed in Nazan Bay:

     John H. Brumfield, S1c
     Lawrence L. Davis, S2c

Missing:

     Cornelius N. Cremer, CMM
     Carl Wilson Manar, F1c
     Dail I. Richard, EM2c

Wounded:

     John W. Jacobs, SC2c
     William W. Porter, RM3c
     Elmer H. Kracke, SK2c

10 May 1943   VB-136—   PV crashes in Kuluk Bay, Adak when returning to base from search:

     Lt.(jg) Malloy and crew

10 May 1943   VB-136—   PV fails to return from search:

     Lt.(jg) Permenter
     Ens. Elton W. Cooke
     Robert S. Matthews, AMM3c
     Frank S. Tall, AMM3c
     John R. McClennan, ARM3c

18 May 1943   VP-62—   PBY missing from patrol:

     Lt. William C. Leedy
     Ens. Earl C. Alter
     Preston Bright, AP1c

18 May 1943	VP-62—	PBY missing from patrol: (cont.)

18 May 1943   VP-62—   PBY missing from patrol: (cont.)
    Walter B. Kerr, AMM1c
    Edwin H. House, Jr., AMM2c
    Allen F. Walker, ARM2c
    Roland L. Hughes, ARM3c

23 May 1943   VB-135—   PV crashes on take-off at Amchitka. Killed:
    Ens. P. P. Patterson
    A. D. Shaver, AMM3c
    Other crew members seriously burned

24 May 1943   VP-62—   PBY crashes in Kuluk Bay, Adak. Killed:
    Lt.(jg) Paul C. Spencer with entire crew

17 January 1944   VP-43—   PBY crashes on take-off from Massacre Bay with all hands lost.
    Lt. Noe and crew

17 January 1944   VP-62—   PBY fails to return from patrol. Missing:
    Lt.(jg) Andrew R. Porter
    Ens. Vincent W. O'Keefe
    Ens. Martin G. Vincent
    Franklin E. Fehr, AMM3c
    Norman R. S. Walker, ARM2c
    Charles W. Gillum, ARM3c
    Thomas H. Durham, AOM3c
    Johnnie I. Couley, AMM3c

25 March 1944   VB-139—   One PV crashes in Massacre Bay.
    Four persons killed
    Three survivors

25 March 1944   VB-139—   PV fails to return from mission to Kokutan Zaki.
    Lt. Walter S. Whitman
    Lt.(jg) John W. Hanlon
    Donald G. Lewallen, AM2c
    Clarence C. Fridley, AMM2c
    Samuel L. Crown, ARM3c
    James S. Palko, AOM3c
    Jack J. Parlier, AerM2c

31 March 1944   VP-43—   PBY crashes at sea. Killed:
    Lt. N. P. Wyman and all hands aboard

24 April 1944   VB-135—   PV missing on training patrol from Adak.
    Lt. McNulty and all hands aboard

1 May 1944   VP-61—   PBY fails to return from patrol from Attu.
    Lt.(jg) Grover F. Heidlage
    Ens. Robert W. Smith

1 May 1944	VP-61—	PBY fails to return from patrol from Attu. (cont.)
		Ens. Philip R. Dering
		James C. McDowell, AMM2c
		Hugh E. Morrow, AOM(B)2c
		Joseph F. Daniels, AMM3c
		Oliver L. Kihl, ARM3c
		Louis E. Palmer, ARM3c

6 May 1944	VB-135—	PV missing on Kurile strike.
		Lt.(jg) Alpheus A. Wheat
		Ens. Wm. W. Schatzer
		Ens. Roger Iani
		Wm. M. Austin, AMM2c
		Theodore Green, ARM1c
		Marion J. Catt, AOM2c

9 May 1944	VB-135—	PV missing on bombing mission to Shimushu.
		Lt. Hardy V. Logan, Jr.
		Ens. Anker K. Jeppesen
		Ens. Raymond Langton, Jr.
		Joseph E. Copeland, AMM2c
		James L. Beaulieu, ARM2c
		Donald J. Farrell, AOM3c

| 18 May 1944 | VB-139— | Mortally wounded in PV by anti-aircraft fire while attacking Japanese picket boat. |
| | | Lt.(jg) Clifford M. Tambs |

| 20 May 1944 | VB-139— | PV crashes and burns after take-off. |
| | | Lt. C. E. Clark and all hands lost |

14 June 1944	VB-135—	Two PV's believed to have made forced landings in Russia following Kurile strike.[1] Crew of first PV:
		Lt. Russell P. Bone
		Ens. Ralph W. Stevens
		Ens. Glenn W. Mantle
		Laurence E. Sommers, AMM1c
		Sam Gelber, ARM2c
		Frank L. Crow, Jr., AMM3c
		John P. Horvath, AOM3c

14 June 1944	VB-135—	Second PV believed forced to land in Russia:
		Lt. Howard P. Schuette
		Lt.(jg) John E. Brassil
		Ens. Byron A. Morgan

---

[1]The PV crews forced to land in Russia were interned until the war in Europe ended. At the same time, however, Russian crews were freely arriving and departing at Fairbanks and Nome, Alaska, picking up Lend-Lease aircraft from the U.S.

14 June 1944	VB-135—	Second PV believed forced to land in Russia: (cont.)

14 June 1944   VB-135—   Second PV believed forced to land in Russia: (cont.)
        Willie A. Donaway, AMM1c
        John F. Beggin, AMM2c
        Walter H. Morris, AOM2c
        John E. Jage, ARM3c

15 June 1944   VP-61—   PBY-5A fails to return from special search for Lt. Bone.
        Lt. Frank A. Woody
        Ens. Norman C. Hill
        Ens. Edward A. Patterson
        Earl O. Brewer, AMM2c
        Bruce S. Haight, ARM1c
        Joseph N. Heldorfer, AOM1c
        Orval D. Lowrimore, AMM2c
        Philip A. Lilly, ARM3c

19 June 1944   VB-135—   PV lands in Russia due to fuel shortage, after night strike over Kurabu Zaki.
        Lt. George A. Mahrt
        Ens. Richard M. Johnson
        Ens. William A. King
        Clifford C. Patzke, ARM3c
        William E. Dickson, AMM2c
        Richard T. Everard, AOM2c
        William D. Strom, AMM2c

22 July 1944   VB-135—   PV lands in Russia after fighter attack and damage over Shimushu.
        Lt.(jg) Jackson W. Clark
        Ens. John F. Mathers
        Ens. Berwyn J. Miller
        Hoyle A. Simes, AMM1c
        John Brennan, ARM2c
        Herbert C. Rowe, AOM2c

23 July 1944   VB-135—   PV lands in Russia due to battle damage after sinking Japanese picket boat.
        Lt. John P. Vivian
        Ens. David R. Wilson
        Ens. Thomas H. Edwards
        Kenneth G. Anderson, AMM2c
        Emil I. Nommensen, Jr., AOM2c
        Paul J. Schasney, AMM2c
        F. A. Virant, ARM2c

12 August 1944   VB-136—   PV lands in Russia due to engine trouble and fuel shortage after Kurile strike.
        Lt. Carl W. Lindell

| 12 August 1944 | VB-136— | PV lands in Russia after Kurile strike. (cont.) |

    Ens. James S. Head
    Ens. Murlin K. Richardson
    Henry H. Williamson, AMM1c
    Cyril J. Brown, ARM3c
    Russel L. Manthie, AOM3

| 19 August 1944 | VB-136— | PV believed to have made forced landing in Russia after Kurile strike. |

    Lt.(jg) Jack R. Cowles
    Ens. Leonard Panella, Jr.
    Ens. Millard B. Parker
    Harold R. Toney, ARM1c
    John R. McDonald, AOM3c

| 27 August 1944 | VB-136— | PV lands in Russia due to battle damage after attack on Kurabu Zaki. |

    Lt.(jg) John A. Dingle
    Ens. Emil M. Petterborg
    Ens. Eugene F. Dulan
    Harvey H. Pollard, AOM2c
    Charles D. Henry, AMM3c
    Daniel Leintz, ARM3c

| 11 September 1944 | VB-135— | PV lands in Russia due to fighter damage during attack on Kuriles. |

    Lt.(jg) Darryl F. McDonald
    Ens. Kenneth G. Miles
    Ens. Donnie L. Broadwell
    John W. Rosa, AMM1c
    Jack G. Ross, AOM3c
    W. F. Nicodemus, ARM2c

| 17 September 1944 | VB-136— | PV lands in Russia due to fighter damage during attack on Kuriles. |

    Lt. Comdr. Charles Wayne
    Lt. John W. Murph
    Ens. John E. Ehret
    Robert P. Baxter, ACRM
    Earl A. Mulford, AOM2c

| 4 November 1944 | VB-131— | PV shot down by enemy fighters in Paramushiro area. No survivors. |

    Lt. Robert A. Ellingboe
    Ens. Roy G. Bird
    Ens. Hoyt J. Overturf
    Gilbert E. Marriott, ARM2c
    Thomas D. Panetti, AMM3c
    Charles E. Rutter, AOM3c

BIBLIOGRAPHY

Agawa, Hiroyuki. *The Reluctant Admiral: Yamamoto and the Imperial Navy.* Translated by John Bester. Tokyo: Kodansha International, Ltd., 1979.

Cohen, Stan. *The Forgotten War.* Missoula, Mont.: Pictorial Histories Publishing Co., 1981.

Costello, John. *The Pacific War.* New York: Quill, 1981.

Creed, Roscoe. *PBY: The Catalina Flying Boat.* Annapolis, Md.: Naval Institute Press, 1985.

Fuchida, Mitsuo, and Masatake Okumiya. *Midway: The Battle That Doomed Japan.* Edited by Clarke H. Kawakami and Roger Pineau. Annapolis, Md.: Naval Institute Press, 1955; New York: Ballantine Books, 1958.

Garfield, Brian. *The Thousand-Mile War: World War II in Alaska and the Aleutians.* New York: Doubleday & Co., 1969; Toronto: Bantam Books, 1982.

Grashio, Samuel C., and Bernard Norling. *Return to Freedom: The War Memories of Col. Samuel C. Grashio, USAF (Ret.).* Tulsa, Ok.: MCN Press, 1982.

Hendrie, Andrew. *Flying Cats: The Catalina Aircraft in World War II.* Annapolis, Md.: Naval Institute Press, 1988.

History of Fleet Air Wing Four (11 August 1941-30 June 1948; April-December 1962). Prepared by officers of Fleet Air Wing Four. Washington, D.C.: Naval Historical Center.

Layton, Edwin T., with Roger Pineau and John Costello. *And I Was There: Pearl Harbor and Midway—Breaking the Secrets.* New York: William Morrow and Company, 1985.

Morgan, Lael, ed. *The Aleutians.* Alaska Geographic series, vol. 7, no. 3 (1980).

Morrison, Wilbur H. *Above and Beyond: 1941-1945.* New York: St. Martin's Press., 1983. Reprint. New York: Bantam Books, 1986.

Potter, E. B. *Nimitz.* Annapolis, Md.: Naval Institute Press, 1976.

Poulos, George. "At War in a PBY." *Fighting Wings of the Navy: 1911-1941* (Canoga Park, Calif.) (Winter 1984): 96-101.

Prange, Gordon W., with Donald M. Goldstein and Katherine V. Dillon. *Miracle at Midway.* New York: McGraw-Hill Book Co., 1982.

Quinn, D. C. "Confessions of a PBM Pilot." *Fighting Wings of the Navy: No. 2* (Canoga Park, Calif.) (Spring 1985): 76-79, 98-99.

Russell, James S. Floatplanes and Flying Boats. Unpublished manuscript (August 1984).

__________. Personal files containing unpublished documents detailing the Aleutian Campaign.

Scarborough, W. E. *PBY Catalina in Action*. Illustrated by Don Greer. Carrollton, Tex.: Squadron/Signal Publications, 1983.

Smith, S. E., comp. and ed. *The United States Navy in World War II*. New York: Ballantine Books, 1966.

Thorburn, Lois, and Don Thorburn. *No Tumult, No Shouting: The Story of the PBY*. New York: Henry Holt and Company, 1945.

United States Strategic Bombing Survey (Pacific), Naval Analysis Division. *Interrogations of Japanese Officials*. 2 vols. Washington, D.C.: United States Government Printing Office, 1946.

Wagner, Ray. *The Story of the PBY Catalina*. Aero Biographies, vol. 1. San Diego, Calif.: Flight Classics, 1972.

War Diary: Patrol Squadron Forty-Two (28 May 1942-31 July 1942). Prepared by officers of Patrol Squadron Forty-Two. Washington, D.C.: Naval Historical Center.

Films

Alaska at War. Anchorage: Aurora Films and Alaska Historical Commission, 1987. Produced, edited and directed by Laurence Goldin; written by Bradford Watson and Laurence Goldin; narrated by Peter Thomas.

Report from the Aleutians. Washington, D.C.: U.S. War Department, August 1943. Produced by Darryl F. Zanuck; written and directed by John Huston; narrated by Walter Huston.

Personal Interviews

Amme, Carl, Capt., USN (Ret), Commanding Officer VP-45. Palo Alto, Calif.

Babbitt, A. K., ADCS(AP), USN (Ret), Second Mech and Plane Captain, VP-42. Fallon, Nev.

Birchman, A. A., ex-AMMC, Plane Captain in Lt. C. E. Perkins' crew. Tacoma, Wash.

Brady, W. J., ex-AMM2c, Navigator, VP-42. Minneapolis, Minn.

Dickey, W. M., Capt., USN (Ret), Patrol Plane Commander, VP-42. Palm Springs, Calif.

Johnson, M. E., Capt., USN (Ret), Second Pilot and Patrol Plane Commander, VP-42. Pensacola, Fla.

Peer, Boyd, ex-AMMC, Second Mech in Lt. C. E. Perkins' crew. Los Altos, Calif.

Russell, James S., Adm., USN (Ret), Commanding Officer VP-42. Tacoma, Wash.

INDEX